The Art of Information Writing

Lucy Calkins and M. Colleen Cruz

Photography by Peter Cunningham

HEINEMANN ◆ PORTSMOUTH, NH

This book is dedicated to Nadine—cockroaches are forever. —Colleen

This book is dedicated to Hareem Khan, who sees the mountains beyond the mountains. —Lucy

DEDICATED TO TEACHERS™

firsthand
An imprint of Heinemann
361 Hanover Street
Portsmouth, NH 03801–3912
www.heinemann.com

Offices and agents throughout the world

The authors and publisher wish to thank those who have generously given permission to reprint borrowed material:

Reprinted with permission from the book: *National Geographic Readers: Deadliest Animals* by Melissa Stewart. Copyright © 2011 National Geographic Society.

Excerpted from the work entitled: *VIP Pass to a Pro Baseball Game Day*, by Clay Latimer. © 2011 by Capstone Press, an imprint by Capstone. All rights reserved.

From Mary Pope Osborne's speech *A Bridge of Children's Books* at the United Nations, April 2011. Used by permission of Brandt & Hochman Literary Agents, Inc. Any copying or distribution of this text is expressly forbidden. All rights reserved.

Cataloging-in-Publication data is on file with the Library of Congress.

ISBN-13: 978-0-325-04733-1
ISBN-10: 0-325-04733-2

Production: Elizabeth Valway, David Stirling, and Abigail Heim
Cover and interior designs: Jenny Jensen Greenleaf
Series includes photographs by Peter Cunningham, Nadine Baldasare, and Elizabeth Dunford
Composition: Publishers' Design and Production Services, Inc.
Manufacturing: Steve Bernier

Printed in the United States of America on acid-free paper
17 16 15 14 13 ML 1 2 3 4 5

Acknowledgments

THIS BOOK WAS A FEW YEARS IN THE MAKING. It started with the simple question, How can we improve the Teachers College Reading and Writing Project's best thinking about informational writing? and grew from there. Over the past few years, we turned again and again to each other and to colleagues to ask questions, pilot new ideas, reflect, and try again. In the end, the unit you hold in your hands is a combination of many talented educators' and hard-working students' best work.

We would like to especially thank the original guinea pigs for this unit's work: the advanced participants in sections both of us led at the Project's July and August writing institutes. Thanks also to the literacy specialist students in Writer's Craft, fall 2011. We are also grateful for the Thursday think tank dedicated to reimagining the trajectory of this CCSS–aligned unit and of the organization's work with information writing. Anna Gratz Cockerille co-led that group and did a great deal of behind the scenes work.

We are grateful for the pioneering spirit of Jane Hsu and the upper-grade staff and students of PS 116. They were incredibly generous with their time and support while working through the earliest stages of assessment for information writing and the connections to the content areas. We are appreciative of the work of the third-grade team at PS 199Q for their contributions of invaluable student work. We thank the third-grade team at Hope Street Elementary School in Huntington Park, California, and their coach Lily Hernandez for their contributions, particularly their willingness to work through some of the crucial work around organization and language. Additionally, we thank Sandy Pensak and her third-grade team at Hewlett Elementary School in Long Island, New York, for opening their classrooms to us. We are indebted to Celina Bialt, an inspirational educator, whose flexibility and keen attention to detail made her an MVP when piloting this work. We are also appreciative of principal Darlene Despeignes and her third-grade team at PS 63, especially Lauren Cohen, Jen Schilling, Judith Colon, and Cindy Brooks, who took a special interest in creating accommodations in this unit for students who need additional scaffolding. We also want to give our heartfelt thanks to Rebecca Fagin and PS 29, especially Alice Pack and Marissa Nealon-Noiseaux, who flew in during the last possible moments to try final changes to the unit and provide access to students and their work to include in this book.

Thanks to our colleagues Julia Mooney, Kelly Boland, Ali Marron, Amanda Hartman, and Hareem Khan for all their many contributions.

We would also like to thank the entire Heinemann production team. Jenny Jenson Greenleaf has once again designed beautiful interiors and covers. Sarah Fournier, editorial coordinator, has managed permissions, contracts, and student writing and edited the CD with impeccable care. Teva Blair, lead editor, has overseen progress throughout the entire effort.

The class described in this unit is a composite class, with children and partnerships of children gleaned from classrooms in very different contexts, then put together here. We wrote the unit this way to bring you both a wide array of wonderful, quirky, various children and also to illustrate for you the predictable (and unpredictable) situations and responses this unit has created in classrooms across the nation and world.   —Lucy and Colleen

From Colleen:

This is the second book I have had the privilege of coauthoring with Lucy Calkins. In the process of designing the unit and writing this book, Lucy has taught me much about the power of constantly reflecting on and revising your best thinking, to find something even better. I am particularly grateful for her dedication to making this work as kid-friendly and teachable as possible and encouraging my unique peculiarities, which brought fun to the endeavor.

Contents

BEND I Organizing Information

In this session, you'll help children think of information writers as teachers. You'll teach them that information writers organize information as they write, like organizing for teaching a course.

In this session, you'll teach children that writers often brainstorm several different ways to organize their information writing. You'll suggest different ways writers structure subtopics and explain that doing this is an important part of planning.

In this session, you'll teach students that by considering different organizational structures, writers can allow themselves to think about a topic in new ways. You will guide them through a process of trying to structure their writing in various ways instead of settling immediately on one way.

In this session, you could teach students that writers of information books take all the information they have and layer those pieces, one on top of the other, to teach their readers as much as they can about their topics.

In this session, you'll teach students that the organizational skills writers use for their tables of contents can help them plan their chapters as well.

BEND II Reaching to Write Well

In this session, you'll teach students various strategies to develop their informational books. You'll suggest using mentor texts as a way to learn more about elaboration and help them apply these ideas to their own writing.

In this session, you'll teach children how to connect the information in their chapters using different transitional strategies and phrases. You'll suggest they look to a mentor text for ideas about how best to transition in their own informational books.

In this session, you'll teach children the art of balancing interesting facts with engaging style. You'll highlight revision strategies that encompass both structure and word choice that will enhance their voices in their drafts.

In this session, you'll teach children that informational writers are actually researchers, and you'll also suggest resources for finding more information to enhance their informational books.

BEND III Moving Toward Publication, Moving Toward Readers

BEND IV Transferring Learning from Long Projects to Short Ones

Welcome to the Unit

THE GENRE OF INFORMATION WRITING is a remarkably wide-open one. Crystallize in your mind, if you will, an information text. To do this, your mind probably casts over the options. You consider pamphlets, feature articles, nonfiction books, websites, textbooks, research reports, encyclopedias, atlases, guidebooks, blogs, and recipes. You think, Of all these many forms, is there one that captures the essence of informational writing? Chances are good that no single image surfaces. While you ponder this, let's go a step further. Try crystallizing a short list of the most important qualities of good informational writing. Again, chances are good that you will not easily settle on a list. The genre that is referred to in the Common Core State Standards as information writing is staggeringly broad.

There are reasons why information writing is harder to define than most genres. Information texts, for starters, exist to carry information that is, itself, constrained by the discipline to which that information belongs. For example, informational writing written by a field biologist takes on some of the traditions of that person's discipline, as does informational writing written by an artist, a travel commentator, or a chef. For years, because of the breadth of this genre, my colleagues and I taught information writing by inviting children to survey the whole wide world of options for this genre. We encouraged children to draw from that entire array of choices to make teaching texts. "Go to it," we'd say. Students would write question-answer pages and fact pages; they'd write fictional stories that made their information juicy. We encouraged them to put information into their own words, to use text features, to include a bibliography of their sources. But frankly, when the class was producing texts that were as different, one from the next, as all the colors of the rainbow, it wasn't easy to know qualities of good information writing that would make a difference, so our instruction tended to illuminate options and to be clearest when addressing peripheral topics like bibliographies or text features.

As a result, there was a striking contrast between our methods of teaching narrative writing and our methods of teaching information writing. For decades now, when students write narratives, we have channeled them to write in a very particular way—zooming in on a focused episode; starting by showing themselves or the character saying or doing something; writing a tapestry of thoughts, actions, and dialogue; using new paragraphs to show time moving forward. In contrast, for years, when our students wrote information texts, we emphasized the importance of noticing what other writers had done and drawing from a wide array of possibilities.

Eventually, however, we began to realize that while students' narrative texts improved in ways that were palpable and obvious to all, when they wrote information texts, progress was much less striking. Whereas one could walk into a classroom and know in a glance whether narrative writers were studying writing under the tutelage of a Teachers College Reading and Writing Project teacher, there was not the same crystal clear effect when students wrote information texts. Research by Hattie, Petty, and others who synthesized more than 500,000 studies to illuminate the factors that support increased student achievement helped us understand why our students were progressing in more dramatic ways as narrative writers than as information writers and led us to alter our approach to teaching information writing.

Hattie's research shows that students progress more quickly when they are given a crystal clear goal that they can fix their eyes on and when they receive feedback that provides them with concrete, specific next steps they can take toward that goal. We came to realize that for our students to have equal success in information writing as in narrative writing, we needed to construct an image of good information writing that, like our image of good narrative writing, could provide children with a crystal clear goal to work toward and could provide teachers with a clear image of the pathway on which children travel toward the goal of more effective informational writing. Of course, it requires some audacity to create a single image of effective information writing (when actually the genre is so wide open), but we realized that in truth, narrative writing is far more varied and complex than the prescribed template that we have taught to young kids and that there is nothing stopping us from eventually teaching writers that neither narrative nor information writing is as simple as we first teach.

This unit, then, teaches students to write in one particular template for informational writing. That template is illustrated in the mentor texts that we highlight. A handful of qualities of strong informational writing are taught with vigor and clarity, and students' progress toward producing this sort of informational writing is tracked, supported, and expected. The results have been as dramatic as the results we commonly see from units of study in narrative writing.

As with all units in this series, the unit begins by asking students to do a quick on-demand piece of writing that you can use to assess where your writers are in their trajectory of development as information writers. We detail more about this later in this introduction. For now, the important thing to say is that based on this assessment, you will be able to tweak and adjust your plan for the unit so that these sessions are a guide and not a prescription. You will also want to introduce your mentor text (or texts) that will be used throughout the unit. The ones mentioned in this book were carefully chosen to be a close matchup to the kind of writing work we are teaching third-graders, as well as to be engaging and aspirational.

While every unit in this series is Common Core State Standards aligned, this is one of half a dozen units in the series that has been directly influenced, from its conception, by the standards. The framers of the Common Core State Standards have made it clear that the standards are designed to prepare students for college and careers. One of the important ways we can prepare students for the world outside of school and for later education is to be sure that they grow up comfortable using writing as a tool to synthesize, organize, reflect on, and teach knowledge. In fact, the ability to write information texts has received a spotlight recently as the number one most desired job market skill. Unfortunately, way too many high school graduates struggle with this crucial genre. The stronger the foundation we can give to our elementary school students with these writing skills, the better prepared they will be.

In the second-grade unit on nonfiction writing, *Lab Reports and Science Books*, students learned valuable writing skills that can be built on in third grade. Second-graders spent time learning how to group information together, create simple introductions, elaborate using a few sentences for each topic, and use domain-specific vocabulary. In this third-grade unit, those skills are built on and extended, and the fourth-grade CCSS skills are introduced. In many ways, the instruction in this unit goes beyond the Common Core Standards. Because we have worked extensively with third-grade nonfiction writers and know what they can do, and are poised to learn to do with a bit of direct instruction, we couldn't resist including that skill work in this book.

There are several standards that we think are especially important to call to your attention. In this unit, you will find that Common Core Writing Standard 2, "write informative/explanatory texts to examine a topic and convey ideas and information clearly," is met in its entirety. Students will learn to write introductions, organize information, and include text features that help their readers (W.3.2.a). In fact, we would argue that third-graders are capable of more than simply grouping information together, as the standards call for, so we teach students how to *logically* organize their pieces. This skill is not required until fifth grade, but the CCSS provide no precursor work that allows students to approximate this goal, and we are convinced both that third-graders are ready for the opportunity to explore this challenging idea and also that this is work that takes a number of years before all students will achieve mastery, so we are comfortable introducing it at this point.

Students will also be taught many different ways to elaborate on their topics, not only learning to include facts, definitions, and other important details, as called for by the third-grade standards (W.3.2.b), but also reaching for the kinds of elaboration called for by the fourth-grade standards. These include concrete details, such as descriptions, and what the standards describe as "other examples," such as anecdotes (W.4.2.b). We transfer these elaboration techniques from our reading units of study, knowing that as the nonfiction texts that students read grow in difficulty, one of the areas that expands is the amount and variety of ways authors elaborate. While the Common Core asks for students to "use linking words and phrases (e.g., *also, another, and, more, but*) to connect ideas within categories of information" (W.3.2.c), we ask for more. In addition to the standard, students will learn various ways to connect paragraphs and chapters across their books, as well as ways to connect words and phrases. Teaching third-graders how to confidently use the kinds of transition words called for by the fourth-grade standards (*another, for example, also, because*) helps them aim for more sophisticated connections in their writing. This work goes hand and hand with the heavy emphasis on structure you will see throughout this unit. The unit also teaches students a few ways to provide a satisfying conclusion (W.3.3.d).

As in all of the units of the series, this unit delves into "development and organization" as students are guided through the writing process, with guidance from teachers initially (W.3.4), and then learn how to develop and organize their pieces with the maximum amount of independence possible (W.4.4). There is also an extensive amount of time spent on teaching students various strategies for "planning, revising, and editing" (W.3.5). In the final bend of the unit, when students are working on informational texts within social studies, students' work will be aligned directly with Writing Standards 7 and 8, which asks students to conduct brief research projects that build knowledge of a topic and recall information from experiences or other sources, as well as to take notes and sort that information.

Of course, this unit involves more standards than the ones included in writing. This unit also targets specific language, speaking and listening, as well as a few crucial reading information standards.

OVERVIEW OF THE UNIT

This unit, like all of the units in the series, is divided into parts, or bends, each offering a new portion of the journey. Bend I is brief in this unit. The bend opens with the assumption that students have already chosen at least the broad umbrella topic they'll be writing about during the first two bends of the unit. That's unusual, but most of your students probably have just a few topics for which they are famous, and those will be the topics students take on in this unit. There is no reason to search high and low and to take days doing so. After conveying to students that they will be writing texts that aim to teach others about topics on which the students have expertise, you will position students to write with authority, for real audiences, by inviting them to actually do some teaching on their topics. Students also learn how powerful a table of contents can be as a tool for structuring an expository piece. You then spend a few sessions teaching students to rehearse various structures, to crystalize the organization of the piece before drafting. Through this process, students learn how to heavily rely on structure in the early drafting process. They also learn ways in which the base structure of the text can also become the base structure for each fully fleshed subsection.

Bend II emphasizes drafting and revising, braided together in such a way that it is sometimes hard to tell when a writer is doing one or the other—which

is exactly the way it goes for professionals who are writing information books! Students will revise by learning concrete strategies and using those strategies to lift the level of all the work they have done to date. They will also rely on their prior knowledge, gathered in the primary grades, to improve their writing in ways they studied long ago. Many revision strategies are easy to talk about, and hard to pull off, and become increasingly challenging as the topics and texts increase in complexity. As this portion of the unit proceeds, students will merge slowly into the fast lane, learning newer, more complex revision strategies such as using grammar with meaning and tapping research for elaboration.

Bend III guides students through preparing for publication. You will emphasize the importance of being aware of one's audience. You will also want students to keep in mind the sorts of things a nonfiction author attends to while preparing for those readers: using text features, fact checking, and being aware of grammar and conventions. These, not incidentally, are skills that third-graders need to practice again and again throughout the year and across the disciplines.

During the final bend, there is a distinctive push toward independence and transference. Students will learn how they can write informatively in a variety of genres about a topic they've been studying at school. They do the work of this final bend connecting with their social studies work to further emphasize how transferable writing skills can and should be once they are learned. Students have an opportunity after publishing to teach their writing skills to younger students as their form of celebration and as a way to bring full circle the theme of teaching with which this unit opened. Throughout the entire unit, you will see a renewed commitment to grammar, vocabulary, and conventions, all carefully aligned with the Common Core State Language Standards.

ASSESSMENT

Our expectation is that at the start of the year, you will have assessed your students as information writers, and we assume their information writing has grown stronger since then, because work in one type of writing enriches what students can do in other types of writing. Also, presumably your students will have done some writing and a lot of reading of information texts outside of writing workshop, in the content areas. If you did conduct an assessment at the start of the year, you'll be able to track the progress students have made from then until now in information writing. On the other hand, this is only the second unit of the year; if you suspect that your students have not developed very much in information writing since the beginning of the year, use the on-demand writing they've already produced to orient yourself to the teaching of this unit.

If you do spend one class period conducting another on-demand information writing assessment, we recommend you use the same prompt and the same conditions as before, and the same as other teachers, so that the pieces your writers produce will be comparable. On the day before the assessment, you can let your students know that you will be conducting the assessment, so they can be prepared. Say to them:

> "Think of a topic that you've studied or that you know a lot about. Tomorrow, you will have forty-five minutes to write an informational (or all-about) text that teaches others interesting and important information and ideas about that topic. If you want to find and use information from a book or another outside source to help you with this writing, you may bring that with you tomorrow. Please keep in mind that you'll have only forty-five minutes to complete this. You will have only this one period, so you'll need to plan, draft, revise, and edit in one sitting. Write in a way that shows all that you know about information writing."

Of course, you'll say this again, right before the assessment, and then you'll provide forty-five minutes for writing. Don't worry if your students do not bring source information. They do not need to do so to be at standard for fourth grade. This clause (and some others like it) is part of the prompt simply because the prompt needs to be consistent for K–8 students, and some portions of the prompt become important for middle school students. When students actually do the on-demand writing, you will want to add:

> "In your writing, make sure you:
> - Write an introduction
> - Elaborate with a variety of information
> - Organize your writing
> - Use transition words
> - Write a conclusion"

Once your students have completed this task, you'll want to use the information writing checklists to study their work. At this point in the year, you will expect to see that most of your students demonstrate that they have mastered most of the big work of the second-grade expectations outlined by the checklists and the second-grade Common Core State Standards and some of the third-grade standards as well. If your students are performing solidly at the second-grade level, that should not be a cause for concern.

If your students are, for the most part, doing work that is more closely aligned to the first-grade standards, level 1 of the Information Writing Learning Progression, you may want to teach another information writing unit prior to embarking on this one. The *If . . . Then . . . Curriculum* book provides options.

Most teachers who have done the on-demand assessment have been pleasantly surprised by how much students bring into this unit of study and by the volume of writing students are able to produce in just one day's writing workshop. The work that students produce in the on-demand situation becomes the baseline, and you can increase expectations as the unit progresses.

Early on, we recommend that you introduce your class to the checklists that they will use to study their work throughout the unit. From the other units of study, your third-graders will already be familiar with how to use these checklists. By providing this opportunity to preview what will be expected of them, you allow your students to begin to visualize final products and to reach for lofty goals right from the start. You may even take some class time for your students to study their on-demand writing with the checklist in hand and to set a few preliminary goals for their work. Throughout the unit, you will channel students to study their work, thus providing them the opportunity to celebrate their progress and set new goals to ensure they are continually outgrowing themselves as writers.

GETTING READY

This unit is centered on a particular type of information writing—a structured, written-to-teach, expert-based project. In one earlier incarnation of this unit, some teachers took to calling these texts "all-about" books. That is not exactly right, because this unit does call on students to choose a narrowed and structured focus on a topic and not simply write all about the topic in broad strokes. As you prepare for this unit, you will want to consider gathering a stack of information books and texts that will help familiarize you with the type of writing you are about to embark on teaching, as well as help you to crystallize the goals you will have for yourself and your teaching. We have found a few book series particularly helpful when doing this work: National Geographic for Kids, Sports Illustrated for Kids, and the ever-popular DK Readers (especially the early chapter book varieties). We also suggest you dig through unexpected places, such as your math, science, and social studies materials. Frequently there are hidden gems tucked within the piles of texts that would be perfect.

Additionally, once you have found a small stack you are particularly fond of and plan to use when exposing your students to the genre, we suggest you choose one favorite book that will become the class touchstone text. You and your students will return to this text again and again throughout the unit. We chose *Dangerous Animals* by Melissa Stewart as the touchstone text for this book. It is a text with a strong and clear structure and a variety of writing craft moves and is highly engaging for students.

You will also note that the theme of teaching and informing runs throughout this unit. You might want to watch some nightly news shows, a TED talk online, or observe a gifted colleague as he teaches, to try to wrap your hands a bit around what skills a great teacher employs and which ones you value. This time spent focused on the art of teaching will not only pay big dividends in terms of making this unit richer and more compelling for you, but it will also likely make you more reflective of your own teaching.

Lastly, carve out some time to work on your own information book, a text that will serve as a demonstration text for your students throughout the unit. Choose a topic on which you feel you are an expert. No topic is too small or too esoteric. Refrain from falling into the trap of saying you are not an expert on anything. What are your passions? Hobbies? Obsessions? What do people always ask you about? If you still are struggling to think of a suitable topic for your demonstration piece, think of something you are involved with, somewhere you go, or something you do all the time that your students are likely to be intrigued by. We chose the topic of cockroaches in part because we have developed a good amount of expert knowledge throughout the years, living and working in New York City. We also know that students all over the world are enthralled by the topic, helping to make this an even more engaging unit. Feel free to borrow that topic if you are still at a loss, or else be inspired by it. Perhaps lice is more your area of expertise? Chocolate ice cream? School supplies? No matter what topic you eventually choose, give yourself some time to explore it in writing. Perhaps try the first few sessions in the book one afternoon, or better still, form a writing group with some grade colleagues and carve out some time to write in the company of others.

Teaching Others as a Way to Prime the Pump

IN THIS SESSION, you'll help children think of information writers as teachers. You'll teach them that information writers organize information as they write, like organizing for teaching a course.

GETTING READY

✔ Baton (or pencil) to conduct the symphony share (see Connection)

✔ Your own topic, with several subtopics in mind, to demonstrate using your fingers as graphic organizers. Be prepared to develop a couple subtopics. (see Teaching)

✔ "Teaching Moves that Information Writers Should Borrow" chart, with heading prewritten (see Share)

✔ Chart paper and markers

✔ Students' writing notebooks and pens or pencils

COMMON CORE STATE STANDARDS: W.3.2.a,b, W.3.4, W.3.5, W.3.8, W.3.10, W.4.2.a,b, RI.3.3, SL.3.1, SL 3.3, SL 3.4, SL.3.6, L.3.1, L.3.2, L.3.3, L.3.6

EVERY YEAR, TEACHERS COLLEGE SUPPORTS a new group of student teachers. I spend a lot of time talking to these fledgling teachers about the children they teach, and less time talking to them about themselves. But the other night, I asked them, "How do you like teaching?"

The student teachers talked about the mental and physical exhaustion, about the thrill of engaging with children in ways that made a palpable difference, but above all, they talked about the effect teaching was having on the rest of their lives. "I think about teaching all the time," one said, and others agreed. "I'll be out at a restaurant, or at a show, or reading the newspaper, and I find myself thinking, 'I need to bring that to my kids.'" For these student teachers, the new role they've been given changes their perspective on everything.

And isn't—or wasn't—it that way for all of us? Have we begun to take for granted the transformational power of teaching? Listening to those students, I felt as if they were articulating something I'd almost forgotten. On the topics that I teach, I am a magnet; any related information sticks to me. When I know I'll be teaching a class on a topic, I become a powerful learner. "We are the teaching species," Erik Erikson has written. "Human beings need to teach . . . because facts are kept alive by being shared, truths by being professed." Erikson is right. We need to teach.

What I sometimes forget is that my students are also part of the teaching species. They, too, need to keep ideas alive by teaching those ideas. Perhaps the most powerful thing about nonfiction writing is that it allows students to become teachers—claiming, developing, and sharing what they know.

And in learning what my students know, I give them faces and voices. Don Graves, credited as the man who ignited reform in the teaching of writing, once suggested that a competency test for teachers of writing should be to ask each teacher to list the names of his or her students, and alongside those names, to record four or five topics on which that child is an expert. Harold Rosen has often said, "Every child has a story to tell. The question is, 'Will they tell it to you?' But I think we can also say, 'Every child has lessons to teach. The question is, 'Will they teach those lessons to you?'"

In this unit of study, you'll give students the processes and skills necessary to write information texts that meet the demands of the Common Core State Standards. To allow students to focus on the demanding work of organizing their information, linking diverse bits of information, synthesizing information and ideas, using domain-specific vocabulary, and above all, writing in ways that instruct readers, this unit asks them to write about topics on which they already have some expertise.

"Have we begun to take for granted the transformational power of teaching?"

Today's session assumes that you have already helped each student settle on a topic (a terrain, an area) in which he or she has special expertise, although students may not yet have mined those areas of expertise for more focused topics. Today you will teach your students that writers of information texts often rehearse for writing by teaching others about a topic. You will not worry about helping students divide their topics into subtopics; you won't fret over whether they organize information into neat chapters. Instead, you will help them understand that they have content to teach and the skills with which to teach that content. We hope this session allows you to communicate to children that writers of information books are teachers, trying to convey big ideas and important information to readers.

Teaching Others as a Way to Prime the Pump

CONNECTION

Launch the new unit by recruiting children to call out the topic they have chosen for their informational book as they participate in a "symphony share."

"Writers, today is a very exciting day because we are ready to begin writing our information books. I know that even before today, you have chosen topics that you will be writing about. Let's begin by celebrating those topics. I'll be the conductor of a symphony, you be the instruments, and when I tip my baton your way, will you simply say, loud and clear, the expert topic you've chosen? For this to work, you can't waffle. You can't say, 'Well, maybe this, but then again, maybe . . .' So take a second and crystallize your topic, getting ready to sing it out."

I stood tall, arms raised, like the conductor with a baton, signaling for children to sit up and give me their utmost attention. With a flourish, I tipped my baton at one child, another, and another.

"The Yankees."
"Cocker spaniels."
"Video games."
"Recycling."

After hearing from half the class, I added an ending, saying, "Expert topics, Room 203." Then I added, "All weekend, I kept asking myself, 'What is a way to begin this unit that is worthy of you and of the expertise you already have on your topics? What are the most important things I can teach?'"

❖ **Name the teaching point.**

"This is what I need you to know. Information writers are teachers. When you write an information book, you are teaching a unit of study on your topic, and it helps to rehearse by *actually* teaching real students, watching to see which information especially matters to them."

All the beginning of this book, I suggested that you prepare for the unit by asking students to think about the topics on which they have expertise so they can start this unit with topics in hand. This shouldn't be too hard because hopefully the kids will plan to write on the topics for which they are famous. The goal, for now, is for them to approach this unit with a subject in hand.

Notice that some of these topics are ones that could fit into a curriculum, and many are more personal interest topics. You can, of course, channel some students toward topics that you think will have curricular implications as well as being high-interest topics—volcanoes, the pyramids, hurricanes—but we suggest that you make peace with the fact that this unit is going to carry an enormous cargo of skills. The truth is that you'll be able to move kids' skill development along more if they are deeply engaged in their topics and if they have personal experience and firsthand knowledge to draw upon.

TEACHING

Explain that today's writing workshop will be unusual, with children teaching each other about their topics rather than writing.

"Today, instead of *writing* about your topic, you'll teach (or make plans to teach) others about that topic. Instead of a usual minilesson, you'll spread out to all corners of the room to teach and to attend classes on baseball and cockroaches, curly hair and New Orleans."

Demonstrate how you go about teaching a topic, using your fingers as the graphic organizers to help you structure a list of subtopics, one of which you then develop as an example of how to do this.

"I'll show you a bit about how I go about teaching, in hopes that this will help you do some teaching on your own topic. Like many of you, I was torn between several topics, but in the end, I decided to write about something I feel passionate about—cockroaches.

"Writers, watch me as I get ready to teach you about my expert topic. As you watch, notice things I do as a teacher that could also be things that all of you do as writers. I think you'll find that teaching about a topic and writing about a topic are very much the same."

Switching into the role of writer, I mused, "Hmm, so, let me plan first. Let me think of some big things I know about cockroaches, some things I could say a bunch about. First, I'll teach that," I touched one finger, "cockroaches are the oldest species still living on Earth."

As I listed subtopics, I located each on a different finger and essentially "talked across my fingers."

- ◆ Cockroaches are the oldest species still living on Earth.

- ◆ Cockroaches can cause lots of health problems.

- ◆ Cockroaches have bodies that make it easy for them to survive.

- ◆ Cockroaches are very hard to kill.

- ◆ Cockroach infestations can be prevented.

"Let me tell you a bit more about each of these now. I'm not going to write it for now, just say it. Hmm, let me think of an important point I can make about the first subtopic ('Cockroaches are the oldest species still living on Earth.') and some details or thoughts to fill out that point. Hmm."

The predictability of minilessons means that students expect a day's writing time to unfold as other days have unfolded. If you plan to break with that pattern, it is helpful to give students a heads up.

You will notice that each of my bullet points could be thought of as a different subcategory of the overall topic and could conceivably be turned into its own chapter. Children who understand the way information books are structured will see and emulate this. Others, those with less sophistication in the genre, may think you have listed facts on your topic, and that is what they will do—list fact upon fact, with no effort to distinguish categories of information. Don't fret about this. In the days ahead, there will be plenty of time for you to teach children to categorize. Today the most important goal is for children to feel what it is to teach others all about a topic.

Cockroaches are the oldest species still living on Earth. I know that scientists think they are over 350 million years old. That means they were on earth almost 300 million years before dinosaurs. That's pretty amazing to think about. Why do so many kids study dinosaurs when cockroaches were here on Earth long before dinosaurs—<u>and</u> they are still alive!

Debrief to highlight the main things you hope students take from your demonstration.

"Writers, did you see that I named the important things I'd teach across my fingers? And when I taught, I first told people a main point I'd teach? Then I filled in some more details or thoughts about that main point?"

ACTIVE ENGAGEMENT

Set children up to teach their partners the topics they have chosen, reminding them to divide their topic into subtopics and to fill in details and thoughts about a subtopic.

"Before you go off to teach, let's try a little of this work here and now. Right now, today, Partner 1 is going to be the teacher-writer. And Partner 2, you'll want to plan your teaching too, though you might not have time to do it today. Partner 1, get ready to use your fingers to plan some of the most important information you might want to teach others about your topic." I left a pool of silence for those children to begin this work. As they thought, I whispered, "Partner 2s, in your mind, think about what subtopics you'd teach if you had the chance to do so." Again I left a little bit of silence.

"Partner 1, would you share your teaching plans with Partner 2? Use your fingers as you go over parts of your topic. Partner 2, as you listen, get ready to give Partner 1 some feedback on his or her plan."

Actively listen to students work with their partners, coaching as needed, and then share overheard comments.

As the students talked through their teaching plans with their partners, I listened in, taking note of the comments they were making that I wanted to highlight as examples for other students, as well as coaching students whose comments were a little off track and needed to be nudged closer to my expectations.

"I listened in as Kayla talked with her partner about babysitting. She was thinking she'd teach about babysitting and that she would talk about different things babysitters do: feeding, playing, putting the baby to bed. I also heard Frank, and he was talking about something completely different. You can probably imagine what it was! Frank wants to teach all of us about dragons! He has planned parts of his topic, and they are the parts of the dragon: wings, tail, fire-breathing mouth, and so on."

Of course, in this minilesson, you are doing exactly the same thing—naming what you'll teach, filling in details and thoughts pertaining to the main point. Every quality of good information writing should also be a quality of good minilessons.

As this minilesson unfolds, you'll see lots of places where you could embed some specific teaching tips. For example, you could coach Partner 2 on some of the sorts of suggestions they might make today. Resist the temptation to load up every portion of this minilesson with a lot of tiny tips. The point really is for youngsters to do the big work of planning and teaching their topics. Most of the smaller tips you find yourself wanting to make will become major points in the days ahead. For now, let a lot of less than ideal approximations be good enough.

You are highlighting the subtopics within your children's topics because you will soon ask them to plan their subtopics. This is less casual than it seems.

LINK

Divide the class into fourths, channeling them to sit with their groups in the four corners of the room. In each group, first one, then another child will teach his or her topic.

Speaking to the children, I convened their attention. "Teachers," I said, waiting for the new title to register. "In a moment you will disperse to the four corners of the classroom." I walked a mid-line through the group of children sitting in front of me, dividing the group into right and left halves, making sure partnerships stayed intact, and then used the same method to divide the halves into front and back quarters. I then assigned each quarter of the children to a corner of the classroom. "When you meet in your corner, will one of the Partner 1s agree to teach the *whole group*? Partner 2s, will you listen to the teaching so that you can give some feedback on it? Remember how I divided my subject into parts and used one finger for each part. Also remember that for each part, I named a big point or two, then filled in some more details and thoughts. After one person teaches, a Partner 2 can give some feedback, and then another Partner 1 can take a turn.

"I know I'm leaving lots of decisions in your hands, but you guys can handle it. Off you go!"

The teaching work that you are instigating will occupy time usually reserved for writing. Today is reserved for writing aloud, writing-in-the-air, and so it is highly unusual in that way.

Helping Children Become Powerful Teachers and Listeners

TODAY YOUR STUDENTS WILL ALL BE BUSY TEACHING EACH OTHER. They won't write at all. So what do you do? Twiddle your thumbs? Not on your life!

For starters, you'll need to do some critical orchestrating. You'll probably want to set things up so that in each corner of the classroom, the child who is teaching other children is given a special seat—a place of honor—at the front of the group. You'll want to encourage those writers to wait until the group is attentive before beginning. The fact that children are teaching each other will assume more importance if there is some drumroll around the teaching. If you happen to be at a child's side when the child prepares to teach other children, you can coach that child to remember to plan out the points he or she will make, to register those points on fingers, and when teaching, to plan ways to elaborate on each point. Then again, if you are listening as a child actually teaches a small group of peers, you can coach in various ways that remind that speaker that he or she can say more by using one of several thought prompts to prime the pump.

> Another thing I know is . . .
>
> Another important idea is . . .
>
> For example . . .
>
> This is interesting because . . .

If you listen in while one child teaches a small group, chances are good that the listeners will benefit from being reminded to listen in more helpful ways. You might say, "Listen in such a way that you can give the writer feedback on what works and doesn't work about the teaching. Notice moves that the teacher makes that writers, too, could make." To a group of listeners, you might whisper, "Did you notice how he said, 'You are probably wondering . . .' and then he answered questions he thought we might have? That was a totally awesome move, and something that writers do as well."

MID-WORKSHOP TEACHING **Using Your Teaching as a Rough Draft and a Source for Insight about This Genre**

"Guys, can I interrupt your classes for just a minute?" I waited. "I want to make a few points, and then I'll let you continue. First, remember that earlier this year when you said your *narratives* aloud, you did that to revise your writing? You said the same story aloud a bunch of times, thinking how you could go from summarizing what happened to actually letting it unroll like a movie in your mind, using dialogue and thoughts and actions to show it, not tell it.

"You need to be thinking, in the same way, about how teaching your topic can be a way to draft and revise how your books might go. The whole point of doing this teaching is to listen to yourself doing it and to think, 'No, that's not the best way to begin,' or 'That really works well. I should write it just that way!'

"So before you go on, talk over the teaching you have heard. Start with the most recent teaching. And think of that teaching as a rough draft. The writer-teacher needs to ask, 'Do you feel like this topic and this way of teaching it will work as an information book?' And listeners, talk over what you felt about the teaching. What did the teacher say or do that was especially interesting or that really helped you learn about the topic? What suggestions do you have? You can decide whether you finish some teaching first, then talk, or whether you talk right away. Go!"

As part of your efforts to orchestrate, you may need to signal to a child that he or she should end in another minute so that others have a chance to teach. Don't expect, however, that everyone will get a turn instructing others. That won't happen, and frankly, it needn't happen. Children will learn almost as much from listening to a classmate's instruction as from assuming the role of teacher.

Although all of this orchestration will be important, above all, you'll want to listen in ways that allow you to help youngsters figure out ways to teach successfully, because that will help them write successfully as well.

Think about it for a moment. Think about times when a principal or a staff developer or a mentor teacher observed your teaching and then later gave you feedback. My hunch is that the feedback that meant the world to you came when a mentor saw potential in you that you'd never seen in yourself and then helped you see and reach for horizons you wouldn't have considered had it not been for that support. So my suggestion is that you listen to a child teach on a subject, knowing that your listening establishes a tone in the classroom and lures others to listen as well. If you lean forward, eyes intent on the child, listening with your entire mind, the child who receives this attention from you will want to write. In *If You Want to Write*, Brenda Ueland (2010) points out that "all people who want to write become anxious, timid, contracted, become perfectionists, so terribly afraid . . . " She writes,

> No wonder you don't write . . . For when you write, if it is to be any good at all, you must feel free—free and not anxious. The only good teachers for you are those friends who love you, who think you are interesting, or very important, or wonderfully funny; whose attitude is "Tell me more. Tell me all you can. I want to understand more about everything you feel and know . . . Let more come out."

> And if you have no such friend, and you want to write, well then you must imagine one.

Listen not only so that the child knows his topic is interesting, but also so that you can later steer the child in ways that make the writing far better. Front-end revision is especially powerful. Try to hear the heartbeat, the center of gravity for that child. What could you imagine the child might do to use and build upon whatever it is that the child seems to know and care about the most? Can *you* imagine a focus or a structure that might work for the child? Take good notes, and then later, perhaps long after writing time is over, catch a minute with the child and convey your sense of possibility.

You might, for example, say something like "You know so much about swimming—and unusual things, too. Did you feel the way the kids were leaning in to listen when you talked about the butterfly stroke? You were practically acting it out, and I actually saw some of the kids trying to do that too. My only suggestion is that you think about focusing your book not on everything about swimming but on one subtopic. You could write just about swimming games or just about the strokes or even one stroke—how to do it, the history, the best swimmers for that stroke. Of course, what you focus on is your choice, but focusing is almost always a way to allow yourself to be more detailed, and it was your details that worked especially today."

Writing Long to Record Teaching

Bring the teaching to a close—in time for a share session that is longer than usual. Channel children to chart moves they made while teaching their topics. These are moves writers as well as teachers might make.

"Writers, I know that only a few of you have had a chance to teach each other, but the truth is that most writers don't actually get ready for writing by teaching real people their topics. Writers are more apt to *imagine* themselves teaching, to teach in their minds, than to actually have a chance to do this.

"Earlier, you gave each other feedback about what worked well, and what didn't work as well, when you were teaching. I overheard you saying some important things. Here is a big idea. Your feedback on teaching is especially important because the things that work for teachers are also things that work for writers. You'll see that I've made a giant chart: 'Teaching Moves that Information Writers Should Borrow.' I'm going to leave some markers here beside this chart, and throughout today, when you have a moment, add suggestions you come up with, or your group comes up with, for moves that teachers made that could also be moves writers make."

Teaching Moves that Information Writers Should Borrow

- Explain what your whole book will be about.
- Tell a bit about the big things you'll teach (kind of like a table of contents!).
- Try to say at least a few sentences about each part of your topic.
- Talk like an expert.
- Use fancy words and explain what they mean.
- Use your hands and your body or make quick sketches to show what things look like.

Ask children to write long on their topics, filling pages with all they know. Explain the value of a throwaway draft.

"While you mull over items that might go on this chart—and any of you can add an item anytime today—I want to teach you one other way that writers of information texts get ready to write. Writers often write long. Writers write long about a topic, filling pages with everything the writer knows. Writers do this as a way to see all the material they have, to sort through it and to come up with ways to put the material together.

"So take the remaining seven minutes of our workshop, and instead of teaching about your topic, write about it, in just the way you would teach about it. This is a throwaway draft just for yourself, where you throw onto the page everything you can remember about your topic. Go!"

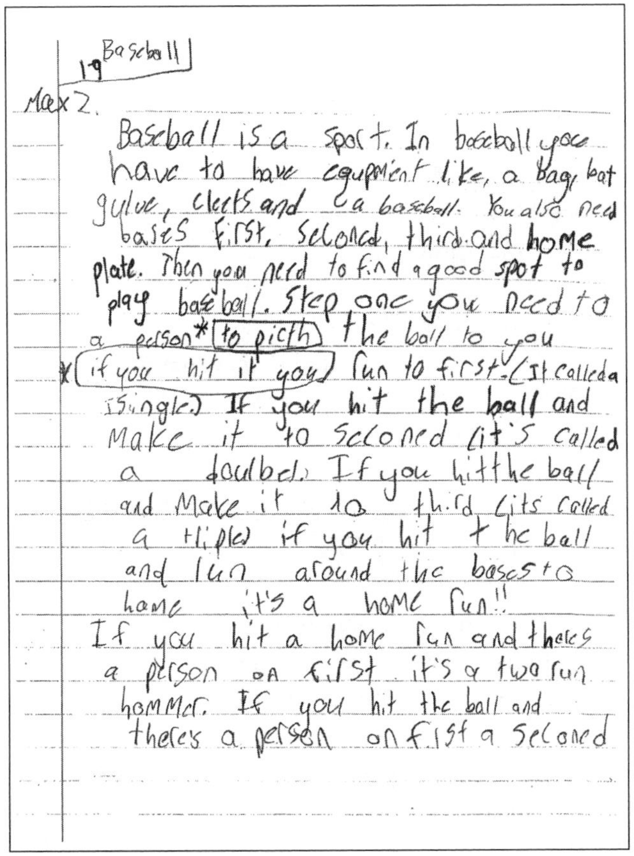

Baseball

Max 2.

Baseball is a sport. In baseball you have to have equipment like, a bag, bat gulve, cleets and a baseball. You also need bases first, seconed, third and home plate. Then you need to find a good spot to play baseball. Step one you need to a person* to picth the ball to you *if you hit it you run to first. (It called a single.) If you hit the ball and make it to seconed it's called a doubel. If you hit the ball and make it to third its called a tripled if you hit the ball and run around the bases to home it's a home run!! If you hit a home run and there's a person on first it's a two run hommer. If you hit the ball and there's a person on first a seconed

FIG. 1–1 Max works on his throwaway draft.

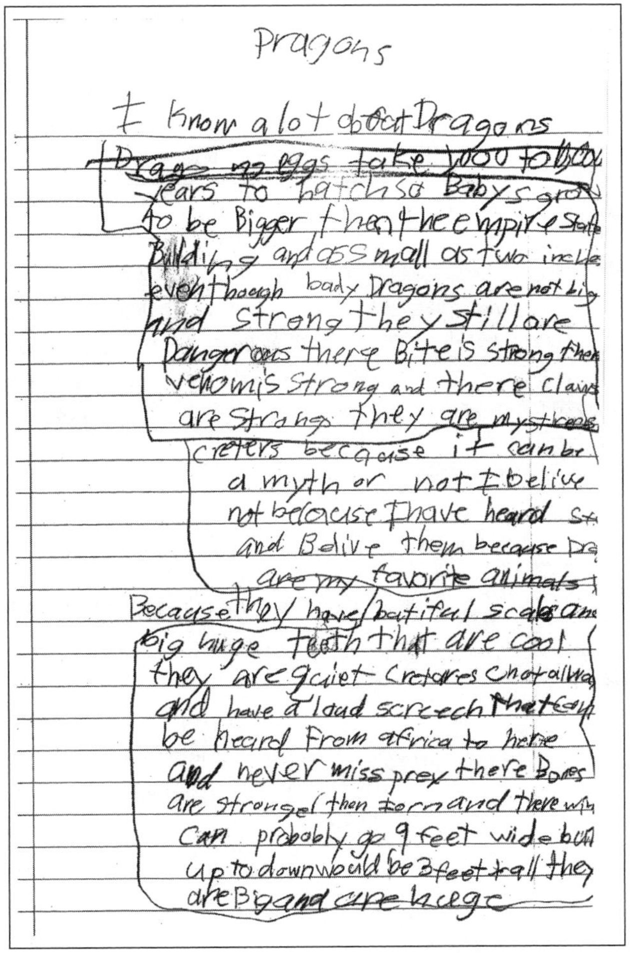

Dragons

I know alot about Dragons

~~Dragons eggs take 1000 to 1000~~ years to hatch so Babys grow to be Bigger then the empire State Building and as small as two inches even though baby Dragons are not big and strong they still are Dangerous there Bite is strong there venom is strong and there claws are strong. They are mystreous creters because it can be a myth or not I belive not because I have heard st and Belive them because Dragons are my favorite animals Because they have beatiful scales and big huge teeth that are cool they are quiet creatures that allways and have a loud screech that can be heard from africa to here and never miss prey there Bones are stronger then iron and there wings can probably go 9 feet wide but up to down would be 3 feet tall they are Big and are huge

FIG. 1–2 Frank shares his expert topic—dragons.

The Power of Organizing and Reorganizing

IN THIS SESSION, you'll teach children that writers often brainstorm several different ways to organize their information writing. You'll suggest different ways writers structure subtopics and explain that doing this is an important part of planning.

GETTING READY

✔ Your own writing in your writer's notebook, based on yesterday's topic, written without an organizational structure (see Connection)

✔ Two different organizational structures for your topic, for example, kinds, ways, examples, parts (see Teaching)

✔ Table of contents pages on each writing table or in the writing center (see Link)

✔ Mentor text with an interesting table of contents, such as *Deadliest Animals* (see Conferring and Small-Group Work)

✔ A table of contents for your topic, organized in a logical sequence (see Mid-Workshop Teaching)

✔ "Strong Tables of Contents" chart, prewritten (see Share)

COMMON CORE STATE STANDARDS: W.3.2.a,b, W.3.4, W.3.5, W.3.10, W.4.2.a,b, RI.3.2, RI.3.4, RI.3.8, SL.3.1, L.3.1, L.3.2, L.3.3, L.3.6

WHEN PLANNING K–5 UNITS ON INFORMATION WRITING, my colleagues and I thought long and hard about what the focus of the unit at particular grade levels would be. We know that children will be engaged in information writing every year throughout their schooling. Rather than trying to teach every aspect of information writing repeatedly, year after year after year, it was important to us to think carefully about the big goals we wanted to highlight in each grade.

The Common Core State Standards do not offer a lot of guidance on this topic because the expectations for information writing are very low for grades K–3 and then rise precipitously starting in grade 4 and, especially, grade 5. I believe—and the entire staff of the Teachers College Reading and Writing Project believes—that the Common Core vastly underestimates what K–3 youngsters can do within this genre. Furthermore, we believe that for students to be prepared for the ambitious information writing expectations they'll encounter in middle school, it is imperative that in the K–3 grades we teach toward an image of information writing that far exceeds that represented in the Common Core.

Most of all, we are concerned that children cannot wait until fifth grade before being introduced to the idea that information texts should have a logical structure. It is no small thing for a writer to discern the possible infrastructure that underlies a body of knowledge. We are convinced that children need several years to wrestle with this challenging concept if they are all going to master this by the time they are fifth-graders. For this reason, you'll see that this unit highlights organization and structure.

The unit assumes that children entering third grade have already been taught to focus on a topic and to make sure that the information they include in their writing all pertains to that focal subject. That is, prior to now, children will have been taught to reread their writing and notice that their book on hamsters has a whole section on summer vacation in it. Children have already learned that when they spot such a thing, they think, "Oh no!" and delete that section unless they want to give their book a more inclusive title. The *new* work of this unit revolves around developing subsections that are parallel, one to another, and that are logical, reflecting the structure of the content. A book about the history of a baseball team probably would be organized in a then-to-now fashion. A book comparing two teams should probably contain a chapter on ways the teams are the same and a chapter on ways the teams are different.

"Writers who do not worry about structure remind me of carpenters who build a home thinking about window shades and not foundations."

More than this, the unit emphasizes the importance of revising one's plans for a book, suggesting that one of the most important ways to revise is to consider alternative structures. Of course, structure is important in every unit, every year. Writers who do not worry about structure remind me of carpenters who build a home thinking about window shades and not foundations. This unit emphasizes the importance of structure more than it emphasizes the importance of research, citations, critical reading, and the like. Those will become important goals in the fourth-grade information unit, *Bringing History to Life*. For now, the message is that before doing anything else, a writer needs to build a sound structure; that structure then allows the writer to elaborate without the text becoming a swamp.

It is not a small thing to teach youngsters to write in ways that use expository structures. Imagine that you were asked to write about the literacy curriculum at your school. How would you structure that text? It's a complex question. Any subject that a person knows well ends up containing parts that are all tangled up together. One writer described a subject as resembling the clothes inside a dryer. Each item is wound up with everything else, and one can grab at a loose end, but things don't separate easily or fall into neat piles.

Although the work of today's lesson is complicated, the actual lesson is not hard to teach. It is, however, hard to do, hard to pull off. And the hard part is not the volume of writing that children are expected to produce. In fact, the sum total of writing they do today is pretty limited. After all, you are simply asking children to write a few different versions of a table of contents. The hard part is helping children fly above the terrain of a topic like an airplane flies above the earth, allowing for a bird's-eye perspective. You will teach children that when looking at their topics to consider ways to subdivide them, it's helpful if they can be flexible. "Could I divide my topic into parts by thinking about different ways? Times?" a child can ask. If the topic is baseball, dividing that topic into kinds of baseball won't yield many ideas, but dividing the topic into kinds of plays or kinds of equipment might. Then again, the same topic—baseball—could be divided into *ways*: ways to be a strong team or ways to win every game.

Today, then, help children to be flexible and to resist the urge to begin writing their chapters without planning. Encourage children to imagine the multitude of ways their books might go. And perhaps the greatest challenge of all for you in this session will be to resist the urge, no matter how tempting it might be, to simply tell your students the structures that you believe are best for a particular book. So much of what makes a writer strong, not just in grade school, but her whole life through, is the ability to envision a variety of structures her work can take and then to choose and implement one of those structures.

The Power of Organizing and Reorganizing

CONNECTION

Read a snippet of the writing you did during yesterday's share, choosing a passage that contains many possible subtopics and ways to organize the information.

"Like you all, I grabbed my pen yesterday and started writing everything I know about my topic. I didn't worry about the order of my information or if things sounded perfect. Instead, I just recorded everything that came to my mind. This is part of what I wrote." I revealed this, written on chart paper.

> Cockroaches live almost everywhere in North America. They are hardy insects that live well with people because they have adapted over time to diets made of human food and objects. For example cockroaches eat paper, glue, fruit, and French fries–to name just a few things. People try to get rid of cockroaches all the time. They try traps, poison, cleaning, storing food differently. Because of their bodies, cockroaches are very hard to kill. They can live for two weeks without their heads!

"But here is the thing. As I was writing all that stuff down, and especially now as I reread what I have written (which is a lot longer than that), I find myself thinking about smaller topics within the large one. Like, I have been thinking that I might want my whole book to be about cockroaches' incredible bodies. Or I might want to write a whole book about ways people try to kill cockroaches—what works and what doesn't work. Or maybe a book about the history of cockroaches."

❖ **Name the teaching point.**

"Today I want to teach you that information writers often make plans for how to organize their information writing. Writers make one plan, then they think about a different possible plan, and they keep doing this over and over. Each plan includes a different way to divide a topic into parts."

The topic—cockroaches—weaves throughout most of this book. You can absolutely write on your own topic instead, but make sure you understand that doing so will require you to comb that new topic through many upcoming sessions, which means that you will need to read ahead because sometimes we deliberately "mess up" so that later we can address the issue in a minilesson. You may want to save your energy for responding to student work, keeping records of what students do, reading their drafts, and so on. But, of course, it's spectacular to use your own writing instead of ours.

TEACHING

Demonstrate, using your hand as a graphic organizer, considering several ways your book could be structured. Perhaps list different kinds and then list different ways.

"Let me show you how I try this out with my topic, cockroaches. I'm going to use my hand to plan my subtopics. (A writer doesn't need fancy graphic organizer sheets to make writing plans; a hand will do just fine!) My topic is cockroaches, so I'm going to touch my palm and say, 'kinds of cockroaches,' and then plan *kinds* of cockroaches across my fingers." Using my hand, I proposed the categories.

Kinds of Cockroaches

- German cockroaches (these are the ones everyone knows about)
- American cockroaches
- Madagascar hissing cockroaches
- Termites (I know–people forget they are cockroaches too!)

"But remember, the important thing to realize is that I could organize a cockroach book in lots of different ways, and it is wise to try one way, another, and another. Before, I mentioned I could organize my book into ways to get rid of cockroaches. Let me try that."

Ways to Get Rid of Cockroaches

- Traps
- Poison
- Environmentally friendly
- Prevention (to keep the cockroaches from ever getting into your home in the first place!)

Debrief to highlight the work that could be replicated with another topic, on another day.

"Did you notice what I did? Using my hand, I thought of smaller parts—subtopics—that go with my bigger topic. When I came up with a subtopic, I made a list of all the points or categories that fall under that subtopic. I could have also tried other ways, like listing parts, kinds, famous examples. The possibilities are endless!"

If your students have grown up within these units of study, they'll be accustomed to planning across their fingers, so you can glide past this extra quickly, emphasizing instead the particulars of your various plans.

As I teach this, I want to convey that the construction of the text will follow a plan. The frame needs to be just right before the materials can be added in. Fixing the structure now is much, much easier than trying to revise a nearly complete draft.

ACTIVE ENGAGEMENT

Channel students to consider alternative ways to divide up their topics, coaching them to generate parallel topics illustrating ways, kinds, examples, or parts.

"Writers, right now you can try this strategy with your own topics. Like me, you wrote long and strong about your topic yesterday, and you probably already looked over what you wrote to think about a way to divide your topic. But here is a hint. It wouldn't really have worked if I had just *one* kind of cockroach in Chapter 1, and just *one* way of killing in Chapter 2, and *one* part of history in Chapter 3. Readers look to see that you have at least a couple of chapters that go together in a way—like four chapters on the kinds of cockroaches, each telling about a different kind of cockroach, or three chapters on ways to kill cockroaches, each telling about a different way. That is, it is usually helpful to have an overall way to organize at least parts of the book.

"So keep in mind the ideas you already had for how your book could be divided up, but let's try out some other possible ways you *could* organize your topic. Let's start with *kinds*. Work with your partner, trying to see if you can plan a book on your topic, across your fingers, with each chapter being a different kind. Partner 1, go ahead."

I listened in as Vitaly talked to Anisa. "For my book on colors," Anisa said, "I could write chapters on the different *kinds* of colors. There's primary colors and secondary colors."

"How about other kinds of colors?" Anisa coached. "Do you know about any other kinds?" I called the children back together.

"Now try organizing your topic so you divide it into totally different parts. Like, if the topic is soccer, it could be different parts of a soccer field, or parts of the team, or parts of the game. You choose one. Partner 2s, are you ready? Say aloud one way your book could be divided into parts."

LINK

Let students know that they will most likely want to put tables of contents on paper.

"Today, writers, you'll probably want to move from thinking through possible structures on your hands to doing this on paper. I've put table of contents pages in the center of each of your tables, and I suggest you make a bunch of possible tables of contents. Once you have one that looks possible to you, try saying aloud what you'd write in each of the chapters to make sure you have content for each chapter and that the plan would allow you to write the things you really want to write. You'll probably want to jot some notes, too, about what sorts of information you'd put into each chapter. I've left an example them a student who did that work on your tables as well."

This is information that most adults could profit from understanding. Annie Dillard once said that when writing, it is a problem if you have a whole lot of Christmas tree ornaments and no Christmas tree. We've thought of that advice often when drafting these units of study. It is helpful to kids if a few sessions fit together as variations on a theme rather than each one being an isolated tip. Readers won't be able to get their mental arms around too many loose unrelated tips. In the same fashion, information writing is better if the text is sectioned into parts that have some cohesion.

When you listen in, you are checking on children's comprehension and preparing to offer more support, if needed. For example, if the partners I'd overheard were silent, as if stumped by the question, I might have grabbed any examples I did hear and broadcast those as a way to prime the pump. "So Rufus just said that in his book about cars, he could add makers—Toyota, Ford—or categories like sports cars and SUVs." A little move like that can provide a leg up for some who need it.

If you've noticed there aren't as many alternatives as usual suggested in this link, then you are becoming a discerning critic of workshop teaching. Sometimes, early in a unit, there hasn't yet been enough teaching or enough work for there to be lots of viable alternatives in play.

Plan Ways to Channel Students to Revise Now

ON ANY GIVEN DAY, IT'S HELPFUL TO HAVE IN MIND a few of the main things you might want to look for as you assess your students' work. Revision that occurs early in the writing process and sets writers up for productivity is very important if students are going to encounter success with subsequent work, so you'll probably want to check on whether students are already revising or whether some of them are still thinking that revision only occurs once the piece of writing has been written.

(continues)

MID-WORKSHOP TEACHING **Considering Whether Your Book Has a Logical Structure**

"Writers, many of you have planned a table of contents and started to jot some of the information you'll put into each of your chapters. Before you get too committed to whatever plan you've got going, I want to emphasize that as soon as you have begun to settle on a plan for how your writing will go—you will want to *revise* that plan! Some of you used to think about revision as something that happens late in the process of writing, after you had written a whole draft, but actually, the most powerful revision is the revision you do at the start of writing. Strong writers revise right from the start. When writers do that, they not only save themselves from doing more work later, but they also start with stronger pieces so everything that comes after the beginning is stronger, too.

"Specifically, there is one question you need to ask yourself as you look over your table of contents. So please choose your best table of contents and get ready for the one question. I waited. Here is the question you need to ask: 'Do my chapters follow a logical sequence?'

"You are probably asking, 'What's a logical sequence?' It is an order, a sequence, that makes sense enough that at least for parts of the book, the reader can almost predict what the next chapter might be. For example, if I was writing about food, one logical sequence in a book on food could be breakfast food, lunch food, and . . . If this is a logical sequence, you can guess what comes next. Breakfast food, lunch food and . . . ?"

The kids chimed in with, "Dinner food."

"You got it! Another sequence in a book on food might be pasta, rice, fruit . . . and what else?"

The kids chimed in with "Vegetables," "Meat," and so on.

"If I want to organize my book around ways to kill cockroaches, I might organize those ways from the least to the most effective ways of getting rid of them. And I might even start the book with stuff about cockroaches' bodies, because that could show how hard it is to get rid of them, and then move to ways to get rid of cockroaches."

Chapter 1: Built for survival–the cockroach body

Chapter 2: One way to get rid of them that doesn't work too well

Chapter 3: A better way to get rid of them

Chapter 4: An even better way to get rid of them

Chapter 5: The best way to get rid of them

"We have about ten more minutes of work time. Will you and your partner use this time to look over possible tables of contents and to ask, about each possible one, 'How could we change this so that it follows a more logical sequence?' Help each other fix your various plans."

The most important revision work that writers can do when working on information texts involves revising the overall structure of a piece. For example, you may find that some children think that their books must have just one organizational structure spanning the entire book. It is helpful to think about books having parts (Part I, II, III), with each of those parts containing chapters. For example, a child writing on soccer could devote one part of the book to positions on the team, with different chapters for different positions, and another part of the book to famous soccer players, again with chapters on specific players. The book could end with a chapter called "Why Soccer?"

Then, too, you may want to help students take more into account as they devise alternative plans for their books. Eventually you will teach the whole class that the plan for a book often needs to be revised once the writer considers the information he or she has on hand. If the writer knows tons about one chapter and almost nothing about other chapters, those depleted chapters may need to be combined and the crammed-full chapter may need to be divided. You might preteach that concept now, which will mean that when you want to teach this to the entire class, you can refer to work some children in the class already did, which is a great way to cement their knowledge.

For example, Sherry was writing about the process of making a pond, and she had categories like these:

Preparing the location
Starting to build
Getting rocks and other things for the pond
Getting plants for the pond
Planting in the pond
Getting fish for the pond

She wasn't sure, however, that she had enough to say to actually fill six chapters, so she considered combining the first three categories into "First Things First: Building the Pond" and combining the next categories (the plants and fish) into "Bringing the Pond to Life."

Writers often consider their readers when thinking about plans for an information book. One of the most important questions to ask is "How can I make sure that readers learn what they want to know, when they want to know it?" To answer this question, a writer has to think really hard about what readers will want to learn. What is the really interesting stuff?

It can help for students to think about their tables of contents as notes for a course they are going to teach. This can lead writers to realize that sometimes readers need background information or need to learn one subtopic before another.

Finally, you may also want to approach today imagining that some of your conferences and small-group work will lean on published information texts. The good news is that children do not even need to know a text really well to be able to study the table of contents and to try to discern whether there is a logical structure informing the book's organization. For example, I suggested the children at one table look together at the National Geographic book *Deadliest Animals*. These are a few of the chapter titles in order.

◆ Deadly Surprises

◆ Scary Snakes

◆ Ferocious Fish

◆ Deadliest of All

Children will immediately notice that the author jazzes up the titles. Chapter 1 tells about lions, but instead of naming this chapter "Lions," the author names it "Deadly Surprises." That title is not just exciting; it also is a title that goes with the main idea of this book—that animals can be deadly.

It is not always easy for children to discern whether there is a logical structure undergirding a book. In this instance, the answer is yes. Each successive chapter describes an animal that is a notch more deadly. This discovery can inspire children to imagine ways that they, too, can organize their book so that the chapters follow a logical sequence.

Considering the Structures of Tables of Contents

Share a few examples of student work that show logical structures.

"Writers, there were so many interesting tables of contents being worked on today! I was especially impressed to see you consider which chapter should go first, which should go second—almost like you were building a block tower and you were making sure your base was strong before deciding exactly which blocks should be placed next and next.

"Max, as we all would have expected, is writing a book about baseball, and his latest table of contents goes like this." (See Figure 2–1.)

Chapter 1: The first position is first base

Chapter 2: The second position is second base

Chapter 3: The third position is third base

Chapter 4: The fourth position is home plate (not your real home)

Chapter 5: Pitcher's mound

Chapter 6: It's right field for you, a left for batter

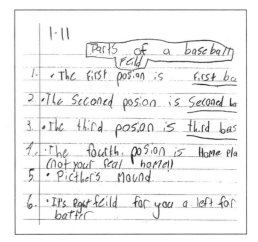

FIG. 2–1   Max drafted a table of contents with logical structure in mind.

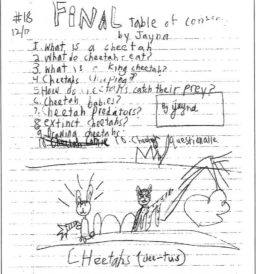

FIG. 2–2   Jayna's early and revised attempts at a table of contents

"I am completely loving the logical structure Max is using here! He's taking us around the baseball field. It makes me think there are so many ways to think about logical structure that I haven't even considered yet."

Tell the students that it might be helpful to see everything they are learning from their tables of contents work on a chart so they can refer to it as they work.

"I thought it might be helpful to write down just a few tips from what I learned from Max and others of you about making strong tables of contents." I displayed a chart on the easel.

Strong Tables of Contents

- Have a logical structure (least important → most important, first → last, parts, types, reasons)
- Contain chapters of almost equal weight and importance
- Cover the whole topic (or angle of the topic)
- Don't repeat information included in other chapters

New Structures Lead to New Thinking

YOU WILL PROBABLY BE SURPRISED TO SEE that although the previous session was a brimful session on writing a table of contents and planning the structure of one's book, this session dives right into that same arena. You'll probably think, "My kids already have reasonable plans for their writing," and you'll probably be itching for them to get a volume of writing done to make up for Session 2's paltry haul. If you are thinking in these ways, know we shared all these feelings coming into this session.

And yet you'll see that we have written another session on writing a table of contents as a way to plan a book. Let me first say that of course you have the option to skip this session. You always have that option. And the work ahead is intellectually challenging work, so there might be a good rationale for some of you to bypass it. But I also want to explain the rationale for an added session on planning.

We came to realize that when people have expertise on a topic, they tend to think about the topic in a particular, set way. The topic comes with labeled categories. For example, if I was to write about my home, I have a way I tend to approach that topic. Perhaps I tend to talk and think about my home in a chronological way, starting by thinking about when we moved in, when we remodeled five years later, when we refinanced ten years later, and so on.

Readers, pause here. Try this for yourself. Think of a topic you know so well that you take that topic for granted: your car, baking, your son. Now review what you know about the topics. Do categories come to mind? We suspect so. If your topic was a well-worn rug, you would no doubt see places your metaphorical feet landed most often. Those places would be mashed down and faded, with other areas pristine and almost new.

We found that when thinking about our topics, we do tend to have categories that we go to almost automatically. Take the topic of conferring. I tend to talk about kinds of conferences or about the architecture of conferring. If someone nudged me to think of conferring in terms of comparing and contrasting or in terms of problems and solutions, I'd not only have new *structures* into which to organize my content, but I'd also generate new *content*.

Try it with your topic. Think of it in a compare-and-contrast way. To what would you compare and contrast your topic? As you mull that over, you may notice pieces of your

IN THIS SESSION, you'll teach students that by considering different organizational structures, writers can allow themselves to think about a topic in new ways. You will guide them through a process of trying to structure their writing in various ways instead of settling immediately on one way.

GETTING READY

✔ Your own metaphor to describe how writers can use the same material in many different ways (see Connection)

✔ Your topic from Session 1, organized in a variety of structures: boxes and bullets, causes and effects, pros and cons, compare-and-contrast (see Teaching and Active Engagement)

✔ Chart paper and markers, or a means of enlarging text to display the different structures

✔ Students' writer's notebooks and pens or pencils

✔ The title of one of your chapters, with jotted notes for information to include in it, written in your writer's notebook (see Mid-Workshop Teaching)

COMMON CORE STATE STANDARDS: W.3.2.a,b, W.3.4, W.3.5, W.3.8, W.3.10, W.4.2.a,b, RI.3.3, RI.3.8, SL.3.1, SL.3.3, SL.3.6, L.3.1, L.3.2, L.3.3

topic you never noticed before. For example, if your topic is your home and you generally think of it chronologically, you might now compare and contrast it with the homes of your friends. Does your home have junk everywhere, while your friends' homes tend to be sparser? What if I asked you to consider problems and solutions? You might think of problems you have with your home and ways you do or do not have for solving those problems. Or you might think of life problems you used to have but that have gone away now that you have your home.

"I believe that the truly revolutionary work in this exploration of structure is that students learn to outgrow their own best thinking very early in the writing process."

When writers do this work, when writers explore possible structures for texts, the payoff is that they end up thinking about aspects of topics that feel fresh because those aren't the topics that usually rise to the surface.

The structure work we ask third-graders to tackle in this session and in this unit is significantly above the Common Core State Standards for third-graders. The CCSS simply call for third-graders to write information texts that have some sort of a structure. However, as mentioned earlier, we know from years of working with students on informational writing that third-graders are capable of much more than that.

The truly revolutionary work in this exploration of structure is that students learn to outgrow their own best thinking and to do that very early in the writing process. Additionally, students begin to train their minds to look at things, especially familiar things, in new ways.

Today's lesson will take longer than a typical minilesson. It is a guided practice minilesson, designed to give students many opportunities to practice a variety of structures before they go off to work with independence. The active engagement is interwoven into teaching.

New Structures Lead to New Thinking

CONNECTION

 ◆ COACHING

Tell a short story about people using one material—perhaps sand—and shaping that material into unique, different things.

"Have you watched a kid playing in a sandbox? Walking past the park the other day, I paused to watch kids in the sand box. I expected they'd have buckets that they fill and dump, fill and dump, and I expected they'd use those buckets to make sand castles. But what I saw blew me away! There were three different kids, all in the same sandbox, each doing something completely different from the others. And none of them were making sand castles.

"One of the boys packed sand into a square mold and then used this method to make bricks that he stacked into a brick wall made out of sand. One of the girls had created these hills and valleys, and was running her toy car over a mountainous road. The third kid was creating a sand person—you know, like a snow angel, but made out of sand. Although they were all using the same material, each child was structuring the material in an absolutely unique way."

Tell students that their topics are material and that it is wise to explore alternative ways to structure the material.

"That made me think immediately of the writing you are planning to do on your information books. For the past couple of days, you've been playing in the sand of your topic, filling buckets and building castles. You've tried out one or two familiar ways to think about your topic. But you might want to take a lesson from those kids in the sandbox. Instead of just filling and dumping buckets of sand to make the castles you've made a millions times, you might want to work with really new structures, structures you might not have thought to use before now."

❖ **Name the teaching point.**

"Today I want to teach you that writers try different organizational structures on for size. They explore a few different structures, noting how those structures affect the way they think about a topic."

This connection moves away from writing to bring home a point about writing. You'll want to cull from these books a set of transferable techniques that you can use when you write your own minilessons. One of the challenges you'll face is that you'll need to help children grasp big concepts that underlie the discipline you are teaching—which in these units is the discipline of writing. It is often helpful to use a familiar topic to teach a less familiar one. That's what this use of a metaphor does.

TEACHING AND ACTIVE ENGAGEMENT

Explain that you will model this, and then guide students to try several structures on for size.

"To do this, we're going to try something different from our usual minilesson. I'm going to tell you a structure I'd like us to try. I'll try that structure on with my topic, and then you'll give it a quick go, trying the structure on with your topic. Not every structure will work for every topic. But give each structure a quick try, jotting in your notebook how your table of contents might go if you were writing in that structure. If a structure doesn't work for you, when others are planning a new table of contents, you can go back to whichever structure *does* work for you, or you can come up with your own possible structure.

"We're going to move fast, so be sure you're ready."

Introduce the first structure: boxes and bullets.

"First, let's try boxes and bullets. I'm going to try boxes and bullets this way. I'll jot down a big topic." I jotted, "getting rid of cockroaches." "Now I'm going to jot supporting subtopics. We've done the organizational structure of boxes and bullets before, so this is really just to warm up our brains." I wrote my first attempt on chart paper.

> ### Getting Rid of Cockroaches
>
> - Traps
> - Poison
> - Green methods
> - Prevention

Ask students to try a boxes-and-bullets structure for their own topics.

"Now, you try it with your topics—just a quick boxes and bullets." I moved quickly through the meeting area, scanning to see what students were doing. I expected what they'd plan would be similar to the organizational plans they'd been making over the last couple of days. I gave them just a minute or two.

I didn't say this, but could have: "Keep in mind that a new structure might replace the table of contents you planned earlier, or it might become a subsection of that original plan. You could use one of the structures I suggest for just a chapter or two or for your whole book."

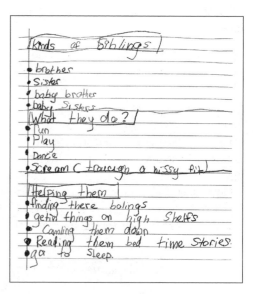

FIG. 3–1   A student tries out a boxes-and-bullets table of contents.

Introduce your next structure: cause and effect.

"Great! Now let's try another way of looking at it—cause and effect. For some writers, it might be easier to look at this as problem and solution." Unveiling chart paper on which I'd already explored causes and effects, and problems and solutions, I said, "For me it might look like this."

Causes	Effects
If I trap cockroaches . . .	**Then** I will get rid of a few cockroaches temporarily. But I won't get rid of all of them or of the eggs.
If I poison cockroaches . . .	**Then** I will kill most of the cockroaches, but if I have pets or small children, I could poison them, too. Some cockroaches build up a resistance to poisons over time that they pass on to their offspring.

Problem	Solution
cockroaches on my kitchen counter	clean up the food in the kitchen, even the crumbs
cockroaches in my bathroom	clean the bathroom and make sure there are no drips so that there is no food or water available

Ask students to try fitting their topics into a cause-and-effect template.

"Now it's your turn to try."

When I saw the students were struggling a bit, I called out sentence prompts and jotted some of them onto chart paper.

"Try 'If _____ , then _____ ,'" I said. "Or 'When _____ , then _____ happens.'" I jotted those onto chart paper, then gave another few alternatives.

"'(Blankety blank) happens because some other (blankety blank) happens.' Or 'If the problem is _____ , one solution is _____ .'"

After a few minutes, I moved on to the next structure.

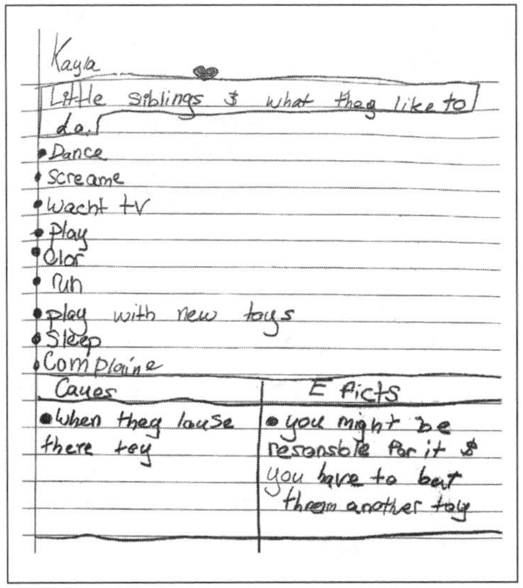

FIG. 3–2 Kayla experiments with cause and effect.

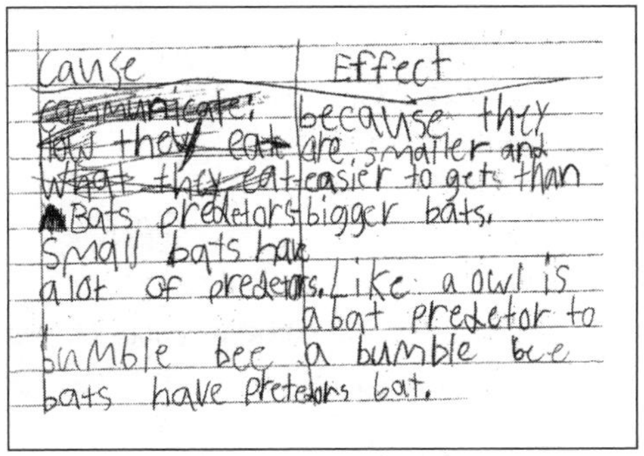

FIG. 3–3 Marquis tries out his topic, bats, with a cause-and-effect lens.

Introduce the next structure: pros and cons.

"We can also consider pros and cons. I may not be able to think of pros and cons of cockroaches as a whole topic, so I need to think, 'The pros and cons about *what part* of my topic?' So, let me think. Do I want to do pros and cons of different methods of killing cockroaches? Or of killing them in general? Once I've decided which pros and cons I want to explore, I can start thinking how this would shape a plan."

Pros of Killing Cockroaches

- You get rid of them!
- They won't eat your food.
- You won't be embarrassed when people come to your house.

Cons of Killing Cockroaches

- Cockroaches are living creatures.
- Cockroaches are part of the food chain.
- Cockroaches take care of crumbs and other leftover food and garbage that would go to waste otherwise.

Encourage students to try pros and cons.

"You can see how considering pros and cons can give you a whole new perspective on your topic, can't you? Why don't you try out the pros and cons of your topic, really fast."

I crouched in the meeting area, leaning over to take a peak at what the students were doing. Many students naturally seemed to place their pros and cons in a T-chart format, and others made them list-like. I encouraged students who were struggling to go ahead and move back to an earlier structure with which they had found success.

Let students know you are going to show them one more structure: compare-and-contrast.

"Let's try one last one: comparing and contrasting. We need to start by thinking, 'What will I compare and contrast?' I could compare and contrast my whole book—so that I'm writing in every chapter about how cockroaches are and are not like other animals. Or I could take a subtopic and compare and contrast just that subtopic. So, for example, I could compare and contrast ways to get rid of cockroaches versus ways to get rid of mice." I revealed a page on which I'd scrawled some thoughts.

Getting Rid of Cockroaches and Mice

Similarities: Getting rid of cockroaches is similar to getting rid of mice because both cockroaches and mice live in people's homes, and are unwanted. Both creatures are killed by similar methods: traps, poison . . .

Differences: Getting rid of cockroaches is different than getting rid of mice because not everyone wants to kill mice. In fact, there are humane traps that allow humans to catch mice without

As students worked, I looked from one student's try to the next, noticing the ways that students were exploring all the nooks and crannies of their topics. When I saw one that I thought might turn out to be particularly fruitful I made sure to give the student a thumbs up or another indication that I thought the student was on to something.

killing them so that the mice can be set free in a field or someplace else. No one really wants a humane trap for a cockroach. Also, there are people who do not want to get rid of mice, or at least don't care about getting rid of mice because they think mice are cute. However, hardly anyone thinks cockroaches are cute, and almost everyone wants to get rid of them.

Ask students to try compare-and-contrast with their topics.

"How can you compare and contrast your topic? What are the similarities and differences? Think for a few seconds. When you have an idea or two, jot it down as fast as you can so you don't lose the idea. If you don't feel like doing this work at all for your topic, after you give this a quick try, go back to the work you began earlier today."

LINK

Send students off to choose between revising their tables of contents, writing long about an unexplored aspect of their topic, or picking up where they last left off in their pieces.

"Wow! This room feels electric. Thumbs up if you're surprised at some of the new thinking you did on your topic." Many so indicated. "Writers, do you see that you only came up with these fresh new plans because you did what those kids in the sandbox were doing? You took the risk to try new ways of approaching the entire project. Lots of times you have waited to revise *at the end of* your writing process, but front-end revision actually helps much more. The first step is to resist what people call 'premature closure' or 'early settling on one set way.' From this day forward, always remember to push yourself to imagine new possibilities.

"Will you star the structures you might want to use for your book? Once you've done that, you have a few choices you might make. You may want to go back to your original table of contents and revise it by including some of the new ideas and structures you just explored. Remember to use the chart 'Strong Tables of Contents.' Or you might decide you want to go back and write long about an aspect of your topic you haven't yet explored. Or maybe you were in the midst of working on something yesterday that you're dying to go back to today, or you feel ready to begin collecting information that you'll put into each chapter. Doing that is a way to check if your plan is going to work."

"Whatever you do today, try to carry with you the idea that by looking at something in a new way, you can get fresh ideas. Off you go!"

FIG. 3–4 Marquis then explores similarities and differences between bats and birds.

FIG. 3–5 This student explores his topic, basketball, by trying out different structures.

Contrast the number of options you present to your students today with the number you could offer just a day ago. Expect that in your teaching, there will be some instances when you don't have as many choices available to kids as you might ideally like.

Keeping Individual Students' Needs and Goals in Mind

THE WORK YOUR STUDENTS WILL BE DOING TODAY WILL BE VARIED. The minilesson you just taught ended with you suggesting lots of options, and by today, some students will be at the vanguard, working at a pace that pushes you to keep moving forward with your teaching, while others will be lingerers. This is a good thing. Resist any temptation to wrangle everybody back in line so that the entire class moves forward at the same pace. Writers do work at different paces, and *should* do so.

It would, of course, be much simpler to have all students working on the same strategies at the same time. During work time, you could just move from seat to seat, prodding students to finish the work that the minilesson highlighted. Carl Anderson, author of *How's It Going?* (2000) and many other texts about the art of conferring, emphasizes, "Let the student set the agenda." Carl does not mean that literally, you should expect students to know exactly what they want taught. Rather, he means that when you confer, your intention is to learn the goals and needs of the unique writer and to teach in response to that writer. The goals for a writer include that child's particular intentions for that day and also the long-term goals that you and the writer have co-constructed. These long-term goals come, in large part, from the data you gather and from your observations. Of course, nothing is simple in life, and so although it is true that during your conferring and small-group work you'll want to help students develop purpose and agendas for themselves, it is also the case that you'll want to weigh whether you can get behind the choices they make.

In today's session you may see students trying their hands at one structure or another. You would do well to identify what the student is attempting to do and then teach into that. For example, if the student is working on comparing and contrasting, you will first want to see what it means for her to try comparing and contrasting. You might notice whether this student seems to believe that to engage in comparing and contrasting, she is expected to suggest that the two items are equally similar and different. In other words, students often think that they'll need to generate two similarities and two differences. You might let the writer know that it's not only okay, but very likely that she'll want to suggest that two things are "mostly alike but partly different," or just the opposite.

MID-WORKSHOP TEACHING

Helping Students File Information into Chapter Files

"So many of you have revised your table of contents. That is fantastic! Some of you have been gathering information that might go in each of your chapters, too. No matter where you are in the process of planning your chapters, you'll need to move toward collecting the information you will include in each of your planned chapters.

"Nonfiction writers think of chapters as files. You might want to make a section or page in your notebook for each chapter of your book. Once you've done that, it would be smart to jot information you'll want to include in each chapter. You might discover as you do this that some chapters have plenty of information, but other chapters need a little research to fill them out. You might decide some chapters can become part of another chapter or be deleted entirely. You might even decide to break one chapter into two smaller ones.

"For example, under my chapter called 'Using Poisons' I've jotted down a few things I knew I wanted to include about using poisons on cockroaches: aerosol, powder, liquid, gas. And as I wrote those down, I started putting question marks next to ones I feel like I have to jump online to research. As you move from one chapter to the next, make sure that each bit really matches, really fits into, its file."

If a writer is considering structuring his text chronologically—say "birth to death"—then you may want to suggest that this would be a time where equal categories are probably the norm.

Each structure that a writer attempts will pose predictable challenges. As you become more experienced with conferring, you'll find that you develop a repertoire of tips you can give, based on your assessment of what a student is trying to do, and this makes you more able to be flexible and responsive.

Although the minilesson focused on structure, and topics haven't been the focal point for your instruction, it is likely that you will have a handful of students whose topics are a bit challenging. Some topics will seem to you to require more research than you believe the student will be able to do during the writing workshop. Other topics will deal with imaginary things, such as fairies, monsters, and aliens. Some topics will come from pop culture, and perhaps these will lead you to worry that writing about the topics could lead a student to write about violence that isn't what you regard as age-appropriate.

Our advice to you it to be ready to talk with students about their topics today. You won't want to wait too much longer to question their choices. And yes, sometimes it may seem necessary for you to redirect a student to change a topic, and it is okay to nudge a writer into a topic you think will be a better match. ("You play soccer. Why not write a book on that?") However, this can also work against you. If you recruit a student to write about a topic you think would be a good one and the student is begrudgingly appeasing you, sometimes the resulting piece can lack spirit. So keep in mind that a student could take a topic that he is fascinated by—say, video games— and end up using a whole host of writing techniques to do a very admirable, even scholarly, job with that topic.

Preparing to Draft

Let students know that they will be moving to drafting tomorrow, and channel them to spend time before tomorrow collecting stuff to help them be ready to draft. Ask partners to discuss.

"Writers, while some of you are still organizing your information into chapter files or figuring out what to do if you don't have much for some chapters, most of you are ready to move on to the next step—drafting!

"Can I tell you a little secret about drafting? The more you get your mind ready for it by planning and thinking and dreaming, the better the draft, and the process of drafting, will be. I'm going to ask you to spend some time this afternoon and this evening preparing for tomorrow's drafting. You've done that before for other writing projects. But today will be different, because today I want you to get not just your mind ready for drafting, but also to get your hand ready. Can you collect things you see, hear, read, feel—really, anything that you can imagine fitting into your book—and jot them down in your notebook? Live the life of a writer, getting ready to draft. Max, when you go to baseball practice after school, don't just go to practice as a baseball player. Go to practice also as a baseball writer. Notice anything that might go well into one of your chapters—and especially notice information that might go into the chapter you'll tackle first.

"Right now, tell your partner how you can live differently tonight because you are preparing to draft. Tell your partner also what you'll put into your notebook tonight that will help you."

Laying the Bricks of Information

 **ear Teachers,**

We hope this letter scaffolds you to design and teach this session. You are the expert on your children, so we hope you tweak whatever we suggest so that your teaching is home-grown, reflecting the needs of your students. It should reflect your data, too, and your knowledge.

You'll want your children to know they are entering another phase of their writing process. When they worked on narrative texts, they entered the phase of writing we refer to as "drafting" with an entry in hand. This time, most of them will approach the work of drafting with just a table of contents in hand, which really means with an outline in hand. This outline will represent a lot of work, but it will not promise that the writing children do today will turn out especially well. In fact, it is fairly likely that today's writing *won't* be particularly strong. That's okay. The plan for the entire next bend is for writers to cycle continually between drafting and revising. As your children learn more ways to make their information writing strong, they'll return eventually to chapters they will write today, revising those chapters with new tools and strategies in hand. So today's work will probably go through successive revision treatments.

The important thing for today is that your children will have spent three days talking, planning, and outlining. Today, they need to write and to write a lot. Fluency, stamina, and speed are all important for writers, and kids grow rusty when they don't write a lot. So today your real goal is to let the starting gun go off and to make sure that all your children write up a storm, working on whichever chapters feel easiest to them. You'll want the minilesson to end by you channeling writers to choose a chapter that they know well and just dive in. Perhaps you will suggest that children look over their tables of contents and star one chapter that they think they can write pretty easily, starting immediately. Then you can send them from the minilesson saying, "Get started. It will probably be a page long, or more. If you finish that chapter, shift to another."

COMMON CORE STATE STANDARDS: W.3.2, W.3.4, W.3.5, W.3.10, W.4.2, RI.3.8, SL.3.1, SL.3.4, SL.3.6, L.3.1, L.3.2, L.3.3, L.3.6

Of course, prior to sending children off, you'll want to teach them something. Early on in every unit of study, it is important to give students a vision of good work, a concrete goal that they can aim for. Exemplar texts do a lot of work, so you may decide to show students a published mentor text, an information book you or another adult wrote, or an especially well-written text by a student their age. In deciding which features of the text you want to highlight, you'll want to ask yourself, "What are the main features of this text?" So whereas the text may contain colons, dashes, and parentheses—kinds of punctuation that are especially vital to this genre of writing (information writing)—you probably will postpone any mention of the exemplar text's punctuation and decide instead to emphasize something more fundamental. For example, I recommend you consider highlighting the information in the text. At the end of the day, the goal of writing an informational text is to inform. If you agree, then in this minilesson you could teach students that writing an information text is like laying bricks. A writer takes pieces of information and lays them, one alongside the next, to form a chapter. Then the exemplar text could help you make this point.

MINILESSON

In the connection you will want to get the students fired up for starting their drafts. It might make sense to start with a bit of a drumroll wherein you extol the fun and adventure of drafting, or you might feel it's more important to name the elephant in the room: sometimes the blank page is hard to face. No matter which way you choose, it's important that you remind them to review their tables of contents and start with the chapter that feels easiest to begin with. Your teaching point might go like this: "Today, what I want you to notice is that the unit we're in is called *Information Writing* for a reason. It is made up entirely of information! The book you will be making is lot like a brick wall, only the bricks are pieces of information. You write information books by taking those chunks of information, your bricks, and then you lay those pieces of information alongside each other."

Set children up to listen to and study a brief part of a text. Choose a passage that includes a wealth of information, with one fact set alongside another: a quote, a statistic, an anecdote, or an observation. If you analyze the contents of one paragraph in the teaching section of the minilesson, students can do the same with another passage in the active engagement section. Give them time to talk in pairs about what they notice. Perhaps they'll add descriptions, lists, and vocabulary words to your list.

Another alternative for the active engagement could be for you to give children a text you composed earlier, comprised of sweeping generalizations. We've found that it can be very helpful if the text is about something the students know well, such as their class. You could then ask them to rewrite-in-the-air, studding the new draft of this text with specific information. As they work with a partner to do that work, call out reminders. Your voiceovers might coach them to vary the kinds of information they include. Later in the workshop, you and a small group might practice this more, and that small group might produce a small bit of shared writing. If you label the text produced, it will be a nice visual to put on the wall. Consider ending the lesson by restating the teaching point and also letting them know that the goal for today is to write fast and furiously, knowing the writing won't be perfect.

CONFERRING AND SMALL-GROUP WORK

You are becoming something of an expert by now on working with writers. Your growing expertise will help you realize that everything is more complicated than you once believed. And so although, yes, it is absolutely true that a good teacher of writing gives the reins to the writer, it is also the case that as a teacher of writing, you need clear goals for your students. Some of those goals will be ones students have chosen; others will be ones that you choose.

The biggest priority for today will be to make sure that every child produces at least a page of writing and probably more. Start by creating a tone in the classroom that says this will happen. You won't want to fuss over one particular reluctant writer until you have conveyed confidence that every child is no doubt dying to write up a storm and have created a tone in the classroom that is conducive to that writing. You'll want your children to settle down today to writing a lot, and this means you'll need the classroom to provide them with a space that is quiet enough that you can hear the scratch of pens. Once you have sent kids off to write, you will probably want to get out those roller blades that you used at the start of the year when you needed to travel quickly from table to table, and you'll again want to circulate among them. Use nonverbal cues to settle kids down: a tap on one child's empty booklet, a gesture that says, "What gives?" to another, a firm, decisive thumbs up to a third. You will probably also say brief voiceover prompts that channel the whole class toward writing "Your hand should be flying down the page." "Andrew's finished one page and is onto his second!" "Pretend to be teaching someone in your mind. Hear the words, then write like all get-out to get them down."

As you move among the writers, channeling them all to write up a storm, you'll no doubt find a few children who need more help to get themselves started. One of the things we know from teaching reading is that whereas successful readers are somewhat similar, less successful readers differ from each other in dramatic ways. In reading, we say it like this: "Struggling readers are all sitting on a three-legged stool that is missing one leg, but the leg that is missing won't always be the same one!" In writing, too, struggling writers are very different, one from each other. For example, in this instance, some of your strugglers will be writers who are so dedicated to the idea of making their chapters perfect, that they are paralyzed by their high standards. These writers may simply need to be told that just as they tried a few leads for their narrative writing, they might try a few leads for this kind of writing. Or they may need to be encouraged to dictate one possible slant to a draft and to have you say, firmly, "Oh my goodness! Capture that on the page before you forget it!"

Other strugglers will not be worrying about writing well. Their worries may be over what to say in the first place. As you teach and confer, you may want to generate a list of the kinds of information that information writers include:

- quotations
- statistics
- anecdotes
- observations
- descriptions
- vocabulary words
- lists
- labels

MID-WORKSHOP TEACHING

You will want to use your mid-workshop teaching to directly address strengths and issues you noticed during the day's drafting session. You might decide that instead of stopping the students to teach, you will want to take on the persona of a basketball coach and call out from the sidelines, offering tips, suggestions, and pokes. In that instance, if you notice that some students are lagging, you might call out, "Keep it going! Push that pen down the paper!" If you notice some students' writing is getting muddied and confused, you might remind them, "Remember your table of contents. Don't forget to check on your order as you write." These voiceovers can happen throughout the period.

SHARE

In today's share, you might find it important to remind students of the technical and logistical needs of drafting, such as where and how to get drafting paper or what color of pen they should be using to draft. Alternatively, you might decide to make this share a mini-celebration of process and have the students go around a circle sharing their favorite sentences they have written so far or their proudest achievements on this project.

Good luck,
Lucy and Colleen

Organization Matters in Texts Large and Small

TODAY IS THE LAST SESSION of the first bend in this unit. In other words, today you will be wrapping up the first stage of developing these pieces before moving into more detailed and focused drafting and revision work. You will recall that earlier in this book, we mentioned that one of the biggest goals of this unit is to teach expository structure to students. Your first three minilessons provided students with strategies for thinking about the structure of nonfiction texts. Our hope is that your teaching not only helped students learn strategies they could use during this unit, but that it also helped them develop skills and strategies they will be able to draw upon anytime they write information texts. It is important for teachers to explicitly teach transference, or else it doesn't happen. Students are often willing to transfer what they learn on one day to their work on another day, but they need to be explicitly taught to always think, "What have I already learned to do that can help me now in this new endeavor?"

Today, for example, your students will need you to explicitly teach them to transfer all that they have learned about planning information books to the new work of planning information chapters. Although it probably seems obvious to you that when you taught students that it is helpful to prepare for writing an information book by weighing alternative structures, you were teaching them something you hoped they'd transfer to any information text, it is almost certain they will forget to do any sort of planning at all for what will go into their first chapter. That is, the goal is always for teaching to be transferable to another day and another text. And it is almost certain that most students will have approached the challenge of writing a chapter without relying on any of your prior instruction. This makes today a wonderful day to emphasize the importance of transference. "What you learn about planning an entire text can be recycled, transferred, so those lessons are applicable to planning a part of a text."

Because structure continues to be an important concept, you'll want to be sure that when you read aloud to your class, you help your students think about the structures of texts. If your class has read the National Geographic Kids book *Cats vs. Dogs* (2011) for example, you might want to revisit that text now, looking this time for ways the authors

IN THIS SESSION, you'll teach students that the organizational skills writers use for their tables of contents can help them plan their chapters as well.

GETTING READY

✔ Sample tables of contents, first written without a logical structure and then revised two ways (see Connection)

✔ "Strong Tables of Contents" chart from Session 2 (see Teaching)

✔ Sentence strip with the heading "Strong Information Writing," to place over the "Strong Tables of Contents" heading on the chart (see Teaching)

✔ Table of contents for one of your chapters, to draft in front of students (see Teaching)

✔ Information Writing Checklist, Grades 3 and 4 (see Share)

COMMON CORE STATE STANDARDS: W.3.2.a,b, W.3.4, W.3.5, W.4.2.a,c,d, RI.3.5, RI.3.10, SL.3.1, L.3.1, L.3.2, L.3.3

of this published text handled some of the challenges that students are working on in their own writing. For example, you could say, "Wow, look at how that table of contents works. It seems like in each chapter, the author pits cats against dogs in an attempt to see which one is the 'winner' of a particular category (sharpest senses, best communication, and so on). Also, is anyone else noticing how the start of each chapter

"The goal is always for teaching to be transferable to another day and another text."

poses a question, like 'Whose nose knows best?' It's as if the writer is setting us up to think about the comparison before it even happens. Then the chapter is full of facts about each animal, showing how that animal fares in that category. At the end, the writer includes a text box with the winner (in 'Senses,' the winner is dogs)."

Organization Matters in Texts Large and Small

CONNECTION

Convey to children that you expect their written products will be very different than they were before because of what they have learned about organizing a table of contents and organizing a text.

"Have you watched any of those TV shows where they do make-overs? On one of them, a person comes in, looking fairly plain . . . and then specialists go to work—the hair dresser, the make-up artist, the fashion expert—and lo and behold, the person emerges as this dazzling beauty. Or the TV show adopts some junky old car or house and then three hours later, the car or the house has been transformed.

You could, of course, vary this. For example, if you have a photo of yourself from long ago and a more recent one, you could talk about "then" and "now" photos.

"I'm mentioning these miracle make-overs because over the first few days of this unit, your tables of contents have gone through similar make-overs."

Show children two fictional tables of contents—one exemplifying a novice way to organize an information text and the other exemplifying a more proficient plan.

"Many of your first tables of contents have gone from this . . . to this."

It is probably not actually the case that many of your third graders have undergone such a transformation this early in the unit. But celebrating their progress and providing a mentor text such as this can help steer the way.

From . . .	To . . .
<u>Dogs</u>	<u>From Beginning to End: Life with a Dog</u>
Chapter 1: Getting a dog from the pound	Chapter 1: Deciding if you should get a dog, and if so, which kind
Chapter 2: Famous dogs	Chapter 2: Getting a dog: Possible places to find one
Chapter 3: What dogs need	Chapter 3: Setting your house and life up for a dog
Chapter 4: Kinds of dogs	Chapter 4: Training your dog
	Chapter 5: When your dog dies

Discuss the difference between novice and more proficient organizational plans. "Some people might not be able to tell the difference between the first version and the next version. Talk to your partner about how that second table of contents—from beginning to end—shows a logical order that is really important. Then talk about whether *your* newest table of contents is logically organized as well."

I listened in as children talked. Kayla said to her partner, "The first one was just all about getting a dog. But the second plan has a way it goes that makes sense. Like, it goes in order—from the first thing that happens when getting a dog to the last. It's sad, but it's good."

"Yeah," Frank agreed. "And it's based on things that happen, and how those things go in order. When I look at my first one, it's sort of more like the first one. I just put down everything I knew, not thinking about the order, exactly. But, my next one, I really tried to think of why I should put things in a certain order. It's a lot better."

After a minute, I said to the whole class, "You all should pat yourselves on the backs over the speed at which your tables of contents got better. Congratulations."

Point out that although the chapters they've written *should* reflect their learning about building logical structures, it actually seems like many kids overlooked structure.

"But here is the thing. We're not just aiming for logical structure in the table of contents. We're also looking to make sure that what you learned affects *every bit* of information writing you ever do for the rest of your life."

❖ **Name the teaching point.**

"Today I want to teach you that everything you've learned about organizing a table of contents applies also to the work of organizing any chapter or any information text you write. Whenever you write an information text, start by making a miniature table of contents—even if it is just in your mind."

TEACHING

Let students know that organization skills transfer. The way kids go about organizing the whole book can be transferred so that it is also the way they go about organizing any chapter.

"Now, I know some of you may be thinking, 'But wait! When you make a table of contents for a whole book, that makes sense. It is a long book. You can't make a table of contents for just one chapter.'" But here is the thing. The way you go about planning the organization of a book is *exactly the same* as the way you plan the organization of a chapter. It is almost like you need a table of contents not just for the book but for the chapter."

"You see, there is a temptation to think, once you've put together a really strong table of contents, that you can just put your information in each chapter in any way it comes to mind, as long as it pertains to the title of your chapter. But when you do that, it's almost like you go into a really neat-looking home, open the closets, and everything is in a jumble."

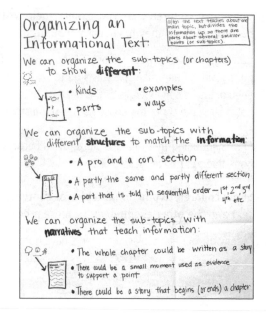

Organizing an Informational Text

Often the text teaches about one main topic, but divides the information up so there are parts about several smaller points (or sub topics).

We can organize the sub-topics (or chapters) to show **different**:
- kinds
- parts
- examples
- ways

We can organize the sub-topics with different **structures** to match the **information**:
- A pro and a con section
- A partly the same and partly different section
- A part that is told in sequential order — 1st, 2nd, 3rd, 4th etc

We can organize the sub-topics with **narratives** that teach information:
- The whole chapter could be written as a story
- There could be a small moment used as evidence to support a point
- There could be a story that begins (or ends) a chapter

Explain and demonstrate that planning for a short text can be quick. Remind students they can draw on all they know even while planning quickly.

"It need not take long to plan a short text like a chapter. Right before you start writing, just quickly jot a sort of mini–table of contents, or plan, for how the chapter will go. You already know so much about the different ways you can organize information. You just need to apply that to your plans for a chapter," I said, gesturing to the chart "Strong Tables of Contents." I pulled out a sentence strip with the title "Strong Information Writing" on it and, placing it over the existing title, I said, "The planning for a strong table of contents is exactly the same as planning the organization of any information writing, so we can rename this chart!"

> ### Strong Information Writing
>
> - Has a logical structure (least important → most important, first → last, parts, types, reasons)
> - Contains chapters of almost equal weight and importance
> - Covers the whole topic (or angle of the topic)
> - Doesn't repeat information included in other chapters

"Let me try making quick plans with my chapter 'Cockroach Bodies Are Built for Survival.' I'm going to use the chart that we renamed to remind me of what I know, and the first bullet reminds me that I need a logical structure. I'm not going to just slap everything I know about cockroach bodies down on paper. So why don't I start with the cockroach head, then talk about the rest of the body from there." I jotted:

Cockroach Bodies Are Built for Survival
- Head
- Abdomen
- Legs
- Cerci (that's kind of like their tails)

"Okay, this looks good. And I would say, if we look at the second bullet on our chart, each of those things are of almost equal weight and importance, yes. The third point on our chart says that it needs to cover the whole topic. Hmm, have I mentioned everything about cockroach bodies? I think I left out their wings and antennae, but wings could go with the abdomen, and antennae could stay with the head, so that covers the whole topic. And this last bullet point—well, you all see what I'm doing here."

"Now I'm ready to start drafting this chapter. I'll just put my little plan right next to my drafting paper and get started. Let's see, I know that I need to write an introduction to my chapter and then move right into talking about the head because that comes first in my plan."

> Cockroaches have managed to survive for millions of years in part because of their incredible bodies, which are built for survival.
>
> The cockroach's head is built for survival in many ways. All cockroaches have antennae at the top of their heads which they use to taste, smell, feel for obstacles, temperature, and moisture.

Debrief in a way that pops out the transferable aspects of what you have just done.

"Did you notice how I made sure to place my plans for my chapter right next to my draft paper? And how I kept looking back at it to spot whether or not I was sticking to my plan? By doing this I was making sure that the organization that I planned will actually come out in my drafted chapter."

ACTIVE ENGAGEMENT

Ask students to verbally practice their plans for one of the chapters in their books and write-in-the-air the first line or two of their chapters.

"Writers, I want you to all think for a second about a chapter you would like to work on today. Thumbs up when you know which one it will be. Now, quickly plan across your fingers how you will organize this chapter to write it well. Don't be afraid to look back at our new chart to make sure you're doing everything you want to do." I left a pool of silence. "Now, partners, turn to each other and share your plans for your chapter. If you have time, go ahead and rehearse the first sentence or two of your new chapter." I listened as children spoke, and then channeled them to start writing.

LINK

Channel writers to either consider another alternative structure for the upcoming chapter or to decide and draft it—or else to revise previous chapters.

"Writers, today you've planned your next chapter one way. Before actually starting to write the chapter, will you remember that you have also learned it helps to push yourself to imagine other possible ways to structure your chapter, and consider a second way?

"The other things you need to decide, writers, is whether you actually want to start using today's reminder on new chapters—or whether you first want to look back on the chapters you have already written to see whether they have a logical structure to them, and if not, you may decide to take the first portion of today to rewrite these chapters and only then move onto the new chapter. Those are a writer's choices. Off you go!"

You need to decide on the mechanics of your demo writing. If you have the technology so that you can write quickly while children watch, that's great. If you would need to do this writing with a marker on chart paper, only do that if you can be speedy. Otherwise, write on a clipboard, voicing as you write, and do the chart-paper version when children needn't all wait for you.

If this seems like a minute active engagement, you're right. But the work your children will do is essential.

FIG. 5–1 Marquis' draft, following his plan for the chapter.

Using Checklists to Find and Set Personal Goals

SOMETIMES YOU'LL USE YOUR CONFERRING AND SMALL-GROUP TIME as a chance to trial-run something so that you can test the instruction out first with a small group before you bring it to the whole class in the mid-workshop or the share. Today, for example, you many want to use some of the work time to coach a small cluster of children to use the third-grade Information Writing Checklist as a guide for assessing one of their chapters, doing this in advance of the share, when the whole class will get involved in this work. This will allow you to see the predictable misunderstandings that you'll want to address when you do this with the whole class.

You are almost sure to see that when you send children off to self-assess, they'll proceed along through the checklist in a very perfunctory fashion, going check, check, check. You'll want to be ready to intervene, telling them that the whole point of using a checklist like this is that it helps them find goals for themselves, and they can only find goals if they are really tough and exacting on themselves. "Did I really *master* that?" they should ask. "Did I do that work as well as I can in every chapter?" Be sure the writers annotate their text.

MID-WORKSHOP TEACHING **Using Code Words to Help Planning**

"Writers, we're going to have a longer share session than usual, so you have just eight more minutes to write. If you have been revising your chapters from yesterday, write like the wind so you'll also get a chance to start a new chapter today.

"All of you, will you remember that it often helps to write the plan for your text on your actual page? Alex has put little code words down the margin of his chapter—so for example, he's writing about the parts of the castle, and he's got *hold* written in his margin, and *tower*, and *moat*. Those code words remind him of his plan.

"Marquis has made a little list of subtopics he'll address in his chapter, 'What Bats Eat.'

"No talking for the next eight minutes so you get a whole lot done. Go!"

> Friday December 14
> Aim: Writers plan how the writing will go
> Topic-Bats
> Table of contents:
>
> Different Kinds of bats   page 1
> Bats predetors   page 3
> How bats communicate   page 4
> What Bats eat   page 5
> What bats do   page 7
> Where they live   page 9
> ~~My topic is ba~~
>
> What Bats eat
> -small bats eat fruit.
> -bigger bats eat small mamals.
> -Bumble bee bats eat fruit
> -bighst bats eat small mamals
> like rats or mice.
> -bumble bee bats eat fruit
> like oranges and apples.

FIG. 5–2   Marquis organized his table of contents. Then he planned one chapter, "What Bats Eat" before he drafted.

Looking Back on the Past to Set Goals for the Present

Channel students to think back on their experiences with writing checklists and how the checklists helped them to not only assess their current writing but also to set new writing goals.

"Writers, you already know that when people want to get good at something, it helps to find ways to look back and ask, 'How have I been doing?' and it helps to look forward and to ask, 'What can I do in the future to get better?'

"During the last unit of study—narrative writing—I was really proud of the way you used the narrative checklist to not just help you assess your own writing, but also to help you set goals for yourself. Today, what I want to tell you is that researchers have studied how kids zoom ahead in skills—on anything. How do kids zoom ahead as basketball players, as rock climbers, as trumpet players—and as writers? What the researchers have found is that it is really important for a learner to have a huge feeling of 'I am working like the dickens to reach these huge goals that I've set for myself.'

"So, today, I want to show you a checklist that third-grade teachers around the world suggest can be an end-of-the-year goal for third-grade information writers, and I'm going to suggest you all try to be not just so-so at these goals, but to actually *master* them. Later, if you want, you coud also study the end of *fourth*-grade goals—and you maybe could work toward some of those goals as well."

Information Writing Checklist

	Grade 3	NOT YET	STARTING TO	YES!	Grade 4	NOT YET	STARTING TO	YES!
Structure								
Overall	I taught readers information about a subject. I put in ideas, observations, and questions.	☐	☐	☐	I taught readers different things about a subject. I put facts, details, quotes, and ideas into each part of my writing.	☐	☐	☐
Lead	I wrote a beginning in which I got readers ready to learn a lot of information about the subject.	☐	☐	☐	I hooked my readers by explaining why the subject mattered, telling a surprising fact, or giving a big picture. I let readers know that I would teach them different things about a subject.	☐	☐	☐
Transitions	I used words to show sequence such as *before*, *after*, *then*, and *later*. I also used words to show what didn't fit such as *however* and *but*.	☐	☐	☐	I used words in each section that help readers understand how one piece of information connected with others. If I wrote the section in sequence, I used words and phrases such as *before*, *later*, *next*, *then*, and *after*. If I organized the section in kinds or parts, I used words such as *another*, *also*, and *for example*.	☐	☐	☐
Ending	I wrote an ending that drew conclusions, asked questions, or suggested ways readers might respond.	☐	☐	☐	I wrote an ending that reminded readers of my subject and may have suggested a follow-up action or left readers with a final insight. I added my thoughts, feelings, and questions about the subject at the end.	☐	☐	☐
Organization	I grouped my information into parts. Each part was mostly about one thing that connected to my big topic.	☐	☐	☐	I grouped information into sections and used paragraphs and sometimes chapters to separate those sections. Each section had information that was mostly about the same thing. I may have used headings and subheadings.	☐	☐	☐

Introduce the checklist and read through it with the students.

"Here is the Information Writing Checklist, Grades 3 and 4, that you'll be using to check on your own writing and how you think you're doing." The Information Writing Checklist, Grades 3 and 4, can be found on the CD-ROM.

"A few things about this checklist probably already caught your eye. For example, you might have noticed that many of the things on this checklist we have worked on over the past few days. Or you might have noticed that some of the things are exactly the same as items on the last unit's checklist on narrative writing, and that some are even things you already learned as second-grade informational writers. This is great because there are things that you already know you can do! Other things on the checklist, though, will seem harder. Since these are end-of-the-year expectations, you won't have mastered all of these things just yet, but you will be working toward them.

"Will you all look at the third-grade checklist and this piece of writing to see how it meets the third-grade goals? Start by studying what the checklist says, with your partner, and then will each of you look at the exemplar piece I gave you and also at your own writing? Be really hard on yourself—like the top basketball coaches are hard on their star players. Then mark off on your chart whether you are not yet doing this, you are starting to do it, or you have mastered it. When you find items you aren't doing or are starting to do, you are finding possible goals. Once you arrive at a goal, make a display of fireworks on your paper to celebrate!"

Read through a piece of student work together, using the checklist as you go along.

"So, writers, Jeremy has been reading over his chapter titled 'Parts of a Turtle' (see Figure 5–3), and he's first looked to see if he wrote a beginning that got readers ready to learn a lot of information about the subject. His lead goes like this, so think whether you'd say, 'Not Yet,' 'Starting To,' or 'Yes!'"

> A turtle have lots of important parts. Each part do something very important jobs.

The children agreed that it absolutely did get readers expecting to learn many important parts of the turtle. "You are right, and let me tell you what else Jeremy did. He said, 'Do I do that usually or just this time?' and he looked at other chapters and found that he often didn't do that. Jeremy wants to be tough on himself, so he checked, 'Starting To.' Nice work, Jeremy!"

And then I turned to the whole class and said, "Try to push yourselves in those same ways!"

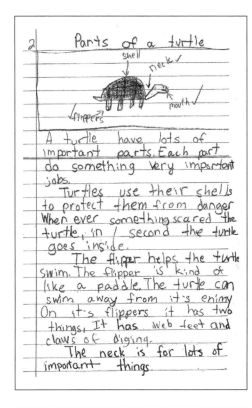

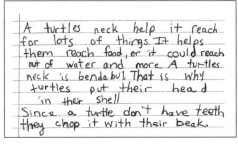

FIG. 5–3 Jeremy's lead sets readers' expectations to learn a lot about turtles.

Studying Mentor Texts in a Search for Elaboration Strategies

IN THIS SESSION, you'll teach students various strategies to develop their informational books. You'll suggest using mentor texts as a way to learn more about elaboration and help them apply these ideas to their own writing.

GETTING READY

✔ Your own story to demonstrate how you can learn elaboration from other people (see Connection)

✔ A section of your information text that needs more elaboration (see Teaching)

✔ Mentor texts, *Deadliest Animals* and *VIP Pass to a Pro Baseball Game Day*

✔ Class book, possibly about your school

✔ Students' writer's notebooks and pens or pencils

✔ An exemplar student text that shows elaboration, to share with the class (see Share)

COMMON CORE STATE STANDARDS: W.3.2.a,b,c; W.3.4, W.3.5, W.3.8, W.4.2.b,c; RI.3.1, RI.3.2, RI.3.10, RFS.3.4, SL.3.1, SL.3.2, SL.3.4, SL.3.6, L.3.1, L.3.2, L.3.3, L.3.4, L.3.6

TODAY BEGINS THE SECOND BEND in the journey of this unit. Teachers, on this day you'll help writers draft by teaching them to elaborate on the various sections of their texts.

In this unit, Bends I and II are not as distinct from one another as is usual. Unlike most other units, there is no mini-publication to mark the end of Bend I. Still, you'll want to let children know that today starts a new bend in the unit. While the first bend taught children to plan and structure, this bend teaches other qualities of good information writing. Children will draft and revise with these qualities in mind. This will give them more opportunities to practice whatever you have taught. Because a majority of third-grade writers need to elaborate more, many of the sessions in this book are dedicated to teaching children different ways to elaborate. Today you will enlist the help of an esteemed and beloved author to help you bring home this lesson.

To prepare for this lesson, do a quick scan of your students' recent checklists and work. In what ways are they already elaborating? What methods of elaborating need some fine-tuning? This prep work will help you tailor your teaching for maximum impact.

Although we mention mentor texts that we've found effective, you may find others that are a better match for your classroom. Choose well-written texts that students will find interesting, texts that meet the standards of your community.

In this minilesson, you'll expand earlier teaching, when you asked students to notice all the kinds of information an author has included. The list of kinds of information can be co-opted as a list of ways to elaborate. You'll want children to know that information writing is made with the bricks of information: numbers, descriptions, quotes, and facts. In your mid-workshop teaching, you may want to teach writers to quote and cite sources, starting with familiar sources (e.g., their friend Chloe, who also happens to be an expert on caring for curly hair). Show them how to quote, name the source, and say a bit about what makes that person an expert. By the end of today's session, your students' elaboration toolboxes should be filled to bursting.

You'll notice that in the active engagement section of this minilesson, students practice what they have learned on a class text. We have found that when a class is able to use what we teachers sometimes call a practice text, this can give students support. That is, we engineer a customized text that allows children to practice something they've learned. These texts are usually written on a topic pertaining to the classroom or the school so that every student has knowledge to draw on. If the whole class participates in a ballroom dancing extracurricular activity, for example, this might be about that topic. If you have not previously used a class text for active engagement, you might need to introduce one, explaining that you took some of the conversations students have had about the topic and wrote a quick chapter.

"By the end of today's session your students' elaboration toolboxes should be filled to bursting."

Also included in this session is a mid-workshop teaching that focuses on grammar, specifically on using transition words between and within sentences (CCSS W.3.2c). Depending on data from your assessments of your students, this could very well become its own session. On the other hand, it could just as easily be small-group or conference work if most of your students already have a good handle on transitions.

Studying Mentor Texts to Learn Elaboration Strategies

CONNECTION

Orient students to the new bend in the road of the unit.

"Writers, today we begin the second bend in our unit. If you think of the bends in the unit almost as chapters in your work, today's chapter is not radically different than the work you've been doing. You'll continue working on your same book, following the table of contents, and you'll continue to shift between drafting and then revising those chapters. But the focus of my teaching and your work will change. Instead of focusing on the organizational plan for the writing, we'll focus on the qualities of good information writing."

Methods of teaching are also methods of learning. Just as it is helpful for teachers to grasp the big goals of a new bend in a unit and to have some orientation, it's also helpful for kids to be let in on the curricular plans.

Tell a story that illustrates how being able to learn about elaboration from other people can be helpful in life.

"You all know that I'm a horrible eavesdropper. I listen in to other people's conversations all the time. Well, yesterday evening, I was on my way home on a very crowded bus. I heard a mother ask her son how his day at school was. And, of course, you know I couldn't resist leaning in and listening. I bet you can even guess what he said. 'Fine.'

When you tell this story, ham it up. Make the son sound especially taciturn and abrupt in his one-word answers.

"Then that mother tried again to talk with her son. She jumped to another topic this time and asked what he planned to do that weekend. He answered, 'Play.'

"She jumped to yet one more topic. 'What do you want for supper?' You can guess what he answered. 'Food.'

"I realized that what that boy was doing was a really extreme example of what some information book writers do as well. The boy kept telling just one thing about a topic, and then the conversation jumped to another, then another. What that boy needed to learn to do is to *elaborate*, or to say more. My hunch is that although none of you are like that boy, I bet each of you could elaborate more."

❖ Name the teaching point.

"Writers, today I want to teach you that when informational writers revise, they often consider ways they can add more, or elaborate. Information writers can learn to elaborate by studying mentor texts, taking note of all of the different kinds of information that writers use to teach readers about subtopics."

TEACHING

Explain that just as narrative writers elaborate by sketching out the "heart of the story" and telling key points bit by bit, information writers also have ways to elaborate.

"Writers, when you were working on stories, you learned that instead of taking giant steps through the event, it is important to tell the story bit by bit, including details, dialogue, and thinking. When you learned to write bit by bit as narrative writers, you were learning to elaborate.

"Information writers also need to elaborate. Whereas narrative writers sometimes reread a draft, decide on the heart of the story, and then stretch that part out by adding in what a character said or did, information writers elaborate in very different ways. In this unit, you'll learn lots of ways to elaborate.

"Whenever I want to do something as a writer, I find it helps to look at a text I like and to search for instances when the author did whatever *I* want to do. So I've been rereading *Deadliest Animals*. Melissa Stewart already taught us about a logical sequence for a table of contents, and I knew she could also teach me new ways to elaborate. Remember earlier, we listed the kinds of information that information writers include?"

◆ quotations

◆ statistics

◆ anecdotes

◆ observations

◆ descriptions

◆ vocabulary words

◆ lists

◆ labels

◆ different punctuation: colons, dashes, parentheses

"So I read a bit of this book and found in this passage that she has elaborated not just by telling facts but also by including an image. She uses what she knows about the topic to make a picture in her mind, an image, and use that image to help readers picture her topic. Listen."

> *Hippopotamuses are usually gentle giants. During the day, they lounge and snooze in shallow water holes. At night, they lumber onto land and munch on grasses and leaves.*

The truth is that whenever I am asked to under-take a new kind of writing, I search for examples that can help me envision the tone, structure, and voice that I want to assume. When I study a mentor text at this very early stage in the process, I'm not apt to notice the decorative details in that text; instead, I hope to gain an overall impression.

"Hmm. I'm noticing she's not picturing one day, one time. She's picturing her subject doing something typical. Let me try that. My chapter on this history of cockroaches could use that kind of elaboration.

"It starts like this."

> Cockroaches have been around for a long time. There are many different kinds of cockroaches. However there is only one species of cockroach that most people think about when they think about cockroaches–the German cockroach.

"Let me try to picture cockroaches—I know they won't be wallowing in mud holes like hippos!"

> Cockroaches have been around for a long time. When the earth was young, even before dinosaurs walked, about 350 million years ago, cockroaches were skittering across the land.

Name the elaboration strategy you borrowed from your mentor.

"Did you see how I made sure that I said more about one of my key points? But I didn't do it any old way, I tried to use the move my mentor author used, which was using facts and imagery.

"Now I can keep studying this part of my mentor text to help me elaborate on the rest of my chapter, or I can find another section that uses another elaboration technique I admire and try that."

ACTIVE ENGAGEMENT

Revise a previously written chapter from the class book.

"Now, it's your turn to try. We, of course, know our school very well. And we have spent some time talking about the different places in the building. In a book about our school, the table of contents might go something like this."

Places in Our School

- Chapter 1: The Main Office
- Chapter 2: Our Classroom
- Chapter 3: The Gym
- Chapter 4: The Nurse's Office
- Chapter 5: The Cafeteria

"Imagine that we are elaborating on one of these chapters—say, the chapter about the gym. Carlo has already taken a stab at this. He has a draft we can look at."

Notice that these are tiny excerpts of writing. The first is already written, so you have only to write the revised version in this minilesson. Time is of the essence, and this is a long, complex minilesson, so it's important to move along briskly.

Here you are using what we refer to as a practice text. That is, children can't help you elaborate in your cockroach book because they don't know the content. But you've created a text on a topic the whole class knows well to use as text.

Show the students an excerpt from another mentor text that does different elaboration work than was shown in your demonstration, asking them to work with their partners to name techniques they notice.

"Now, I'm going to put up a page from another section of *Deadliest Animals*, and I want you and your partner to look at and see if there are ways our author elaborates that we can use when we are trying to elaborate on our chapter about the gym. Let's look at an excerpt from this chapter, 'Small but Deadly.'"

> Scorpions
>
> *A scorpion's huge, claw-like pincers are its weapon of choice. But if a predator attacks or its prey puts up a fight . . . ZAP! A swift strike with the stinger on its tail usually does the trick.*
>
> *The stinger contains a hollow tube connected to two sacs full of venom. The scorpion controls the amount of venom its stinger delivers, so bigger victims get a bigger dose.*

"So, first, Partner 1, can you just name to Partner 2 some of the ways the author has elaborated? Be sure to give evidence from the text."

I listened in as the students talked to their partners. "I heard Sarah say she noticed that the author includes a little story of something happening, to help readers really picture what's going on. Instead of using an image, a picture, this writer uses a micro-story, a vignette, and it's not just a fun razzle-dazzle-for-decoration vignette. It's a vignette that teaches us something about the topic.

"Others of you noticed that the second paragraph has a topic sentence that tells the reader what to expect. Some of you noticed some other things as well."

Give students an opportunity to work with their partners to revise the class chapter using those techniques they just noticed.

"Now, Partner 2, with a little help from Partner 1, can you use "scorpions" to help revise the chapter Carlo wrote on the gym?" I showed the chapter. As students talked, I guided them to imagine ways they might apply the techniques they admired to this piece.

The Gym

Gym class is one of our favorite classes. We need to leave Room 303 and go to the gym. Once we're there we need to sit in our special spots. When Ms. Heinz is ready we do warm-ups. Then we learn about the activity for the day. Usually Ms. Heinz divides us up into groups so we can all get a turn.

The Common Core State Standards expect children to be able to talk about the craft moves that writers make to forward a central meaning. The work of studying a mentor text in order to name what the author has done and why she has done it is fundamental to the reading standards.

As children talk together about ways to revise the excerpt, take notes on a clipboard; later you'll share out a compilation and you can use or pretend to have used these ideas in its construction.

Celebrate and share the students' collective work to revise the class chapter, naming some of the moves they made while elaborating.

"Can I have everyone's eyes back up here? I listened closely to many of you as you were talking, and this is what I think I have now as our newest version of our chapter, using everything we learned from Melissa Stewart."

Gym Class

In a giant room, surrounded by basketball nets and sports equipment everywhere, we wait, sitting on pieces of tape stuck to the floor, imagining how we might get to use that equipment today. We are in our favorite class, gym!

Ms. Heinz teaches us how to do a lot of exciting things in gym class. In the fall we learn how to play football. In the winter we learn how to play basketball. In the spring we get to practice our soccer skills. In May and June we get to play baseball.

"Wow! So it looks like we uncovered even more ways we can elaborate by using our mentor texts and then applying them to our own topics. Fantastic!"

LINK

Channel writers to plan whether they want to revise previously written chapters or to draft a new chapter.

"Writers, today and every day throughout this unit, when you learn something new, you will decide whether you'll use it first to revise chapters you've already written or whether you'll use what you've learned to create new writing in your next chapter.

"If you are revising already-written chapters, I have a few suggestions. First, think of which parts of a chapter deserve more elaboration. When writing stories, you stretched out—you elaborated—on the heart of the story. Now, too, you'll want to elaborate on important parts of a chapter. And second, I suggest you don't try to use just a caret to elaborate. You need to give yourself space to add on a paragraph, not just a word. So I suggest a whole new draft, or a code inserted into the draft and then again at the end of the text, or a big flap of paper, taped on."

Warn students of one of the pitfalls of elaboration: repeating oneself.

"As you go back to your seats to revise your pieces, I want to give you one last tip about elaboration. Elaboration means to say more, to give additional information that hasn't been mentioned before. It *does not* mean saying the same thing twice, using different words. Like I wouldn't say, 'Cockroaches have been around for a long time. They are very old. They've been on earth for ages.' That's not giving more information. That's just repeating myself!"

You need not write this on chart paper yet. Instead, you can read it off from your clipboard. Of course, this is not a verbatim compilation of what your children suggested to you. Naturally, you may want to alter it or just pretend it represents the students' list.

Leading Students Away from Unintentional Plagiarism

BECAUSE THIS UNIT IS BASED ON STUDENTS' WRITING about topics on which they have expertise, the unit has built-in safeguards to keep students from copying books. As you encourage elaboration, however, they'll begin to rely on sources outside themselves, and you might find some students beginning to slide on that slippery slope.

Your knowledge of your students will help you make sense of this. It is very common for English language learners (ELLs), for example, to copy chunks of text as a scaffold for learning the language. They are not intentionally doing anything wrong, but rather they are trying to understand the language from the inside out. Then again, some ELLs may be barely holding on to what the text is saying at all, so without a more extensive vocabulary on the topic, paraphrasing becomes extremely difficult. It is also true that most third-graders who do copy from a text are not trying to "get one over" on anyone. Rather, they are trying to make their writing sound good, and sometimes, especially when sentences are very simple, it is hard to paraphrase the author's words.

One way to combat all of these situations is to make sure that students are using outside sources as additions and embellishments, not as the meat of the work. The students' own wording, structure, and phrasing should be the bulk of the writing. If they are adding a quote, a fact, or a number here or there, they will not be in danger of plagiarism. You can model this with your demonstration text by showing that when you are unsure of a specific fact or know you need to clarify a point, you leave a blank line or a question mark as a placeholder.

Additionally, you might pull a small group of students who have shown a particular need for more technical language or might have more facility with understanding the difference between their own words and a source's words. You can then teach this group how to use direct quotes and then attribute those quotes to their sources.

MID-WORKSHOP TEACHING   Using Transition Words

"Writers, can I interrupt you for a minute? Everywhere I look people are asking themselves, 'Do I need to add more?' and then cracking open their mentor texts to get ideas for ways to elaborate. Such nice work!

"When chapters and books are loaded with information—with examples, lists, descriptions—writers know that glue matters. For writing, we glue our work together with special words. Some people call these words *transition words*, or *connecting words*. These are words and phrases that you have used and read a million times. Words and phrases like *also, because, and, another reason,* and *for example*.

"Some writers who are newer to writing make the mistake of thinking they can just slap these words on in any old way. They don't think it really matters which words or where you put them! But you know that when you're applying glue to paper, and you put it in the wrong place, or it's a little bit sloppy, it can ruin the whole project. Transition words are the same way. It's important to read back your word and think, 'Are there ways I can make sure that this part is connected to that part? Are there ways I can smooth out the bumpy parts?'

"You can revise to add transition words in ways that glue a text together. And you can study how mentors use glue. Back to work!"

Studying Mentor Texts for More Elaboration Strategies

Channel writers to revisit the conversation you described at the start of the minilesson when the boy gives only one-word answers. Can they rewind and role-play a more elaborate response?

"Writers, your first challenge was just learning to say more. Remember that boy who answered his mother that his day was 'fine' and on the weekend he'd 'play'? Partner 2, pretend you are that boy. Partner 1, be the mother and see if you can rewind their conversation. This time, Partner 2, use all you know about elaboration to provide *your* answer to the questions."

The kids talked. Then I said, "As you elaborate, you'll find you'll learn ways to do this really well. Alessandra learned something today that can help the rest of us. She's been working on a book about soccer. Alessandra noticed that in her mentor text, the author would often say a fact. But then instead of going right on to the next fact, the author would say a little more about that first fact. So Alessandra tried that with her writing. She wrote this sentence":

The yellow card is when you get a penalty.

"Now, Alessandra could have stopped there, but she realized there was more to say about yellow cards and penalties. So she elaborated, adding more information about penalties."

It happens when you push, kick, trip, or even punch someone. You can get very aggressive when you fight too.

"I think we can all learn something important from Alessandra. We can find all sorts of things we can learn from our mentor authors that can help us elaborate and make our pieces the best they can be."

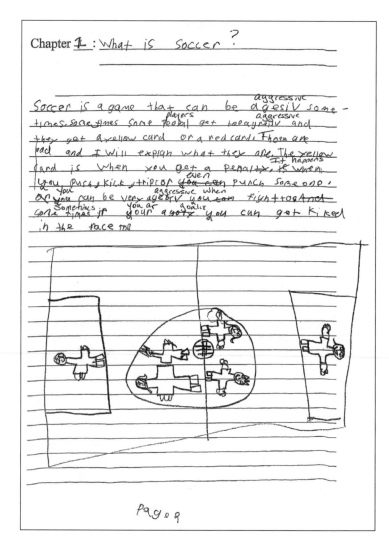

FIG. 6–1 Alessandra uses a mentor text to work on elaboration.

Session 7

Making Connections within and across Chapters

YOUNGSTERS WILL ALWAYS THINK THAT A UNIT OF STUDY is about the topic you name—in this instance, writing information books. But you will always know that within the broad scope of a unit, you will address a few goals that seem especially important. These goals will be multifaceted. After all, you can't teach a child to ride a two-wheeler by saying, "For starters, we'll focus on just the brakes or just on balancing." Neither braking nor balancing can be taught save within the context of pedaling, accelerating, holding handlebars, and so forth. Similarly, your focus when teaching this unit can't be too narrow. As soon as you focus on writing with lots of information and with a variety of information, you'll need to focus also on writing within a structure and on linking one piece of information with another. That's the topic for today's session.

Approach this teaching with proper humility. The truly great nonfiction writers are able to weld disparate pieces together to create a cohesive draft, and the techniques they use are far more complex than the admonition "Add linking words!" Listen, for example, to the start of E. B. White's passage on J.F.K., and notice the tongue-and-groove fit between one sentence and the next.

John F. Kennedy

When we think of him, he is without a hat, standing in the wind and weather. He was impatient of top coats and hats, preferring to be exposed, and he was young enough and tough enough to confront and enjoy the cold and the wind of the time, whether the winds of nature or the winds of political circumstance and national danger. He died of exposure, but in a way he would have settled for—in the line of duty, with his friends and enemies all around, supporting him and shooting at him. It can be said of him, as of few men in a like position, that he did not fear the weather.

Do you see the finesse? The theme that synthesizes the text, the deft use of repeating key words, the way sentences overlap with each other, so a new sentence restates the former content and then adds new content? This is nothing to sneeze at.

IN THIS SESSION, you'll teach children how to connect the information in their chapters using different transitional strategies and phrases. You'll suggest they look to a mentor text for ideas about how best to transition in their own informational books.

GETTING READY

✔ Your own metaphor to describe how writing is made up of different connected pieces, for example, a paper chain (see Connection)

✔ Your own information text, to model rehearsing across fingers and drafting in a way that connects all the parts (see Teaching)

✔ Class book, to draft a chapter together with students (see Active Engagement)

✔ Chart paper and markers

✔ Mentor texts or other reference books in which students can check their spelling (see Mid-Workshop Teaching)

✔ Index cards or Post-its® (see Mid-Workshop Teaching)

✔ Information Writing Checklist, Grades 3 and 4

COMMON CORE STATE STANDARDS: W.3.2.a,b,c; W.3.4, W.3.5, W.3.7, W.4.2.a,b,c; RI.3.3, RI.3.8, RI.3.10, RFS.3.3, SL.3.6, L.3.1, L.3.2.e,f,g; L.3.4.d, L.3.6

Making Connections within and across Chapters

CONNECTION

Describe an object that is made up of various connected pieces.

"A writing teacher once told me that writing is like making paper chains. Has anyone here ever made a paper chain?" I held up a paper chain I had constructed to illustrate the point. If you have made one of these, you know that each piece of paper becomes a link and that link connects directly to another link. When the connections are weak, the chain breaks apart."

Name the teaching point.

"Today I want to teach you that writing chapters is like making paper chains. Writers know that each chapter needs to connect to the chapter before it. Actually, each paragraph connects to the one before it as well. There are two secrets to this. First, the order needs to make sense. And second, the author uses transitional words like *because* and *also* to glue parts of the text together."

TEACHING

Before demonstrating how to link pieces of information, explain that you first need to have compiled information. Review yours.

"Today I want to show you how I link my writing together, just as paper chains are linked together. Let's think about that while we work on an important chapter about ways to prevent cockroaches from getting into a home in the first place. Before a writer can think about making the pieces of writing (and information) link together, the writer needs lots of information. So I have already collected things I want to say." I revealed a piece of chart paper on which I'd listed my points.

◆ COACHING

If a picture is worth a thousand words, an artifact is worth even more! If you don't have time to make a paper chain, channel a child or two to do this prior to the minilesson. That chain will link the chain makers to your lesson in a powerful way.

Reviewing my list, I said, "Okay, so I know I want to talk about keeping your home clean so cockroaches aren't tempted to come in. I also want to talk about keeping all food in plastic, glass, and metal containers. And I want to talk about making sure your home is drafty, keeping air flowing, because cockroaches don't like a lot of dry air. Oh, yes, I also want to be sure to include something about plugging up any gaps or holes that are thicker than a dime.

"So, writers, remember that the first step to linking all information is to do what you already learned to do, and that is to plan the structure of the writing. The first thing is to think, 'How will the miniature table of contents for this part go?' Help me think about that for my chapter on preventing cockroaches from coming in. Hmm." I scanned the page on which I'd jotted information.

"Which order?" I held up my hand so I could show ticking off fingers in order. "I think plugging the holes goes first. That keeps them out. Then I need to think of ways to make them not like my house, for example keeping the house drafty and putting food away. Oh! I like that! My progression is like almost following the cockroach's journey into a home.

"Now I'm ready to draft the chapter. As I draft, I'm going to remember the next way to link information—that is, to use transition words as glue."

> There are many ways that you can keep cockroaches from ever becoming a problem in your home. You would want to keep them from even walking in to begin with by plugging gaps.
>
> Also, you can make the space uncomfortable for cockroaches by making it drafty. Another way to keep cockroaches from being a problem in your home is to be sure they can't survive. Cleaning up all food and storing foods in cockroach-proof containers accomplishes this.

Review your writing and highlight the replicable things you did to link things together in your writing.

"So did you guys see how I checked to make sure my order was logical? Did you notice how I thought carefully about how to connect one sentence to the next by using transitional words (*also, another*) and by using words and phrases that were mentioned in earlier paragraphs (like *problem in the home*)?"

ACTIVE ENGAGEMENT

Return to the class book, choose a chapter to draft together, and have the students try a quick rehearsal.

"So, let's all try this right now with our class book. Let's try writing about the nurse's office. First, we need to think about a logical structure for our information. Let's tick off on our fingers the things we think are important to include about the nurse's office."

This list needs to be jotted on chart paper because you'll later scan it—and will want children to do so as well.

Notice that here I am linking one section of the minilesson with another. In this instance, the phrase "once you have a lot of information" references and repeats something I said earlier.

Notice that when debriefing, I describe these things in ways that are replicable and that can be used another day in another text.

I took the lead, pantomiming ticking off on my fingers and taking on a quizzical look. "When you feel ready, talk it over with your partner. What should we include? How should we organize our chapter? What should go first? How are we going to link the parts?"

Max turned to his partner. "I think we should include the things she does to see if we're okay—like take your temperature. Then write about what she gives us, like band-aids and ice packs."

"I agree." Carlo nodded. "But we probably want to say something first, before all that stuff. Like a mini-introduction. Maybe something like 'When you don't feel well, you should go to the nurse's office.'"

Once students have orally rehearsed, record on chart paper a combined version of their various ideas, which you have modified to match your goals.

"You have a lot to say about the nurse's office! Kayla and Vitaly were saying that it felt like this chapter should be organized by the things the nurse does for you in the nurse's office. So it seems like you are saying the chapter might go like this," and I wrote-in-the-air, stressing the portions that showed a logical order and those that included linking words. I dictated:

The Nurse's Office

Our nurse is very good at making us feel better. When we go to the office, she makes us feel better. If we bump our heads or arms or anything else, she gives us an ice pack. Another thing she does in the office is that if we have a cut or scrape, she gives us a bandage. She also helps us out of her office. If we have a temperature, she sends us home. If we are sick for a long time at home, she calls us up.

"I'll stop there. I think we all know how this chapter is going to go. I love how each part of this feels connected to the part that comes right before and right after it."

LINK

Rename the teaching point and remind students that this lesson pertains not only to today but also to any day.

"Writers, today and any day that you are writing informational pieces, think about how you can put your chapters and sections together as if you are constructing a paper chain—making sure that each piece connects logically to the piece that comes before it."

Recruit students to reread the work they've done so far in their book, and then to make plans for what they'll do today based on that.

"Writers, let's think for a moment of what you know how to do as information writers. How many of you know how to plan a table of contents like an outline of a chapter you want to write, making sure you have a logical structure? How

The instruction you are giving to students is very high level, so if you notice that students aren't grasping what you are hoping to teach, don't be surprised and don't feel as if you need to reteach right now. It is in fifth grade when students are expected to be able to structure their information texts logically. You are initiating this and helping some members of the class to grasp this today, but you should not worry that it seems beyond some.

Again this won't be written on chart paper yet. Instead, jot it on your clipboard and read from there.

many of you know how to ask questions of the plan before plunging ahead with it—questions like, 'Are the parts of my text going to be equal in weight?' How many of you know how to write with a variety of information—facts, descriptions, images? How many of you know how to think about whether you have used transition words to link one part of your text with another?

"There are other things you know as well. Right now, reread your work, plan what you will do, record your planning on a Post-it, and then you can get started."

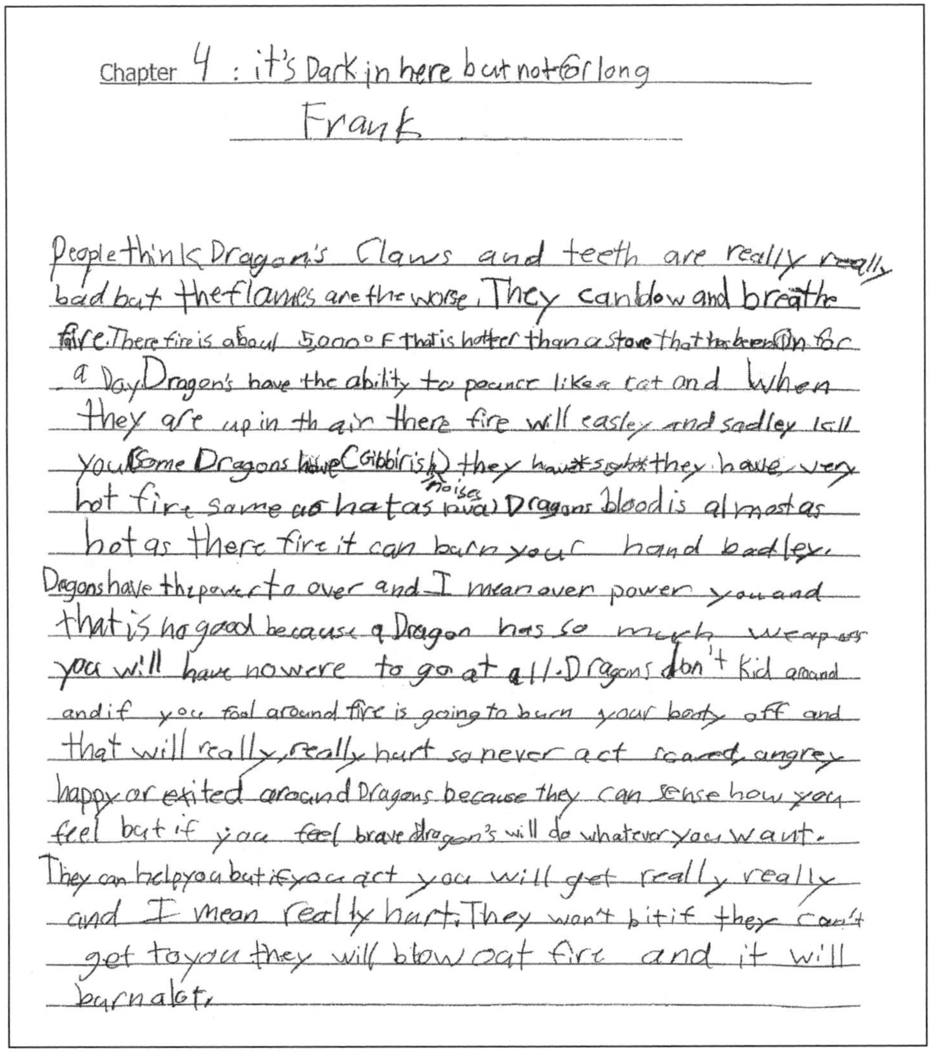

Chapter 4 : it's Dark in here but not for long

Frank

People think Dragon's claws and teeth are really really bad but the flames are the worse. They can blow and breath fire. There fire is about 5,000° F that is hotter than a stove that has been on for a Day. Dragon's have the ability to pounce like a cat and when they are up in th air there fire will easley and sadley kill you. Some Dragons have (Gibbirish) they have sat they have very hot fire same as hat as (noise) Dragons blood is almost as hot as there fire it can burn your hand badley. Dragons have the power to over and I mean over power you and that is no good because a Dragon has so much weapons you will have nowere to go at all. Dragons don't kid around and if you fool around fire is going to burn your body off and that will really, really hurt so never act scared, angrey, happy or exited around Dragons because they can sense how you feel but if you feel brave dragon's will do whatever you want. They can help you but if you act you will get really, really and I mean realy hurt. They won't bit if they can't get to you they will blow out fire and it will burn a lot.

FIG. 7–1   Frank works to connect a chapter to the one that precedes it, as well as working to connect the information inside the chapter.

Making Plans for Work

PETER JOHNSTON, IN HIS POWERFUL BOOK *CHOICE WORDS* (2004), discusses the importance of agency, that is, students' ability and desire to be in charge of their own learning. In the push of standards, deadlines, and time constraints, it's easy to lose sight of the fact that we are teaching little human beings who very likely have their own ideas about how and when to do certain things—especially when it comes to a project on a topic that is near and dear to their hearts.

If you haven't done so already, you will want to make today be the day that your students are following not only your plans for the unit, but also their plans for their pieces. You might find it helpful to break your class up into groups based on patterns that you're seeing: students who currently have their own plans, students who should have their own plans but don't, students who are unsure what a good plan would be, students who make plans but don't follow them, and so on.

You will then want to gather those students together in small groups, perhaps not all today, but definitely across the next few days, to teach them about the value of making individual writing plans and then following those plans. You will want to show some of them ways to pace themselves, perhaps providing them with personal calendars. Others you will want to teach the habit of making a personal assignment for each day they write. Above all, you will want to teach each student that no matter what is going on in class on a particular day, it is important that they have their own writing plans alongside this work. Students' own plans and visions for how they want their work to go is of the utmost importance and should be the most powerful engine in any unit.

MID-WORKSHOP TEACHING
Using Research Resources to Help Fine-Tune Spelling

"Writers, I'm glad to see you are punctuating and paragraphing as you write. Show your partner the paragraphing you've been doing, and if you spot anyone in this class who isn't writing in paragraphs, help that person straight away."

After leaving a few minutes for that, I added, "Because almost all of you are punctuating and paragraphing, I want to remind you of one more thing you must do, and that is, you *must* spell your high-frequency words correctly. We usually refer to high-frequency words as 'word wall words.' Will you quickly check these high-frequency words, because once you are in third grade, you should never mess these up: *then, because, when, which, also, in addition.*

"Now I have one more pointer. You have your own particular list of high-frequency words—that is, words that are very frequent in your writing. *Cockroach* is one of my words—though it's not yours. The thing is, it's really not okay for an expert on a topic not to be able to spell key words related to that topic. It would be silly if I was spelling *cockroach* like this: *c-o-o-k-r-o-a-c-h.*

"Here is a tip. I know that some of you have been taking quick looks at books, checking for facts to add to your writing. You can look in those same places to find the spellings of key words. You could copy the correct spellings from those references onto a Post-it and keep that paper someplace handy so you can check back when you need it."

Using the Third-Grade Checklist to Check if Your Writing Is Stronger

Remind writers of the goals they set earlier and channel them to look between their latest writing and the checklist they previously studied.

"Writers, I almost didn't want to stop you because you were all so engrossed in your writing. But I want to make sure that you are keeping in mind the goals that you set for yourself earlier in this unit and noting ways that your writing is changing. Would you get out the goals you set for yourself and also the third-grade checklist?" I waited for children to do this. The Information Writing Checklist, Grades 3 and 4, can be found on the CD-ROM.

Demonstrate how to look between the checklist and your writing, highlighting the fact that you discover new goals.

I placed an excerpt of my draft on chart paper and looked back and forth between the checklist and the excerpt. "Watch to see the way I study whether my draft shows I can now do an item on our checklist or whether my draft shows that I'm still learning it. Earlier, I decided one goal would be to elaborate more, so I'll start by looking at what I've done to elaborate." I then read aloud a bit of my text.

> There are many ways that you can keep cockroaches from ever becoming a problem in your home. You would want to keep them from even walking in to begin with by plugging gaps.

Information Writing Checklist

	Grade 3	NOT YET	STARTING TO	YES!	**Grade 4**	NOT YET	STARTING TO	YES!
	Structure							
Overall	I taught readers information about a subject. I put in ideas, observations, and questions.	☐	☐	☐	I taught readers different things about a subject. I put facts, details, quotes, and ideas into each part of my writing.	☐	☐	☐
Lead	I wrote a beginning in which I got readers ready to learn a lot of information about the subject.	☐	☐	☐	I hooked my readers by explaining why the subject mattered, telling a surprising fact, or giving a big picture. I let readers know that I would teach them different things about a subject.	☐	☐	☐
Transitions	I used words to show sequence such as *before*, *after*, *then*, and *later*. I also used words to show what didn't fit such as *however* and *but*.	☐	☐	☐	I used words in each section that help readers understand how one piece of information connected with others. If I wrote the section in sequence, I used words and phrases such as *before*, *later*, *next*, *then*, and *after*. If I organized the section in kinds or parts, I used words such as *another*, *also*, and *for example*.	☐	☐	☐
Ending	I wrote an ending that drew conclusions, asked questions, or suggested ways readers might respond.	☐	☐	☐	I wrote an ending that reminded readers of my subject and may have suggested a follow-up action or left readers with a final insight. I added my thoughts, feelings, and questions about the subject at the end.	☐	☐	☐
Organization	I grouped my information into parts. Each part was mostly about one thing that connected to my big topic.	☐	☐	☐	I grouped information into sections and used paragraphs and sometimes chapters to separate those sections. Each section had information that was mostly about the same thing. I may have used headings and subheadings.	☐	☐	☐

Also, you can make the space uncomfortable for cockroaches by making it drafty. Another way to keep cockroaches from being a problem in your home is to be sure they can't survive. Cleaning up all food and storing foods in cockroach-proof containers accomplishes this.

"Let's see." I pointed to the checklist under "Elaboration." "Have I written facts, definitions, details, and observations about my topic and explained them?" I began rereading my draft, annotating evidence or lack thereof for each of these, illuminating items I had not achieved yet. "I definitely don't see any definitions in my writing," I said. "I'm going to look at mentor texts to study how authors do that."

Then I paused. "I could go, on but I think you see that I really check for evidence when I use the checklist, and I'm hard on myself. The whole point of this is to find goals and reach toward them. I'll go on doing this for the rest of my writing."

Ask students to try using the checklist to get a first impression of their piece, to get a sense of where they are as writers today.

"I know that you are still a bit early in the writing process for this piece, but you can use this checklist right now as a way of seeing where you are now so you can make plans for what you might want to do in the future. Can you, right now, read your piece, then look back at the checklist and do a quick check of where you are today?"

I motioned to the students to get started and then moved through the meeting area, looking over shoulders and coaching students who needed help.

Tell students that one great way to make sure their writing from today forward is stronger than it has ever been is to use the checklist to set goals.

"I am so impressed with your honesty about your writing and your willingness to take a serious look at your drafts. I can tell from the buzz in the room that many of you are already chomping at the bit to get back to your seats to start adding and changing things right away. I completely understand and respect that desire. But can I ask you to do one more thing before you get back to work? Can you take just a minute to write at the top of your draft a little note to yourself about what you would like to accomplish as you work on your writing? What are your current goals for this piece of writing? When you have those jotted down, you can head back to your seats."

Session 8

Balancing Facts and Ideas from the Start

THE WRITER'S OWN DEEP INVOLVEMENT with the subject matter leads readers to also be involved with the subject. Consider the great nonfiction writers—Rachel Carson, writing about the seashore; Clifford Geertz, writing about a cockfight; John Muir writing about Yosemite Park—and you'll note that each writer brings a zeal and a wonder for the mysteries of the topic. A writer of information texts sustains the reader's interest by putting his or her own interest, voice, and above all, ideas onto the page.

Children, too, need to be taught not only to collect and convey information, but also to respond to that information. This doesn't mean that they need to add, "I think that's disgusting" or "I never knew that!" as they are apt to do when asked to think in response to information. In fact, there are some kinds of information texts—newspaper reports or business reports, for example—where the first-person pronoun would be out of place. Nevertheless, children need to learn that effective information writing shows the writer's own involvement with and interpretation of a subject. Readers want to read texts in which facts carry and create ideas.

This is especially true now, when information is so accessible. People carry mini-computers in their pockets and call them phones. Just over a decade ago, it was a novelty for a teacher to have a working computer in her classroom, and now it's considered a travesty if there aren't several available at any given time. People, our children included, are used to being able to get facts anytime and anywhere. Accessing information takes no longer than it takes to type in a Google request. The result of this information overload is that now, when readers turn to information books, they want more than the facts. They want the facts with a new perspective, organized in a way that makes them think.

Like the best fiction, the best nonfiction has voice. Facts alone do not convey a voice. The writer's personal voice shines through when these facts are coupled with ideas. The best nonfiction makes something of mere facts. The challenge when teaching information writing is to teach children to generate ideas, align them with facts, and weave both facts and ideas together into a text.

IN THIS SESSION, you'll teach children the art of balancing interesting facts with engaging style. You'll highlight revision strategies that encompass both structure and word choice that will enhance their voices in their drafts.

GETTING READY

✔ Mentor text, *Deadliest Animals*

✔ A paragraph from your informational book, full of facts that need more interesting information or ideas (see Teaching)

✔ Another paragraph full of facts, written on chart paper for students to revise (see Active Engagement)

✔ "Informational Writers Bring Their Writing to Life" chart (see Link)

✔ Chart paper and markers

COMMON CORE STATE STANDARDS: W.3.2, W.3.5, W.4.2, RI.3.4, SL.3.1, SL.3.3, SL.3.6, L.3.1, L.3.2, L.3.3.a, L.3.6

Balancing Facts and Ideas from the Start

CONNECTION

Invite your class into a small inquiry study of the balance of facts and ideas using a preselected information text that shows that balance clearly and well.

"Yesterday someone said to me, 'Oh, your third-graders are writing information texts?' And then she nodded knowingly and said, 'Facts, facts, facts. They must be writing down all kinds of facts.'"

"Writers, she got me thinking. *Do* information texts contain facts and *only* facts?" I held my chin and looked skyward as if pondering the question. "I don't know. Let's check together. Listen carefully as I read aloud from our mentor text, *Deadliest Animals* by Melissa Stewart." I began reading loud and clear.

> *The African lion has all the features you'd expect to find in one of the world's deadliest animals. These powerful predators are skillful stalkers that usually hunt together in groups called "prides" and can take down prey ten times their size. That's why people often call lions "the kings of the jungle."*

"Writers, of the three sentences I just read, two sound like facts. One, that lions are predators that hunt in groups and can take down animals ten times their size. And, two, that they are called the kings of the jungle because of their hunting skills. But the very first sentence . . . Let me repeat it. Listen closely and tell me if it sounds like a fact."

> *The African lion has all the features you'd expect to find in one of the world's deadliest animals.*

I invited children to comment. Kayla said, "That's not a fact. It's like an order on how to think." Max said, "It's like the writer is talking to us." Vitaly said, "It's not a fact. It's like an idea. It's telling us what we expect about lions."

"Hmm," I added. "I think I agree with you about the first sentence. It isn't a fact; it's an *idea*. After that, the sentences do hold some facts—facts that support an idea. Let's take a look at those next sentences again." I read aloud.

> *These powerful predators are skillful stalkers that usually hunt together in groups called "prides" and can take down prey ten times their size. That's why people often call lions "the kings of the jungle."*

When I teach teachers, I often try to begin by naming what I'm sure is on teachers' minds. For example, if I'm teaching about conferring, I don't wait long before addressing the question of how one gets around efficiently to all the kids. I know that teaching involves taking the learner on a journey, and it can help to start where the learner is.

In this start to the minilesson, I try to begin at the very beginning. I believe many kids and many teachers, too, think that information texts are made of facts. So I begin there.

"It seems to me that those sentences contain facts—lions are stalkers that hunt together in groups called *prides* and they can take down prey ten times their size. But the author has used those facts to grow ideas. To this author, all those facts add up to some big ideas. These are powerful predators. The fact that they do these things is why they are called the *kings of the jungle*. Those absolutely are big ideas.

"Writers, here's something you need to know: although at first glance, information texts might seem to be just facts, facts, facts, the truth is that these texts also contain ideas that make sense of those facts. In fact, if it weren't for the ideas, information texts would be nothing more than patches full of jumbled-up facts."

❖ **Name the teaching point.**

"Today I want to teach you that when you write information books, you try to *interest* your reader. Readers love fascinating facts, *and* they love ideas, too. Writers make sure their writing contains both facts and ideas."

TEACHING

Demonstrate a couple of ways that an idea might be added to a fact-filled paragraph.

"Writers, remember that paragraph I wrote about keeping your home cockroach free?"

> There are many ways that you can keep cockroaches from ever becoming a problem in your home. You would want to keep them from even walking in to begin with by plugging gaps.
>
> Also, you can make the space uncomfortable for cockroaches by making it drafty. Another way to keep cockroaches from being a problem in your home is to be sure they can't survive. Cleaning up all food and storing foods in cockroach-proof containers accomplishes this.

"For example, in the passage about the lions, it was almost as if the author asked herself, 'So what?' Or another way to say it is she asked, 'So what does all that make me think?' and she came up with ideas like, 'Lions are powerful predators' and 'Lions' ability to hunt is why they have the name 'king of the jungle.' What ideas might our facts give us about cockroaches?"

We reread the text, and this time I said, almost dictating a new entry:

> It's not an easy job to keep cockroaches out of a house—but it is possible.

"Then again it could end like this."

> Humans can say "No Entry" to roaches by taking these few simple steps.

William Stafford talks about "the importance of plain receptivity" when writing. He describes his process of growing ideas through writing by saying, "I get pen and paper, take a glance out of the window (often it is dark out there), and wait. It is like fishing. But I do not work long, for there is always a nibble—and this is where receptivity comes in. To get started, I will accept anything that occurs to me.... If I put something down, that thing will help the next thing come, and I'm off.... Things occur to me that were not in my mind when I started." (Stafford, A Way of Writing, 1978)

Debrief in a way that highlights the replicable aspects of the work you have demonstrated.

"Writers, did you see what I did? I took my cockroach paragraph that had nothing but facts, and showed you several ways that I could add ideas to this paragraph. You'll recall I asked myself questions such as 'So what?' and 'What does that tell me?'"

The ideas that I gesture toward and demonstrate are very accessible ideas—but that's as it should be. You want to remind writers to do some work they should already be able to do.

ACTIVE ENGAGEMENT

Invite students to study a few fact-filled sentences and develop an idea to go with them.

"Let me see you have a go at this. I'm going to put up a small paragraph that is full of facts, facts, facts. See if you can add an idea somewhere into this paragraph. Remember, you could look the reader in the eye and talk directly to him or her. Or you could paint a tiny descriptive picture to hook your reader's attention. Or add an idea at the end to summarize. Or you could invent a new way to add an idea. Pens and paper ready?"

I put the following paragraph up on chart paper for writers to consider, allowing them a minute or two to pen an idea.

The ideas that I gesture toward and demonstrate are very accessible ideas—but that's as it should be. You want to remind writers to do some work they should already be able to do.

Note that minilessons are very repetitive. If we want to bring home these concepts, it is important to repeat them often.

> The head of the ant has a pair of large, strong jaws. The jaws open and shut sideways like a pair of scissors. Adult ants cannot chew and swallow solid food. Instead they swallow the juice, which they squeeze from pieces of food.

Notice that whenever we include bits of student writing, we keep those texts very, very short. This excerpt is long enough to make the point.

Call out for a few students to share the idea they've added, describing the move that each has used.

Kayla suggested, "At first, an ant looks like any other animal. But actually, its body works differently than the bodies of most animals."

Max volunteered, "It's not just ant colonies that are special. Their bodies are special, too."

"So, writers, you've done some wise work. You've taken a text that contained facts, facts, facts, and you've added ideas. You may not realize it, but in a way, what you seem to have done is to collect facts and then ask yourself, 'So what?' and your answer to that question is your idea."

Here, I want to emphasize that there is no trade-off between facts and ideas. It's the marriage of the two that works.

LINK

Send writers off to draw on all they have learned to do as they draft a new chapter and revise old ones.

"Before you head off to work today, I want you to remind you that you aren't just carrying with you today's lesson about interesting your readers with facts and ideas. You know many other things that you should also pull out of your pockets to use as you draft and revise your chapters. Can you think for a few minutes about some of the other things you know about making your informational writing come to life for your reader? Think about all the things we've talked about so far this year, of course, but also push yourself to remember things you learned last year or things you've learned from mentor authors. Put a thumb up when you have an idea or two."

I waited a few beats, watching to see when most students had a thumb up. I then turned to a blank piece of chart paper. "Let's make a chart we can use now and add to as we go, reminding us of all the things we know to do to bring informational writing to life."

The students took turns sharing their ideas. After a few minutes, sometimes finessing some ideas so they would be more helpful for more students, we had begun a new chart I knew we could add to throughout the unit and the year.

Informational Writers Bring Their Writing to Life

- Add a vignette to illustrate a bit of information or an idea.
- After mentioning a fact, say a bit more about that fact.
- Describe something in detail.
- Compare something that might be unfamiliar to readers with something that's likely to be familiar.

Remember that many great nonfiction writers write with the personal pronoun. Your third-grade teacher may have wagged her finger at you, saying, "Never use the personal pronoun, I," but when one studies effective nonfiction writers, that advice is not borne out. Zinsser limits the use of one. He writes in On Writing Well, *"I don't want to meet 'one.' He's a boring guy. I want a professor with a passion for his subject to tell me why it fascinates him" (1998).*

Conferring with the Checklist in Hand

YOU'LL WANT TO PREPARE FOR YOUR CONFERENCES and small-group work by spending some time studying your students' writing in relation to the checklist and their goals, trying to decide on the most important instruction you can give. When you read over students' drafts, try to look at the work with a particular lens in hand.

I pulled my chair alongside Brady, who was looking between the fourth-grade checklist and her most recent chapter, "Turtles Are Very Cheap." She was struggling especially to decide whether her chapter was well structured. "It says that each section needs to be mostly about one thing," she explained, "so I'm rereading to see if everything in my chapter is mostly about the title—'Turtles Are Very Cheap.'"

FIG. 8–1 Brady's chapter on the cost of turtles delves into their value instead.

MID-WORKSHOP TEACHING
Don't Let Your Writing Be a Trash Compactor

"Writers, how many of you have a seen a trash compactor? In some people's kitchens, there is a machine that scrunches up and squeezes down trash, so tin cans are as flat as a lid, and boxes are sheets of cardboard. There's no air left—just metal, plastic, and cardboard.

"Years ago, the great Pulitzer Prize–winning writer Don Murray led a writing class for me and other writing teachers. In the class, we did what you are doing. We wrote nonfiction texts on topics we knew a lot about. After Don read my draft and the drafts that my classmates had written, he said, 'Writers, I need to tell you one thing. You are writing as if you are a trash compactor. Everything you have to say is scrunched up and squashed down.'

"Class, I'm telling you this because your writing is squashed down, too. And I say this especially because for one topic, you tend to have a sentence or two. Nonfiction writers write in paragraphs, not in sentences.

"Right now, will you take a recent passage or page that you've written and will you rewrite that passage, only this time, let whatever took three or four lines fill a page now. Write with much, much more detail and with more ideas. You can use these thought prompts if you need to do so," I said, and gestured toward a list of phrases, such as "The important thing about this is . . . " and 'This makes me realize that . . . "

I read over her shoulder, noticing immediately that in fact she had many sections of her chapter that explored whether turtles are worth a lot of money or not. She'd explained that they are "not fun" because it feels like the turtle is "not in the house" and because "you don't really play with the turtle." These passages, of course, weren't about the turtle's cost so much as its value.

I wondered if Brady would come to this insight on her own. I asked her which sections felt unrelated to her idea that turtles are cheap, and she pointed to many of them. "You are doing just the work you need to do with your checklist," I told her. "You are using it like a teacher. It's telling you there is a problem here. The contents don't go with what you claim your chapter is really about." I congratulated her for noticing this, and suggested she consider whether perhaps the real topic, and real title, weren't the cost of the turtle, but something close yet different. "So now maybe you take out parts that don't go," I said, "and somehow you rework the umbrella idea."

I told her I knew she'd figure it out, and she'd find yet more work to do with the checklist.

Shifting between Big Ideas and Small Examples

Teach writers that good information writing shifts between big ideas and small examples, details, and explanations.

"Writers, do you remember being taught that when you go to write a true story, it's important to write not about big watermelon ideas but to write instead about small seed stories? Like instead of writing about summer camp, you write about the last bonfire at camp.

"Well, today, I hope you are learning that when writing information texts, it actually works best if you *do* include some big watermelon ideas. And now, your seeds aren't just stories. They are examples, definitions, explanations.

"Ryan is going to read you the chapter he wrote today, and will you see if you can grasp his big idea and some of his small specifics." I made gestures to accompany both the big and the small ideas.

> The reason why most people hate/despise rats is they look at rats like sewer suckers and evil rat eyes and bad things. They don't see how they can make great pets and companions. When you look at something by their down points, you don't see the great things about them. So if you want a loyal, squeaky companion, get a rat.
>
> Rats are curious. They can be taught many tricks like rat basketball. They can also easily tell the difference between two or more people. Even though they are nocturnal, they will adjust their schedule to when you are home. Rats really enjoy the company of people. Some rats may be adventurous and outgoing, while others may be laid back and cuddly. You can train them to sit on your shoulder, to be litter-trained, and come by name.

"Tell your partner what Ryan's big idea is and what his supporting details are." As the children talked, I pointed out to them that Ryan's idea wasn't just stated in a single line. He took his time developing it.

FIG. 8–2   Ryan's chapter showing a big idea and small specifics

Session 9

Researching Facts and Ensuring Text Accuracy

I N THE PREVIOUS SESSION, you reminded writers that their readers want not just facts and information, but also the writer's own enthusiasm for those facts. Readers want the writer's responses to information. Listen, for example, to this famous passage from *The Glow-Worm* (1924) by Jean-Henri Fabre, the French entomologist.

> Few insects vie in popular fame with the glow-worm, that curious little animal which, to celebrate the little joys of life, kindles a beacon at its tail end.... Who has not seen it roam amid the grass, like a spark fallen from the moon at its full?

This session shifts back again to a focus on information, allowing your instruction to mirror the shifts that nonfiction writing itself needs to take: between information and response to information, facts and ideas. More specifically, this session highlights the importance of research. You aren't teaching youngsters to write "Ye Olde Research Report." This is not a time for children to buy three packs of index cards and to begin collecting a file box full of notes. Instead, your message is that while writers are in the act of drafting, they often come to intervals when a quick foray into research is vital.

This basic message—that research is an integral part of a writer's life—is often lost in writing instruction. We can blame logistics: writing is what kids do in the classroom, research is what they do down the hall in the library, and one wants to avoid the brouhaha of moving twenty-seven third-graders back and forth between classrooms and school libraries. We can blame the daily schedule: we're lucky to have a measly x number of minutes per day to teach "writing" without throwing "research" into the package. We can blame resources: the reference material is either too high in reading level or we just don't have research material that is relevant to the specific things children want to know. And let's not even get started on the Internet: how's a kid to know which one of 4,860,000 results to look at first?

IN THIS SESSION, you'll teach children that informational writers are actually researchers, and you'll also suggest resources for finding more information to enhance their informational books.

GETTING READY

✔ Whiteboard and marker (see Connection)

✔ Reference books and resources students can use to research their topics (see Teaching)

✔ Your writer's notebook (see Mid-Workshop Teaching)

✔ Students' writer's notebooks (see Share)

✔ Chart paper and markers to complete a two-column chart titled "Expert Vocabulary," the first column of which is already filled out with examples of domain-specific words used in *Deadliest Animals* (see Share)

COMMON CORE STATE STANDARDS: W.3.2, W.3.5, W.3.7, W.3.8, W.3.10, RI.3.4, RI.3.8, RI.3.10, SL.3.1, SL.3.2, L.3.1, L.3.2, L.3.3.a, L.3.6

The fact remains that "researching" cannot be divorced from "writing." The sooner we make arrangements for children to be able to look things up within their everyday writing space, the more accustomed they'll become to reaching out for the facts and references to bolster their work.

> "The sooner we make arrangements for children to be able to look things up within their everyday writing space, the more accustomed they'll become to reaching out for the facts and references to bolster their work."

Once you know the topics your children have chosen, you'll want to search for level-appropriate reference books on these topics. This might mean borrowing several books from the library or from other rooms. Instead of opening up the whole World Wide Web, you might allow access to certain websites (such as the ones connected to the Smithsonian Institute, PBS Kids, or other reputable sources) that are encyclopedic in nature and at your children's reading level.

In addition, in this session, you'll encourage your young writers to interview experts in their community.

Researching Facts and Ensuring Text Accuracy

CONNECTION

Enlist students' help in listing the tools people in various professions use and then ask the class to suggest the tools writers need.

"Writers, can you tell me the tools that a dentist uses? I need descriptions."

I gave children about forty seconds to fill the room with animated descriptions of mouth mirrors, spit-sucking tubes, and "sticks topped with hooked needles."

"Ouch!" I said, clutching my cheek in response. "Okay, can you give me examples of some tools that a policeman might keep handy?"

I again allowed about forty seconds for students to fill the room with chatter about walkie-talkies, whistles, handcuffs, batons, and flashlights. Summoning their attention, I said, "Now think carefully and tell me—what are the tools that a writer needs?"

Nodding all the while, I jotted down student responses on the white board, from the inevitable cries of "Paper and pencils" to a few who offered "Dictionaries. Notebooks."

"Here's a tip I want to give you: writers do need paper and pencils, but writers also need tools for research. Every writer constantly needs to search for a fact, statistic, definition, name. Can you name some tools for research that writers might use to check on a fact or find out something specific about a topic?" I returned to jotting their suggestions on the white board. Soon I had added suggestions like encyclopedia, the Internet, and reference books to the list of writers' tools.

In this connection, you leave the topic at hand for a moment to help children co-construct what will be an analogy. This needs to be quick. Don't think a longer, more comprehensive list would be a better one!

Again, there is no advantage to making this a comprehensive list throughout the minilesson. You'll add more sources, and you may decide to later recruit a child to make a proper chart of these. But it's more likely that you'll decide children don't need such a reference.

❖ Name the teaching point.

"Today I want to teach you that writers don't just write, write, write all the stuff from their brains. Real writers are researchers. Writers often leave the page in search of the perfect fact or the perfect example."

TEACHING

Let students know that experts don't just magically know everything—they often have resources at their fingertips that they use frequently.

"Just like dentists or policemen or artists have their own tools, writers know how to access—and use—their own tools for research. This is especially true when writers are writing on topics of personal expertise. I don't know who invented the rumor that experts don't need to look stuff up, because it's just not true! Experts seek out other experts. An expert wants to know if other experts have the same things to say about a topic, or if they see another angle. If you visit my home, you'll see tons of books on how to teach reading and writing to third-graders. I'm an expert on that, so I seek out other experts—in life and in books. It's true! I bet if you go to a golfer's house, you'll see books on golf. At an expert chef's house, you'll see recipe books! Experts actually research their topic way more than other people do."

It is helpful to name students' misconceptions and to address them head on. Many will believe that because they've chosen a topic they know well, there is no reason to research the topic.

Point out all the resources for research available in the classroom and outside of it.

"If you look around the room today, you'll see many tools of research that you could be using. If I want to research how to prevent cockroach infestations, I might look up cockroaches or insects or pests in a science book." I gestured toward the science textbooks. "I might look for a book on insects here." I walked over to the nonfiction section of the class library. "Or I might type out *cockroach* or *pest* in the search bar on the computer." I pointed to the class computer. "Or I could walk over after school to the pizza place next to my house and interview the manager about what chemicals they use to prevent roaches. I could interview a principal I know who used to keep an aquarium of cockroaches in her classroom when she taught first-graders. I could interview my grandma because I once saw a roach in her house and saw how she shrieked and whacked at it. She'd know how hard you have to whack them to kill them."

The truth is that your kids will only be able to collect a variety of evidence, as in these examples, if you give them more than a day to do this work. You'll still want to teach a minilesson in which you highlight that researchers value drawing from a variety of sources, but you need to decide whether to make this a priority and, if so, you'll probably need to give children more time for the research involved than this unit provides.

Set up students to watch you research.

"Watch me research." I walked over to the insects basket in the nonfiction section of our library, picked out a thick book, and thumbed through to the cockroach section. "Look here. It says, 'Cockroach Trapping, Baits.' I already know about baits. But further on, it says 'boric acid dust.' Hmm. This is new to me. Let me jot it down in the margin of the chapter I'm making on getting rid of cockroaches." I picked up a pencil and made a show of jotting down "boric acid."

This unit offers a wonderful context within which children can learn a bit about research. The fact that they'll be researching a topic they know well will make it easier for them to be successful as researchers, and more likely, too, that they won't fall into the trap of plagiarizing.

"I'm going to read on, keeping my chapter titles in mind. If I see any fact that will go into one of my chapters, I'll jot it down in the margin of that chapter, if I've written it, or in my notes. And then I'll also note down the book that gave me this information!" I read the book cover name, author, and copyright year aloud.

Debrief about the various quick ways you researched.

"Writers, did you see what I did? When I chanced upon a fact that was new, I immediately thought back to my table of contents, asking myself, 'Where in my book would this fit?' and jotted the information down in the right chapter or the right plans for the chapter. I'm also going to note the reference book's name, place, and year of publication because I will make a list of references at the end of my book, to give credit to the sources that I've used. Then I read on for further new and interesting facts, keeping my table of contents in mind. I will only pick up a fact if it is relevant to my book."

ACTIVE ENGAGEMENT

Ask the students to consider their own subjects and where they might want to look for more information.

"Look through your drafts and think about where you could find more information. Try to list a few different options across your fingers. If there's anything I've learned as a researcher, it's that no one source has all the information I need. Remember to think widely—not just books and websites, but people and places are good sources, too. When you have a few ideas for what and where you can research, share them with your partner. Partner 2, you start today."

As students talked to their partners, I made small suggestions here and there to push them outside of the obvious. When Frank mentioned he could look up dragons in his fantasy reference books, I noted that he might also consider asking one of the clerks at the comic book store down the street who was clearly a dragon expert.

Highlight any ideas for research that students discussed with partners.

"Frank was thinking that he might want to interview some dragon experts. After all, dragons have a lot of fans. He knew our school librarian knows a lot about dragons, and so does the store clerk at Bergen Comics. That made me think we should all consider interviewing people who are experts on a topic. Caitlyn was telling her partner she would go to the public pool, because she knows they have all kinds of posters, pamphlets, and other information about swimming there. Places like museums or dance studios or stadiums or zoos all have information about our topics."

LINK

Tell a short story about an author who regularly uses research in his or her writing.

"Ann Bausum is a professional nonfiction writer and author of *Our Country's Presidents*. She talks about how whenever she is working on a new information book, she collects a small library of books on the topic. That makes researching her topic much easier. Everything is right there at her fingertips."

Let students know that if it makes sense for them, they might consider bringing their nonfiction reading lives into their information writing or vice versa.

"I can tell by the looks on some of your faces that you are already thinking of your small stacks of books and articles you've been reading and gathering in reading workshop, and you're wondering if you might be able to turn some of your reading work to the cause of doing some research for your writing. Of course you can! That's such a great way not only to be an efficient learner, but also to get more out of your work with both subjects."

Set students up for their work today.

"Thumbs up if you are planning to do some research today. Thumbs up if you are planning to do more revision. Thumbs up if you will be writing another chapter. Off you go!"

It is not accidental that we suggest you teach children to research after they've already written lots of chapters. Chances are good that the research will be adding a fact or two to a chapter—making large-scale copying from a book less likely.

It's the mark of responsive teaching when the conversations you overhear lead you to add a qualifier to redirect your students and refine your teaching point with more specifics.

Reminding Students to Respond to Information

YOU'LL WANT TO IMAGINE THE KIND OF HELP THAT CHILDREN are apt to need today so that you don't feel empty-handed when conferring and leading small groups. When doing this, remember to anticipate that youngsters will be drawing on the full repertoire of all that you have taught and not just on today's teaching point—though it is an important one.

For example, you'll surely find some students whose writing looks as if a trash compactor has squashed everything tightly together. Those youngsters will need you to remind them that they know how to address this. They can scissor their work into sections, taping each section onto a piece of paper so there are lots of empty line below the brief bit of writing. These youngsters may need to be encouraged to expand the section of their writing that is information. Pose questions to them, such as, "What else do you know about the goalie in soccer?" "To whom might you talk to learn more?" "What can you read that might help?"

Then, too, the youngsters can be reminded to look at Ryan's writing about rats, in which he shifted between telling facts about rats and writing his major idea—that rats are undervalued and deserve respect. Ryan didn't just say his idea in a sentence, and your writers can learn that they too can expand their efforts to write ideas. Sentence prompts can help.

Some children will not easily grasp what you hope for when you ask for their ideas. Gary, for example, had already written a chapter on his coyote book about a time when he saw a coyote that he believed had rabies. He had written already, "never saw it again" and now after encouragement to think about his information, he added this to the end of his sick coyote chapter.

> I never saw it again. For all I know, it could have died sometime ago. And that's the end of the coyote, for I never saw it again. Disappeared. Somehow disappeared. Somehow.

MID-WORKSHOP TEACHING   **Embedding Topic-Specific Vocabulary to Help Readers Get Smart on the Topic They Are Teaching**

"Writers, Joe is writing about basketball and he just did something really wise, something you'll all want to do. He wrote about how players win a game, but instead of writing, 'The guys that get the most points win,' he used the fancy words that basketball players use to talk about the sport. He wrote, 'The squad that wears down their opponents with a solid man-to-man defense wins.' It's important for all of us to use expert language to describe things. It makes readers trust that the writer is an expert.

"I know a lot of vocabulary about cockroaches, but I'm not sure I always remembered to use those words in my writing. I'm going to revise to be sure I used the language experts use. Let's look at this part of my book," I said, and read:

> Cockroaches don't breathe like we do, through our mouths. Instead, cockroaches breathe through holes on the sides of their bodies. These special holes allow cockroaches to breathe even if something is blocking part of their bodies.

"Hmm, there's a name for those holes. I think I should mention it right here." I reread a bit of my text, adding the domain-specific term.

> These special holes—called spiracles—allow cockroaches to breathe even if something is blocking part of their bodies.

"Do you see, researchers, that just adding the scientific term makes my writing more informative? Try this with your own text. Back to work!"

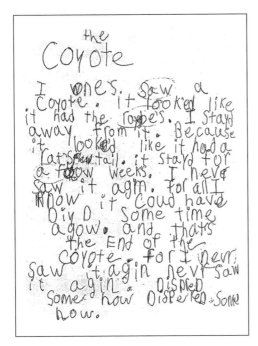

the
Coyote

I ones, saw a Coyote. it look'ed like it had the [rabes]. I stayd away from it. Because it looked like it had a rat's [new] tail. it stayd for a few weeks. I neve saw it agin. for all I know it coud have DiyD some time a gow. and thats the End of the coyote. for I nevr saw it agin nevr saw it agin. OisPeD Somer how OisPeReD. Some how.

FIG. 9–1 Gary added his response to information in the last paragraph of his chapter.

In an instance such as this, be sure to celebrate the writer's effort to respond to information, to record thoughts as well as facts. You might actually address a different chapter in his writing so as not to demoralize him by challenging this one. But one way or another, you will want to help Gary know that elaboration doesn't involve more verbiage, more think-alongs, so much as more information or more thoughts about information. You could coach Gary to grasp ways a person thinks about information, such as by comparing it to something else or by speculating about causes or by thinking about kinds of something (such as kinds of things coyotes might die of) or thinking of pros and cons.

Then, too, you'll find children who are pleased by the invitation to research but end up devoting the entire writing time to reading. These youngsters will need to be reminded that their job is a special kind of reading. The goal is to learn and to add to their writing.

It may be that this child needs to reread her own writing, making almost a shopping list of what she needs to get from her research, and then she may need to spend more time skimming the book, as one might glance over the signs labeling the contents of each aisle at the grocery store.

Yet other students may need to be encouraged to imagine whole new chapters based on their reading. If their research sparks ideas and reminds them of their knowledge, it's a great thing for them to add new chapters to their original table of contents.

Studying Mentor Texts to Emulate the Use of Expert Terminology

Remind writers that mentor texts can help them with whatever they aspire to do.

"Writers, earlier in this unit, we studied the mentor book, *Deadliest Animals*, noticing the way Melissa Stewart organized her chapter so that the animals she described were deadliest and deadlier. I thought that today, we could end our workshop by doing a quick study of how she uses expert words in her book."

Divide the class into small groups and channel each group to study one page of this class mentor text and emulate the use of expert terminology.

"I'm going to ask you and your partner to group with another partnership—the kids sitting at your table or near you—and when I see your group has been formed, I'll give you a copy of the book with a bookmark on a page I'd like you to investigate."

Learning from a Mentor: Expert Vocabulary	
She did . . .	**I did . . .**
p. 5 . . . usually hunt in groups called "prides"	. . . play another team called "the opponent"
p. 5 . . . a text box: Predator: An animal that hunts and eats other animals	. . . a text box: Rabies: a deadly disease that can be passed by animal bites
p. 19 . . . exact descriptive words: huge, hulking, hooked horns	. . . descriptive words: sewer suckers and evil rat eyes
p. 21 . . . a list of names	. . . everyone got divided into groups: a Shake group, a Rattle group, a Roll group
p. 32 . . . a drawing: with the label of "tentacles"	. . . a diagram of a fort, with the parts labeled
p. 46 . . . a glossary	. . . a glossary

I'd soon distributed the books, with different children channeled to different pages. After children talked about the technique Stewart had used, I said, "Now get out your writing, and you have three minutes to emulate—to try out—that same strategy in your book. Go!"

As children work and talk, compile a list of ways the mentor and the children incorporate expert terminology into texts.

As children worked, I circled the groups, gleaning the techniques they'd learned and examples. I made these into a quick chart, which individuals completed later.

Reusing and Recycling in the Revision Process

ear Teachers,

We are, again, leaving today's session in your hands. You will have just taught your students lots of important content, and they need time to put all they have learned to use. Today, then, might be one of those lessons in which your goal is not to add one new tip so much as to rally writers to use all they have learned so far. The particular points that you'll highlight will need to come from your assessment of their work.

To prepare for this session, start by studying your students' drafts in relationship to the third- and fourth-grade checklists for information writing. What gaps do you see between their work and the expectations encoded on the third-grade checklist? You'll want to teach those topics today, perhaps without ever referencing the checklist, because it is meant more as a reminder than as a primary means of instruction.

For example, after we studied our students' work, we noticed that many of them had elaborated by including definitions and details on a topic, but few had included observations, and fewer had "explained" the information. We realized this was a way of responding to information that we hadn't taught, and we resolved to incorporate that into today's teaching. Similarly, we noted that we hadn't stressed graphics—drawings, diagrams, charts. We decided to reserve that for later.

MINILESSON

We then thought over the various ways we could nudge writers to draw on all they'd learned and decided to focus on revision. If you make this same decision, your teaching point might be, "Writers, I'm noticing that when you learn something new about information writing, you often go back to a chapter you wrote earlier and use tiny Post-its or marginal notes to add this or that in your draft. That sort of teeny tiny work is not really revision—that's

COMMON CORE STATE STANDARDS: W.3.2, W.3.5, RI.3.1, RI.3.10, SL.3.1, L.3.1, L.3.2, L.3.3

fixing up an almost perfect draft. To revise, you need to have the courage to try a chapter over again, or to write the first or last half again." That is, you'll want to move youngsters beyond making timid little edits to engage in the hefty work that real revision often requires.

In the teaching section, you might point out that to do large-scale revision, writers first reread, thinking, "Is this the best I could possibly do?" Writers do this, keeping in mind the checklist for strong information writing, and if they are ambitious, they look not only at goals for their grade level, but also for the grade level above. You might demonstrate doing this, showing kids that you glance over the third- and fourth-grade checklist, looking at the categories that are worth double, because they must be especially important. After reading the elaboration and description categories aloud, you could then show children that you reread your draft with these in mind.

If you notice your text doesn't have as much information as you'd like, that it reads like it's been through the trash compactor, show the class that you reach for old class charts to help you. The list of the kinds of information that writers draw on will help, as will sentence starters for writing ideas. If you want to point out that nonfiction authors don't only list information, but they also try to explain that information, show kids that it helps to pause and think, "How can I say that in other words to help people understand?"

Be sure you do this work with just a tiny section of your text. Don't aim to be comprehensive or go on and on about your writing. Pass the baton to the kids and ask them to do similar work with their own writing.

CONFERRING AND SMALL-GROUP WORK

Try sitting beside a child. Watch what she's doing. Chances are good that the writer will not be involved in wholesale revision. Ask, "What are you doing as a writer today?" The writer may well say that she's revising, in which case you'll want to be blunt. "Actually, you are tweaking. You are fixing up." Then ask the child if you can show her real revision, send her off to get a wad of paper (and higher expectations), and then suggest the two of you refer to the checklist and to her goals to get lots and lots of new goals in mind. (Note that goals are interrelated. It's hard to write with more volume without writing with more information, more speed, more paragraphs.)

Perhaps this particular child's entire book is written in an overly folksy fashion with lots of personal responses like, "Ugh! That's boring!" You tell her that the book doesn't yet feel like a nonfiction book that could sit on the library shelf, explain why, and set her up to write a chapter in the air, using a more teacherly tone. "Sit up. You are a professor now," you say, getting her into the role. After a bit of rehearsal, channel her to plan how her chapter will go across the page. The fact that this is a new draft can be almost bypassed. Of course she'll want to rewrite it in a more professional tone! Once she is well underway, working on a whole new draft, you can convene a group to study what she's doing and to think about what their large goals might be so they could do likewise.

MID-WORKSHOP TEACHING

Often mid-workshop teaching feels a little bit like playing jump rope with other people who are turning the rope. You know how you want to jump, and likely any tricks you might do while jumping, but you still need to watch how the rope is being turned and what happens when you start jumping to be 100% sure of how it should go. All this is to say that you should absolutely have a planned mid-workshop teaching, most likely related to revision (but it could just as likely have to do with conventions or something else entirely), but be ready to tweak when and how it goes according to how your students are performing during this workshop. One teaching point that might feel particularly appropriate right now is a return to mentor texts. Many students were on fire about using their mentor texts just a day or two ago and now have barely given them a glance. You might want to teach them how to mark up a text with places they admire and then try some of those things in your own writing.

SHARE

Today's share might be well suited for teaching organization of materials. By this point in the unit the chances are good that students have piles of stuff they are working with on a regular basis: mentor texts, research resources, various drafts, notes from interviews, and so on. You might decide to teach students one particular way you'd like them to organize everything. For example, you might give each student a colored bin with dividers that they can label and use to divide each stack. Or you might decide to teach a few different strategies, perhaps reminding them of a strategy you taught them earlier in the year. Some teachers like to teach students to use filing folders. Others who have access to laptops or digital tablets show students how to organize digitally. Still others clear away space on a bookshelf and let each student have a small piece of real estate to use however they see fit. Whichever you do, it is likely that if you exude energy and offer up some fresh materials to play with (plastic tabs, labels, and fresh markers do wonders for the organizationally avoidant), your students will "discover" new things to include in their pieces and develop a renewed sense of clarity for this project.

Enjoy!

Lucy and Colleen

Creating Introductions through Researching Mentor Authors

IN THIS SESSION, you'll guide students through an inquiry process that asks them to consider introduction strategies of mentor texts.

GETTING READY

✔ Mentor texts (e.g., *Deadliest Animals* or *VIP Pass to a Pro Baseball Game Day*)

✔ "What Do Our Mentor Authors Do When Writing Powerful Introductions?" chart, to be written with students during the guided inquiry

✔ Chart paper and markers

COMMON CORE STATE STANDARDS: W.3.2.a,d, W.3.5, W.3.7, W.4.2.a,e, RI.3.1, RI.3.10, SL.3.1, L.3.1, L.3.2, L.3.3

W HEN YOU WERE SCANNING THE TABLE OF CONTENTS of this book, you might have been surprised to see that a session on writing introductions (and conclusions) was placed in the second half. You might have expected it to have been at the start of Bend II. This lesson is late in a strand of revision work for a few reasons.

• It is very helpful for writers to know what the body of their work will contain before they decide how to best introduce the piece to others.

• Your students have likely learned about writing introductions and conclusions before this unit—if not this year, certainly last year—and already have at least a general sense of ways these can go. It is likely, therefore, that they have probably drafted ones that are adequate placeholders.

• Introductions and conclusions have similar structures and purposes, and teachers have great success teaching them together.

It is also for those reasons that we decided to set up today's session as an inquiry. Inquiry lessons invite writers to explore the unknown. They are energy builders. This might be exactly what you and your students need at this stage in the process.

A good rule of thumb is that a strong inquiry is one where the teacher asks a question to which he or she does not already have an answer. In a strong inquiry, the teacher expects students to discover things he or she never could have predicted. That is, "What are writers' notebooks?" wouldn't be as strong an inquiry question as, "What are some ways youngsters can invent for using their writer's notebooks?" Indeed, the overarching goal of good inquiry work is to foster students' sense of independence and agency in their own learning. There's incredible power and transferability when students realize that when they have a question, any question, they can launch their own inquiries.

Today's inquiry is based on the idea that authors have a variety of ways to introduce information writing. There are many different ways this inquiry could go. If your resources are limited, or you just want to streamline the options, you might decide to limit students' work to your mentor text—the one you've been using all unit long. If, on the other hand, you have

---

"The stance you want to take is that of a supportive coach, who expects the athlete to do most of the work yet will offer a quick tip or word of encouragement or collect information that can be studied with the athlete later."

---

several information texts whose writing you would be happy to have your students emulate, you might opt to have the session go in the way it's described, with students working in small groups to pore over different texts together. A few strong texts

we found particularly easy for kids to access include *Amazing Animal Journeys* by Laura Marsh (2010), *Plants Bite Back* by Richard Platt (1999), *Tomatoes Grow on a Vine* by Mari Schuh (2011), *Cats vs. Dogs* by Elizabeth Carney (2011), and *Fashion Design* by Jen Jones (2007). Two texts we found, *Let's Talk Tae Kwon Do* by Laine Falk (2008) and *Going to a Restaurant* by Melinda Radabaugh (2003), are great for students who are struggling with reading.

Ultimately the stance you want to take during this whole session is that of a supportive coach who expects the athlete to do most of the work yet will offer a quick tip or word of encouragement or collect pertinent information that can be studied with the athlete at a later date. This is a great stance to assume in your teaching, not just today but always, since after all, they will ultimately play in the big game without us.

It is worth noting that the instruction students receive on introductions and conclusions in this session is significantly beyond the Common Core State Standards (CCSS W3.2.a and 3.2.d). In those standards, students are simply asked to "introduce a topic" and "provide a concluding statement or section." Third-graders are capable of much more. However, the beauty of teaching through inquiry is that students can set their own paths and choose one they want to follow. At the very least, they will all learn to write introductions and conclusions that will meet, and very probably exceed, the standards.

Creating Introductions through Researching Mentor Authors

CONNECTION

Explain why now, toward the end of the writing process, you'll channel students to consider their endings and their beginnings.

"Have you ever been asked to introduce someone you hardly know? You are standing with some kids from a different classroom and your mom approaches you. She joins the little group for a moment, then looks at the other kids and asks, 'Aren't you going to introduce me?'

"You stand there with your mouth open, going, 'Uhhh . . .' because it's not that easy to introduce someone you hardly know.

"It's the same with writing. Writers need to write introductions, but it's not easy to write an introduction until you know the piece of writing. So today I'm going to suggest you take time from all the many jobs you are doing on your writing to check the introduction to the whole book and also the introductions to each chapter, and to make them the best they can be. To do that, you can study the introductions in other people's writing."

Name the question that will guide the class inquiry.

"Today, specifically, let's ask, 'What do our mentor authors do when writing powerful introductions for information writing?' Once we figure out the answer to that question, we can ask, 'How can we apply those strategies to our own introductions?'"

TEACHING AND ACTIVE ENGAGEMENT

Set the writers up to investigate a mentor text with you, guiding the work in a series of steps that help them answer the inquiry question.

"Writers, let's begin our inquiry by looking at a book we haven't studied a lot—it's one with a beautiful introduction. Let me show you the start of this book, and will you join me in reading it with the extra powerful lens of someone who

Sometimes kids and teachers alike treat qualities of good writing as if they are celestial. The truth is that writing well has a lot to do with living well. This minilesson suggests that just as it's hard to introduce a person you don't know well, it's also hard to introduce a piece of writing unless you know it well.

Think about the minilessons in this book. Writing is like making paper chains, linking events, information, and understandings. Throughout the unit, we try to demythologize good writing.

needs to notice how this was written? We'll be thinking 'What kinds of stuff did the author put here?' and 'What did this author seem to be trying to do?'"

I displayed the text of *VIP Pass to a Pro Baseball Game Day* and read aloud, slowly, thoughtfully, as if annotating as I read. My intonation stressed the pattern that behind every visible part of baseball, there is an invisible part to it.

> *"Play ball!" Baseball fans love hearing those wonderful words. A Major League Baseball (MLB) game offers fans plenty of entertainment and interesting action. But a lot happens behind the scenes that the fans never see. Behind every stolen base there's a coach that flashes signals to the players. Every relief pitcher has a great bullpen story. During the game, coaches discuss strategy in the dugouts. Grounds crews continually work to keep the field in tip-top shape.*
>
> *To understand the big picture you have to look beyond the field. How do teams travel? What do they do before the first pitch? How do umpires prepare for a game? There's so much more to baseball than just the game on the field.*

"Hmm, so I'm thinking of our first inquiry question—'What do our mentor authors do when writing powerful introductions?' Will you jot silently on that question? Try to ask, 'What's the big, main thing that this author is doing?'" I reread it, then left silence so all we heard was the scratching of pens.

Direct children to get into conversation circles to talk about how the mentor author wrote the introduction.

Then I said, "Let's get into conversation circles—bigger than partnerships, maybe four or six kids—and will you talk about this?" As the children moved into groups, I distributed copies of the text to them. I listened in on the groups, nodding often for writers to name not just one-time moves but patterns the writer did a lot, and to speculate on the purposes. After a bit, I said, "Let me list some of what I've heard you say, and if you said this, or thought it as well, give me a thumbs up."

What Do Our Mentor Authors Do When Writing Powerful Introductions?

- Start with a quote or a bit of excitement
- Go over the big topics that will come up in the book
- Talk about the whole thing and its parts, not just the first part
- Ask questions to get readers curious

When teaching, it is helpful to think about whether you are putting enough cognitive demands on children. Sometimes, you may find that you inadvertently do the hard work yourself. In an inquiry minilesson, you ask youngsters to do work that is intellectually rigorous. Try answering your own questions, and you'll see how challenging the work is.

Channel students to try the same work with another text, then to discuss it in small groups. Coach these groups with voiceovers.

"Writers, let's try this with other texts. I'm going to distribute one text to each of your conversation groups." I did, "And will your group read just the first page and discuss what the author has done?" As the children talked, I made voiceover comments, saying,

"Some of the groups are being quiet. Think aloud." After a bit, I said, "Ask yourself, 'What has the author done here?'" Another minute later, I added, "You should be citing the text, reading parts aloud."

I continued to add to the chart as students worked.

LINK

Compliment students on their sophisticated work, and let them know that the work they did today can be carried with them into future writing.

"Writers, I hope you walk away from today's lesson with three big things. The first thing is that it is reasonable for a writer to hold off on finalizing an introduction until the piece is written. William Zinsser, a great writer, has said, 'The most important sentence in any article is the first one. If it doesn't induce the reader to proceed to the second sentence, the article is dead'" (*On Writing Well*, 1990). "The second thing is that you now have a whole buffet of ways to write powerful introductions for today and whenever you are writing introductions. The third thing is the idea that as a writer, whenever you have a question or a struggle, you know you have a handy tool at your disposal: you can pose a question and set up an inquiry for yourself. You'll probably work today on an introduction to your book, and perhaps to many of your chapters as well, so get busy!"

FIG. 11–1   Kayla writes an introduction that aims to set the reader up for the book.

What Do Our Mentor Authors Do When Writing Powerful Introductions?

- Start with a quote or a bit of excitement
- Go over the big topics that will come up in the book
- Talk about the whole thing and its parts, not just the first part
- Ask questions to get readers curious
- Ask a question the reader will be able to think about and have answered
- Start with a short Small Moment story that paints a picture of the topic
- Include right away that people have different perspectives. "Some people think . . . Other people think. . . . "
- Introduce important vocabulary for the topic
- Start with a description of a tiny detail (like a seed) and then connect it to something bigger about the topic (there are millions of plants)
- Start with a description of something huge (like the Earth) and then connect it to just the focus of the book (zebras, walruses, crabs)

Writing Conclusions that Leave Readers Thinking

PAUSE TO THINK ABOUT ALL THAT YOU'VE TAUGHT your children to do as they work on information writing. You've coached them to combine specific, varied pieces of information, much as a bricklayer lays bricks. You've shown students that the information can include images and descriptions and micro-stories as well as facts, definitions, quotations. You've reminded them to use transitions and other techniques to link one portion of their writing with another. You've helped them study mentor introductions and conclusions.

As you lead conferences and small groups, keep in mind that your job is to help children access all that they've learned. This means, in part, that they need to be willing to shift from writing to rereading, and to reread with a critical eye. Help children know that they can use their Information Writing Checklist on any day, and can reread with an internalized checklist as well. "What more can I do to make this as strong as it can be?" they need to ask. Hopefully your children have checklists, flaps, tape, and scissors on hand, and they're trying a second introduction to a chapter, taping the new version over the old, and doing the same with conclusions.

Today, among other things, you can help your youngsters to reread their leads and conclusions, asking whether they set readers up to learn a lot of information and help readers know ways to respond. Kate, for example, reread her introduction to "Basketball" and saw that she'd emphasized exactly what she wrote about in her book: the length requirements for a basketball court, the safety risks of playing basketball. Her conclusion, however, had focused on the appeal of basketball.

> Now that you know about basketball, you want to play it. Boys and girls can play. It's really fun. I think you could enjoy it....

When I asked Kate to show me where she'd detailed the fun of playing basketball as opposed to the risks, she realized she had choices: alter her ending to fit her report or alter the report itself. For Kate, this led to fast and furious revisions—and you'll find the same happens with your students.

MID-WORKSHOP TEACHING **Writing Conclusions that Leave Readers Understanding What They Just Read**

"Writers, I was just meeting with Vitaly and Anisa, and they came up with a great idea! They were thinking that the work we did with studying our mentor authors' introductions would really work with conclusions as well. I think that is something many of you would like to try, so let me stop you for just a minute to talk about it.

"So Vitaly and Anisa gathered three texts we had in our mentor text basket and just turned to the last page of each of them right away. Then they read just the conclusions, making notes as they read about what they admired that the writers were doing. For example, they noticed that in *VIP Pass to a Pro Baseball Game Day*, it ends by letting the reader know that everything they just read about would happen again."

> Tomorrow they'll return for another game and another day of fun.

"Whereas *The Deadliest Animals* ends by giving a quick summary of the main things it talks about and then gives just one sentence that's a positive spin, which leaves the reader with something unexpected to think about."

> From tiny mosquitoes to gigantic elephants, the world's deadliest animals come in all sizes and shapes. And they live in every habitat you can think of. But each of them has a special way of keeping themselves safe in a dangerous world.

"Many of you know great ways to write conclusions for your information books. But I would like to encourage you to consider learning from Anisa and Vitaly and look at one, two, or even three mentor texts to see if you can pick up any additional ideas you can use."

Celebrating Our Progress

Enthusiastically welcome students back to the meeting area, making a big show of how hard they have worked thus far.

"Writers, you look surprised that I am applauding you as you join me on the rug! But I know you worked so hard today and did such impressive work that it felt like the thing to do. You know, the same way when we saw that play and there was intermission. The curtain came down about halfway through the show so the actors could take a little break. We all broke out into wild applause. We knew the show wasn't over, but we were so appreciative of everything we had seen so far."

Encourage students to compliment their writing partners on the efforts they've put forth.

"Today is the last day in this part of the unit—the part of the process where we were looking to make sure that our writing is matching our visions of how we want our books to be. Tomorrow we will be taking a turn. Instead of mostly looking out for what you want from your writing, you will be moving forward with your readers' needs at the forefront of your minds. But, before we do that, it's important for us to honor the work you've done so far and do some applauding as the curtain comes down on this act and before it goes up on the next act. Could you take a few minutes to swap your work with your partner? I'd like you to look at your partner's work for things to celebrate—strategies they've tried, places they've clearly worked to make their writing stronger. When you find those places, point them out to your partner and make a big deal about them."

Students turned to each other, knee to knee, pieces set between them. I watched closely to see what sorts of things they would notice in each other's writing, and also prepared to chime in, in case a student needed another set of eyes to help him or her give a clear and explicit compliment. I needn't have worried. At this point in the unit, most of my students were easily able to comment well on each other's work both because of the teaching in the unit and because they knew their partners' work so well.

"Your lead has become so much more exciting than it used to be," Frank's partner said. "I like how you tell a little story about dragons to help your reader really imagine them."

If a student whose turn it was to comment on his partner's work seemed to be faltering, I leaned in and whispered that she might want to refer to some of our class charts to get ideas of some things to look for.

Taking Stock and Setting Goals

IN THIS SESSION, you'll teach students how to review their information writing using a checklist and then how to make a plan for revision.

GETTING READY

✔ Information Writing Checklist, Grades 3 and 4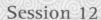

✔ An excerpt from your information book that can be measured against the Information Writing Checklist (see Teaching)

✔ An anecdote you can share to enhance your information text (see Mid-Workshop Teaching)

✔ A metaphor to illustrate a point from your information text (see Share)

TODAY MARKS THE BEGINNING OF THE HOME STRETCH for students' current projects. We want to celebrate this milestone and use it to help improve students' writing. Throughout this unit, and all of the units in this series, we have asked students to regularly look at their writing and to assess what is strong and set goals for ways to improve. These periodic moments of reflection have usually happened as part of mid-workshop teaching, teaching shares, conferences, and small-group work. Today's session puts that work at the forefront, in the minilesson.

You will want to guide students toward looking at their pieces not as good or bad, wrong or right, but rather to ask themselves, "What am I doing well?" and "What can I do better?" Pause for a moment to take note of the importance of what you are doing. Think of your own experience as a child, being assessed. Chances are that you were only assessed when your work was done, and there were no more opportunities to improve on the work. And chances are that your teacher did the assessing, not you. Then again, you probably had no clear sense of what the teacher wanted.

So teach this lesson as if it is precious, indeed. We think it is. You'll be trying to rally students to own their own assessment process. Your goal is for youngsters to understand that writing well is within their reach. Your goal is to create a classroom community of self-reflective, purposeful learners.

COMMON CORE STATE STANDARDS: W.3.2., W.3.5, W.4.2, RI.3.1, SL.3.1, SL.3.3, L.3.1, L.3.2, L.3.3

Taking Stock and Setting Goals

CONNECTION

Give an example of a time when you worked on something, needed to pause to take stock before completing the effort, and did that for yourself.

"I recently had a party for a friend. I made all these decorations and got right to decorating. At some point, after decorating for a while, I thought I might be done. But I wasn't too sure. Maybe I had overdone it and needed to take down some things. Maybe I needed to add more. What I needed to do was to ask someone, 'What do you think?' but I had no one to ask. So I pretended to be a visitor, arriving at my home, and tried to see what I'd done through the eyes of that other person.

"Have you ever done that? You may not have been decorating your house—you may have been working on your Halloween costume, or painting a picture, or hanging stuff on your bedroom wall. You get to a place where you need to take stock, and no one is there to do that for you."

❧ **Name the teaching point.**

"Today I want to teach you that information writers stop, before they are completely done with their pieces, to take stock. They reread what they've done so far and think about any guidelines, checklists, or mentor texts, asking, 'What's working already?' and 'What do I still want to do to make this as strong as possible?'"

TEACHING

Set up the third- and fourth-grade checklists to serve as an elaboration tool with your demonstration text.

"Lots of people use checklists after they've wrapped up their work. At the very end of their writing process, they reread and say, 'Hmm. This part was good. This part could have been better.' Which, to me, seems sort of silly. If they had just used the checklist a little bit earlier, they would have had plenty of time to go ahead and fix those parts that could have been better.

"What I am saying is that the checklist allows a writer to stop working on some things that seem okay, and to make a to-do list of other things that still need to be addressed. Then the writer can make a game plan to start working on

Once again, I'm talking about writing by talking about everyday life.

Notice that the worries I had over decorating are worded so that they can be exactly applicable to writing as well. "I might be done, but I wasn't sure. Maybe I had overdone it . . ."

those things. That's what I'm going to do now, working with my draft of the cockroach book."

I displayed the checklist the students had been working with during the unit next to an excerpt of my demonstration text written on chart paper and then distributed copies not only of the third-grade checklist but also of the fourth-grade checklist. These checklists can be found on the CD-ROM.

"Last time, when I worked on my checklist, I found that I needed to do more work on elaborating by including facts, definitions, details, observations. So as I reread, I'll keep a close eye on whether I did that. Help me:"

> Killing cockroaches using natural methods is not the only way to keep cockroaches out of your life. There are many ways that you can keep cockroaches from ever becoming a problem in your home. You would want to keep them from even walking in to begin with by plugging gaps. Some cockroach exterminators suggest using steel wool to plug those holes. Other people recommend using plaster. You can also make the space uncomfortable for cockroaches by making it drafty and bright. According to the book Cockroaches by Nancy Dickman, cockroaches like places that are warm and dark. Another way to keep cockroaches from being a problem in your home is to be sure they can't survive in your home. Clean up all food and store foods in cockroach-proof containers to accomplish this.

Information Writing Checklist

	Grade 3	NOT YET	STARTING TO	YES!	Grade 4	NOT YET	STARTING TO	YES!
Structure								
Overall	I taught readers information about a subject. I put in ideas, observations, and questions.	☐	☐	☐	I taught readers different things about a subject. I put facts, details, quotes, and ideas into each part of my writing.	☐	☐	☐
Lead	I wrote a beginning in which I got readers ready to learn a lot of information about the subject.	☐	☐	☐	I hooked my readers by explaining why the subject mattered, telling a surprising fact, or giving a big picture. I let readers know that I would teach them different things about a subject.	☐	☐	☐
Transitions	I used words to show sequence such as *before, after, then,* and *later.* I also used words to show what didn't fit such as *however* and *but.*	☐	☐	☐	I used words in each section that help readers understand how one piece of information connected with others. If I wrote the section in sequence, I used words and phrases such as *before, later, next, then,* and *after.* If I organized the section in kinds or parts, I used words such as *another, also,* and *for example.*	☐	☐	☐
Ending	I wrote an ending that drew conclusions, asked questions, or suggested ways readers might respond.	☐	☐	☐	I wrote an ending that reminded readers of my subject and may have suggested a follow-up action or left readers with a final insight. I added my thoughts, feelings, and questions about the subject at the end.	☐	☐	☐
Organization	I grouped my information into parts. Each part was mostly about one thing that connected to my big topic.	☐	☐	☐	I grouped information into sections and used paragraphs and sometimes chapters to separate those sections. Each section had information that was mostly about the same thing. I may have used headings and subheadings.	☐	☐	☐

Model finding something to work on that closely aligns with what a majority of the students still need to work on.

"I'm looking over my piece, and I'm noticing that I do include a lot of facts. I even did most of the fourth-grade requirements—putting facts, details, and ideas in each part. I still need quotes, but the rest of this is done." I underlined evidence that my writing matched the checklist.

"I'm noticing that in this elaboration category, I don't really explain the facts as much as I could or support them with details. I'm going to star those two goals. I think it is really true that sometimes I love my facts about cockroaches so much I expect that the facts alone should be enough to keep people interested. Let me just try to find a place where I can explain more." I reread and added this at the end of the passage.

> Clean up all food and store foods in cockroach-proof containers to accomplish this. <u>Do you have cookies, cereal, or candy lying around the house? If you do, you will want to place them in plastic containers that you can get into, but a cockroach will never be able to open.</u>

Name how you were really exacting, looking for evidence that you'd mastered each item on the checklist and collecting a to-do list for yourself.

"Did you see how careful I was to make sure I truly did each item on the checklist? Did you see that I read the fourth-grade checklist in instances when I'd mastered the third-grade expectations? You can do the same."

ACTIVE ENGAGEMENT

Guide students to look at the checklist first for signs of growth since the last time they used it, then for goals, and to tell partners what they found.

"Let's take those checklists out right now and see how much your writing has improved since the last time you looked at them. Read each item on the checklist and search for evidence to show if you have truly mastered that item. If not, mark "not yet" or "starting to." Push yourself to find ways you can get better.

"Mark those places on the checklist, and if it's possible, also find places on your draft where you can imagine doing that work. Thumbs up when you have found some important goals that you can work on right away." When a majority of the students had their thumbs up, I continued.

"Here is the challenge. I can know I need to work out more, but just saying that doesn't make it happen. Settling on a goal is the first step, but then I know I need a very specific action plan. Talk with partners about the work you need to do over the next few days."

So far in this unit, most of the work involving the checklist has been either inquiry based or guided practice. This is one of the first times we have modeled how the checklist affects our own writing. This is intentional. We want students to have developed their own strategies, but we also want to be sure that they are offered other possibilities through our modeling.

You'll notice that the work during today's active engagement is a first step toward work students will be doing for the next few sessions. At first glance it may look as if students are all doing the same thing—that there is little differentiation. In fact, enforcing the creation of a plan will set students up to create independent and individualized writing plans for themselves in the future. Expect them to eventually come up with differentiated goals for themselves!

LINK

Channel writers to collect the tools they'll need to do the work they've set out for themselves.

"How many of you will be thinking and working to make sure each of your chapters has its own subtopic, and that this is a logical plan for the book and for each chapter?" As some hands went up, I added to those children, "Without structure, you have nothing, and structure then becomes buried when there is a lot of information. So those of you doing this work deserve a cheer! You'll need scissors, tape, fresh sheets of paper—and class, point to the chart that will help the structure group." They did and soon this group was sitting together at the science table.

In the same way, clusters of kids working on other like endeavors headed off together, carrying the pertinent charts or mentor texts.

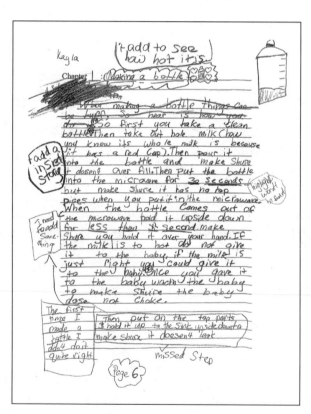

FIG. 12–1   Kayla makes notes to herself for things she plans to revise.

Encouraging Students to Make Individualized Plans for Revision

YOU WILL WANT TO APPROACH TODAY WITH EXPECTATIONS for what the small groups will probably be. If you look over your students' papers and skim the checklists, it will be immediately apparent what the work they need to do is.

Don't channel them toward terribly focused goals, and avoid those that you plan to tackle in upcoming whole-class minilessons. For example, it's almost surely the case that many children will identify leads as an area of need, if only because that item is high on the checklist. Save that for a minilesson.

You'll see from the link section that we sent a small cluster of youngsters off to work on overall structure. That group will certainly need to reread, noting sections that don't fit the central idea of a chapter. Writers often resist subtracting content, but that is a valuable thing to learn. Then, too, there may be times when the work entails not deleting extraneous information, but rather rethinking the focus of the chapter, broadening it to fit the information.

Many children's texts will not yet include quotations. By fifth grade, information writing will include various trusted sources. For now, third graders can explore text citation without pressure. You may find it helps to remind children that just as direct quotes enliven their stories, so too they can enliven a nonfiction book. Transferring those skills to information writing is well within their grasp. Rally those who take on this cause to study exemplar mentor texts, to compare and contrast with how one does this when writing narratives, and after writing information texts, to think about the difference between doing this poorly and doing it well. Ask them to help each other become experts on their topics, with wonderful examples. Once this is accomplished—after, say, a day—recruit the group to become professors of quotations and to teach others.

Notice throughout this session that it is your job to turn the checklist into something collegial, supportive, and rich.

"I cannot believe how far your pieces have come in just a few days! I see such incredible work around structure, use of mentor texts, word choice, research, and now the checklists! It is becoming more and more challenging for me to think of things I need to teach you to help you become even stronger. It feels like you're already doing so much!

"I squeezed my brain to think of one thing I could teach you, and one quick tip I can give you is this: don't just draw on charts from this unit. Draw on all you know about writing. And here is the secret tip. Information writing is actually made up of other kinds of writing. For example, in many nonfiction books, you'll find little Small Moment stories! It's true!

"For example, in my cockroach book, where I tell about ways to get rid of cockroaches. I could tell the story of my grandma seeing one, screaming, and whacking it. I might start it, 'Once, when I was reading my book on the sofa at my grandma's house, I heard Grandma go into the kitchen. She was humming a little song to herself. Suddenly . . .' Notice that I used everything we learned about writing true stories to tell that story well.

"Right now, find a place in your writing where you could insert a small moment and mark that spot. You can do that writing now or save it for a rainy day. Keep working."

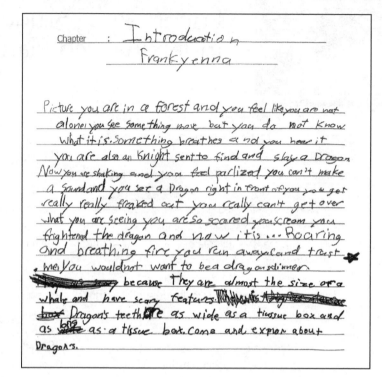

FIG. 12–2 Frank crafts a small moment to pull the reader in and make dragons feel more believable.

Developing Metaphors

Consider a different way to begin and or end writing: with a metaphor.

"Writers, I want to teach you one last way you might possibly start or stop your writing. You might compare it with something else. And if you do that, and you stretch the comparison out as you learned to do long ago when writing poetry, this comparison might become a big part of your first and last paragraphs. Let's say I wanted to compare cockroaches with something else. I might start and end my piece by talking about cockroaches as being almost like the largest living dinosaur. Or, if I was writing about gymnastics and focusing on the lessons gymnasts teach, I could start and end by taking that big idea and comparing. I could write that many kids think gymnastics practice is a lot like school. Seymour Simon does the same thing. He compared whales . . . to a school bus (*Whales*, 2006)! Right now, talk to your partner about comparisons you might make. Turn and talk."

I listened as Kate wondered if she should compare basketball to a different sport, and Marquis wondered if he should compare bats to birds. Conversation turned to whether they might compare the start of the book to the start of a class, the end to closing a door.

Putting Oneself in Readers' Shoes to Clear Up Confusion

IN THIS SESSION, you'll teach children additional revision strategies for clearing up confusion in their work, including imagining a different perspective and role-playing with a partner.

GETTING READY

✔ Sample quotes from professional authors about revision (optional)

✔ A section of your informational text that can be revised for confusion (see Teaching)

✔ Conjunctions and subordinating conjunctions chart (see Mid-Workshop Teaching)

✔ A quote about perseverance from a writer or someone the students admire (see Share)

O FTEN IN MY WORK WITH TEACHERS nationally and internationally, I am surprised to find that third graders are third graders wherever they are on the globe. Whether I'm in Singapore or Jordan, France or the U.S., third graders seem to be free with hugs, small gifts, and compliments, and to have a penchant for tiny toys, plus low frustration levels and thin skins. One of the qualities that can be most challenging for teachers is that the intellectual life of third graders often goes on inside their heads, rather than being shared with spoken or written words. And yet if you nudge a third grader to talk, show, or explain his or her thinking, the youngster will be surprised. "I already did."

Today's session is a tricky one. Whether you've asked third graders to check their multiplication facts or their spelling errors, they are notorious for not being able to see weaknesses in their work. They often have a hard time differentiating what is in their heads from what is showing up on paper. It is almost as if they have written some sections in invisible ink that only the writer can see. When we try to push for more elaboration or explanation, they protest, "It's there."

Even professional writers find it tough to be critics of their own writing, so you'll want to approach this session expecting your children will need your support. Couch the work in this session with as much of a "we're all in this together" feeling as possible. You might also want to collect a few sample quotes about revision from professional writers, especially writers your students know about or admire, as a way to get them to see that when they revise for clarity, they are in good company.

COMMON CORE STATE STANDARDS: W.3.2, W.3.5, RI.3.1, RI.3.6, SL.3.1, L.3.1.h,I; L.3.2, L.3.3, L.4.1.f

Putting Oneself in Readers' Shoes to Clear Up Confusion

CONNECTION

Engage children in thinking about a common experience from a different perspective in preparation for doing the same with their writing.

"The other day I had some friends over for dinner. As we were sitting down to eat, they asked me what happened to my window. I looked over to the window we were talking about and I saw for the first time that it was cracked. Not a big crack, but there was definitely a crack. I have no idea how long the crack had been there, but I knew it must have been a while.

"All at once I looked at my whole apartment with new eyes. I noticed how my bookshelves were a little dusty, and I saw piles of junk everywhere! I thought I had cleaned everything before company arrived. That made me start thinking about how helpful it can be for writers to have a friend come over to dinner!"

 **Name the teaching point.**

"Today I want to teach you that writers know that eventually other people will read their writing, so writers prepare for that by rereading their pieces very carefully, looking for places that are confusing or undeveloped. Writers then revise to make sure that the writing will reach readers."

TEACHING

Remind writers that they need to shift from being writer to being reader, rereading their writing as if seeing it for the first time.

"You already know that writers, near the end of their writing process, start to think, 'How will readers experience this?' Usually, the first thing a writer does is to conjure up a reader in his or her mind. Like I'm going to think of someone who knows nothing about cockroaches—my friend Mike. Now I'm going to go back and reread my piece from the very beginning, asking myself, 'What would Mike think? Where would he be confused or need more information?'"

◆ COACHING

This connection, of course, relates to one in an earlier minilesson when we talked about pretending to be a guest, visiting for the first time, in order to see through the guest's eyes.

I'll never forget the way that becoming a teacher transformed everything in my life, turning it all into grist for my teaching mill. Suddenly, every disaster was a metaphor to bring into my class!

You'll want to fill your minilessons with teeny tiny stories like these—and more importantly, to live your life aware that all the little moments are actually lessons to be shared.

Model reading a few lines of the demonstration text, noting where things might be confusing and thinking of ways to revise those things.

"Usually, I just read to you the part of my writing that we're working on in class, but today I am going to start from the very beginning of my first chapter. Now I'm going to read it very carefully, acting like I haven't read it before. I'm going to be looking for places that are confusing and places where readers might quit."

Imagine it's the middle of the night and you wake up thirsty. You head to the kitchen. When you turn on the light you see a bunch of dark blobs on the floor and the counters running everywhere. Eww! That's what this book is all about.

"Hmm. Now, I know that what I was trying to do was write a small moment to get the reader interested and talk to the reader directly. And I think I was pretty good about that. But I'm pretty sure that if I was reading this for the first time, I would be confused because it doesn't come right out and say what it's about. So let me add a sentence that will explain I'm talking about cockroaches being in homes and trying to get rid of them."

Imagine it's the middle of the night and you wake up thirsty. You head to the kitchen. When you turn on the light you see a bunch of dark blobs on the floor and the counters running every-where. Eww! <u>Cockroaches have taken over your home and unless you do something about it they will be here to stay.</u> That's what this book is all about.

"I like that! I think it's much clearer. Now let me look at the next paragraph to make sure I'm not making my readers go, 'Huh?'"

People hate cockroaches. They have probably hated them for as long as they've been around. They hate them because of many reasons. One reason they hate them is because cockroaches can cause allergies.

"Wait!" I flipped my page over, acting as if I was looking for a missing page. "That can't be it! I say right here that people hate cockroaches *for many reasons*. I set the reader up to expect more than one reason, but I only gave one! That is certainly confusing. And I know all those other reasons too. I could tell them to you, but for some reason I just left them out. Maybe I thought they were on the paper. I'll fix them in a jiffy."

Pulling back, I said, "I think I can stop there. You guys see what I'm doing. I'm rereading like I've never seen this before and going back and coming up with work I need to do to make my writing clearer to my readers."

ACTIVE ENGAGEMENT

Ask students to role-play with their partners, pretending to be someone who does not know the content of the class book.

"Now it's your turn to try. Do you remember that earlier we worked on a class book about school? If you remember, we decided to start with the main office because it's the first place you pass when you enter our school. Partner 1, you pretend to be the reader. Partner 2, you're the writer. Have a conversation about what makes sense and what doesn't make sense and then how you might change it."

The Main Office

When you first come to our school, after the lobby the first place you will stop is the main office. The main office is very important. It's where people who work for the school have desks.

Logan told his partner, "It's like it's not finished yet. I'm confused. It has to be more important than just being the place where people have desks."

Max nodded, "I agree. It is confusing. The first part is okay, but the rest is not exactly right. Teachers work for the school, but they don't have desks in the main office. Only the secretaries and the principal does. So we need to change that. Maybe we can say something else about the people who work there and the work they do before we talk about desks. Like something like, 'The main office has all the information people need about the school. It is also where the principal and secretaries work. We bring our attendance folders there.'"

LINK

Remind students that writing needs to make sense as well as be brimful of facts and information.

"I think we all agree that it's very important to make our pieces exciting and filled with interesting facts. But it is also true that our writing needs to make sense for our readers. If they're saying, 'Huh?' then all the cool facts and great sentences in the world will be wasted. Today when you go off to write, I know so many of you have a list as long as your arms of things you want to accomplish with your writing. I want you to stick with that list. I also want you to keep one eye out for places where the writing might be confusing to your readers and revise those places to clear up any confusion.

"That's not just a tip for today or just for information writing. That's true for all of your writing. You need to take on the eyes of a stranger to look at your work and try to see what you would see if you were new to the piece so that you make sure your writing is as clear and as easy to read as it can be."

Notice that this text is flawed. Our goal is to nudge children to find it easy to be critical readers, getting them into the swing of it.

Preparing Students for Next Steps

MANY OF OUR CONFERENCES address where students are currently in their process. If students are struggling, we make suggestions for support. If students are soaring, we make suggestions for deepening that work. But another option for students who seem to be flying along at a good clip is to teach them ahead of the curve; in other words, it can help to try out future lessons in order to explore possible teaching points. This can serve a few purposes. For one thing, it offers an opportunity to stretch students to the edges of their current abilities. It also helps scaffold them to take steps forward as writers. Also, on a practical note, we can often ask these students to serve as coteachers in our minilessons, allowing them (or their work) to be famous for a session.

Knowing that an upcoming minilesson needs to focus on text features, you might then deliberately decide to work with a few writers around this topic. Before you do this teaching, take a moment to consider ways third graders will tend to use text features, contrasting that with your goals. For example, you might find that children are more apt to insert fun-fact boxes and photographs rather than inserting subheadings. As you explore why this might be the case, you may come to the conclusion that third graders see text features as a way to make their writing look grown-up and legitimate. Their goal with text features is to make their pages look more like the pages in a magazine. If that's what your children believe, you'll want to teach them just how and where one adds text features. You'll want to teach "why" and specifically you'll want children to see this as a way to accentuate main ideas and to pop out the important content in a text. The subheads, titles, captions, and the rest all serve to highlight the central ideas. That's important!

MID-WORKSHOP TEACHING   **Teaching Coordinating Conjunctions and Subordinating Conjunctions through Guided Practice**

"Writers, I really hesitated to stop you today because you were being so productive. However, as I was meeting with some of you and reading over your shoulders, I realized I could teach you something really quickly that will make your writing crisper and tighter. I'm going to ask you to stay at your seats and just listen and practice this as I walk you through the work.

"I know we've discussed coordinating conjunctions in the past. Not just this year, but last year as well. You probably got used to just calling them *conjunctions*. These words—*and, for, but, or, nor, yet,* and *so*—are very helpful when making longer sentences. I see that so many of you are using them while revising today. I want to tell you that there are other kinds of conjunctions writers use as well. They're called *subordinate conjunctions*. These are words that often go at the *beginning* of sentences—almost to let readers know that this is going to be a fancier and longer sentence.

"Here's a chart that lists the conjunctions we already know with a few examples of sentences using them, as well as a short list of subordinating conjunctions with some examples. Will you try using a few from this new list at the start of fancier, longer sentences?"

Conjunctions

Conjunctions we know:

- And
- But
- So
- Or

Examples of sentences using conjunctions:

- Many people have not seen a flying cockroach, <u>but</u> most people don't mind missing it.
- Cockroaches are attracted to crumbs, <u>yet</u> many people do not do a good job of cleaning up after themselves.
- Neither poisons <u>nor</u> traps are as effective as natural methods of cockroach prevention.

More Conjunctions:

- After
- Because
- Before
- If
- Even though

Examples of sentences using these conjunctions:

- <u>Before</u> people decide how to get rid of cockroaches, they should learn the methods that work best.
- <u>Since</u> cockroaches can cause allergies, they are a serious problem.
- <u>Unless</u> food is put away, you'll have insect visitors.

"Run your finger along the sentences in your draft and find one that jumps out at you as being a sentence you might want to jazz up a bit. When you find it, go ahead and write that sentence down."

If you notice students writing fragments or incomplete sentences (a common error when first experimenting with subordinate conjunctions), you'll want to warn them of the danger and guide them toward completing those sentences.

"I see a few of you sort of tacking the words on to the beginning of a sentence. The thing with these words is that when writers use them, the new sentences need to become longer. So if I write, 'After the cockroaches get used to the poison,' I need to add something to the end of the sentence for it to be complete. I know it's funny that by adding a word or two you end up adding a lot more, but that's why conjunctions make sentences longer and fancier."

Dividing Writing Work into Smaller Jobs

Tell students that you know they have been working hard and you are proud of them.

"I can almost touch the energy in this room. It is so strong! The thing that impresses me the most is that you are doing some of the most challenging work for writers in revising. It can be so hard to go back and look again at a piece you spent so much time working on the first time. But you're not giving up—and your writing is fantastic and it shows!"

Share an inspirational quote about perseverance from an author or someone else you or the students admire.

"Some of you are feeling a little tired right about now. You look at your list of things you still want to work on to make your pieces as strong as they can be, and it can feel exhausting just to think about it. There's too much to do! I know that feeling. I feel that way too when I've been working on a writing piece for a long time.

"I want to share one of my favorite quotes. It's from a famous inventor, Henry Ford, who some of you have heard of. He said, 'Nothing is particularly hard if you divide it into small jobs.' That made me think. You know what? I don't think you should get intimidated by looking at how messy and long your drafts are becoming or how many things you have on your To-Do lists. Instead, you should think about how you can divide those things you need to do into smaller, bite-sized chunks and go from there. Can you, right now, before we move away from our writing work today, think of one tiny, five-minute writing job that you can do tonight for homework? Make it a goal tonight to accomplish just that one tiny little job."

Using Text Features Makes It Easier for Readers to Learn

YOUR STUDENTS WILL HAVE STUDIED TEXT FEATURES while reading nonfiction texts, and presumably they studied these also when writing information texts in previous years. They already know that text features exist to help readers navigate through the text. Still, we haven't stressed these prior to now because it's easy for youngsters to become so enamored with text boxes and glossaries, charts and diagrams that they drop all attention to writing.

"The goal of this session is to help children use text features to make texts easier for readers to read."

The goal of this session is to help children use text features to make texts easier for readers to read. You want to help children think of subheads, glossaries, charts, captions, and the rest as methods for making reading easier. Ideally, children will see that many text features help to highlight central ideas.

This session is a good time to bring in technology, if you have access to it. You might invite students to do image searches on the Internet. They can also design their own charts and other graphics. If you have the time, resources, and know-how, you might consider using technology for publishing. Today you could begin to plan ways to do that.

IN THIS SESSION, you'll teach children the ways text features can enhance their information writing. You'll guide them to choose the most appropriate features for their books.

GETTING READY

✔ "Some Common Text Features and Their Purposes" chart, prewritten (see Teaching)

✔ Several ideas for text features for your own information writing (see Teaching)

✔ Blank paper and pencils (see Active Engagement)

✔ Mentor text, *Deadliest Animals* (see Share)

COMMON CORE STATE STANDARDS: W.3.2, W.3.5, W.3.6, W.3.10, W.4.2.d, RI.3.1, RI.3.5, RI.3.7, RI.3.10, SI.3.1, L.3.1, L.3.2, L.3.3, L.3.4.d

Using Text Features Makes It Easier for Readers to Learn

CONNECTION

Acknowledge that the students have become quite the nonfiction experts, invite them to list what they know, and if text features are on their list, exclaim that they've stolen your tip.

"Writers, it feels as if we've been eating, sleeping, and breathing nonfiction texts for a while. Can you right now tell your partner all the things you know about information books, ticking them off on your fingers as you talk?"

Students talked to each other, saying things like:

◆ "Informational texts have tables of contents."

◆ "There are special words that information writers use."

◆ "They have facts and ideas."

◆ "There are text features like subheadings and charts."

Several times in this book, the connection has been a time for the teacher to draw a quick list from the class. This is an easy way to engage the class, and it will work beautifully unless you feel some need to call on all raised hands or to react to every point. Don't!

"You just stole my thunder! You said that information texts contain text features, and that was going to be my point! It's hard for me to stay ahead of you guys!" Then I added, "Okay. I am going to teach you a *really advanced* thing now."

❧ Name the teaching point.

"Today I want to teach you that information writers think, 'Will that text feature help readers?' and they only include the one that will really help readers. They think what the text is mainly about, and that helps them decide what should be popped out or highlighted."

TEACHING

List possible text features and their uses, giving children a few minutes to see which of these are used in a nonfiction text they have on hand.

"Writers, because you are advanced in text features, I'm going to give you this long list of text features that I saw in a fifth-grade classroom. Will you take your book and see if you can imagine adding most of these text features to it?"

The children did this, working by themselves. They hadn't finished looking through their drafts before I convened them and said, "The trick is to choose the one or two text features that might be really important for each part of your writing. More is not better!"

> ### Some Common Text Features and Their Purposes
>
> - Drawings and photographs help the reader to picture the subject.
> - Diagrams include labels and words to help explain parts or ways something works.
> - Definition boxes explain vocabulary words.
> - Maps help the reader to understand more about the places where the topic lives.
> - Timelines show the order of events.
> - Glossaries define key vocabulary from the text.
> - Charts can show how two things compare and contrast.

Then I said, "Let's glance at Jeremy's book and see if we can help him imagine text features he could add." I turned to a page titled "Turtles and Fish" and read a bit of it aloud.

Turtles and Fish

Turtles and fish are both sea creatures. Turtles and fish can be pets or they could be in the ocean.

Turtles and fish both could swim. But turtles and fish use different body parts to swim. Turtles use their flippers to swim and a fish uses its fins to swim.

Turtles and fish are both reptiles. Turtles and fish don't die at the same time. A turtle can live for about more than 2000 years. And turtles were in the time of dinosaurs. Fish can only live 2 months or less.

Turtles have different body parts than a fish. Turtles and fish sometimes also don't do the same thing. House turtles that are small can weigh more than a fish. Turtles have a shell to protect themselves. Also fish can just be eaten.

Then I said, "Hmm. What text features could we add that would help this chapter get its main message out?" I paused on the final bullet "Charts can show how two things compare." "This seems like the best idea!" I said. Then I reread "Turtles and Fish," and as I did, I added to this chart.

How Are Turtles and Fish the Same and Different?

	Turtles	Fish
Sea creatures	X	X
Pets	X	X
Can swim	X	X
Use fins		X
Use flippers	X	
Live a short time		X
Live thousands of years	X	
Have hard shells	X	

When I'd finished charting, I summarized, "Do you see that this chart matches? It goes with the main content of the chapter."

ACTIVE ENGAGEMENT

Use a piece of student work to engage children in thinking about what kinds of text features go with a certain kind of information writing.

"Writers, will you listen to this next chapter from the same book and think if there are text features you'd recommend for Jeremy to use?" I read a chapter titled, "Where Turtles Can Live."

Where Turtles Can Live

Turtles can live all around the world. They can live in sand, mud, deserts, swamps, and more. Sand, mud, deserts, and swamps are in air. Sometimes some turtles live on land, so they can live on land and on water. Sometimes some turtles only live in rivers, oceans, and lakes or ponds. Turtles swim fast in water and walk slow on land. That is why some turtles live under water. Turtles can live on land because whenever a mother turtle lays its eggs, it could lay their eggs on land and in water. If it did not know how to breathe on land, it would be bad. Whenever you sometimes go to the zoo, you might see turtles on a log in a big, damp pond. They breathe perfectly in water and in air. Some only can only live on deserts because in deserts there is no water.

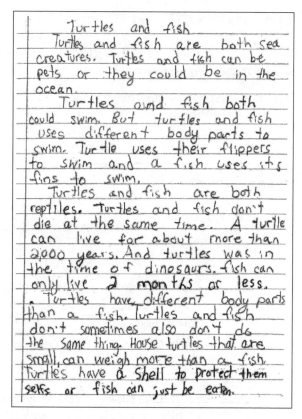

FIG. 14–1 Jeremy compares and contrasts turtles and fish in his text.

Children talked to partners and quickly generated the idea that labeled maps would help.

LINK

Remind students that what they learned about text features needs to fit into the structure of their books.

"For the past several weeks we've been talking about the words we should use in our books. Today we started talking about text features. Some of them (like headings and captions) use words, but lots of other features do not. The thing is, words or not, everything that you include in your book is part of your writing and should fit within your structure and should be treated with the same careful consideration that you are treating everything else."

Convey that you expect they will be doing various kinds of work today. Explain that writers always think about supporting their readers when they write.

"I expect that some of you will be working on text features today. But I also expect that some of you have other work you planned and need to work on today, instead. However, whenever you write, I want you to remember that you're writing for your readers, so pay attention to supporting your readers."

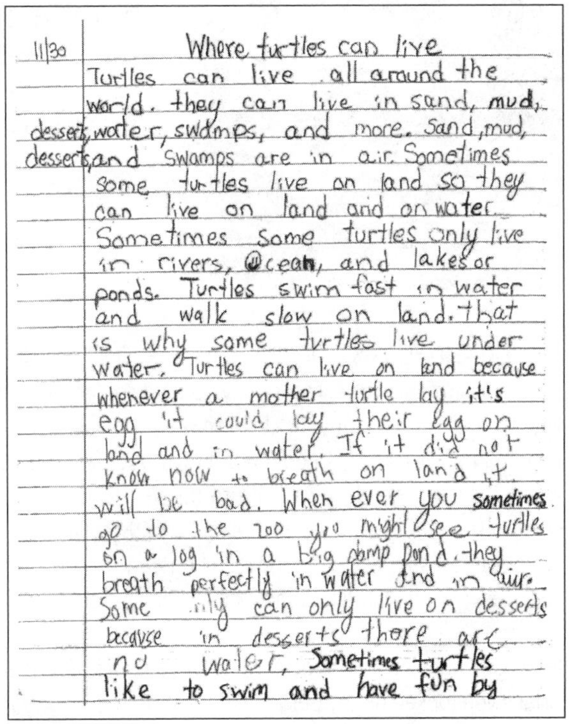

11/30	Where turtles can live

Turtles can live all around the world. they can live in sand, mud, dessert, water, swamps, and more. Sand, mud, dessert, and Swamps are in air. Sometimes some turtles live on land so they can live on land and on water. Sometimes some turtles only live in rivers, @cean, and lakes or ponds. Turtles swim fast in water and walk slow on land. that is why some turtles live under water. Turtles can live on land because whenever a mother turtle lay it's egg it could lay their egg on land and in water. If it did not know now to breath on land it will be bad. When ever you sometimes go to the zoo you might see turtles on a log in a big pamp pond. they breath perfectly in water and in air. Some nly can only live on desserts because in desserts there are no water. Sometimes turtles like to swim and have fun by

FIG. 14–2 Jeremy's chapter on where turtles live could be supported by a map with labels.

Reminding Students of Their Resources for Revision

YOU AND YOUR STUDENTS ARE CLOSE TO FINISHING THIS UNIT, and very close to finishing this piece. Most likely, today's conferring and small-group work will take you on a global tour of your classroom with quick tips and stops along the way. This is probably not the day to do long, drawn-out conferences that require major revision work. They are too close to done to be able to make large-scale changes without it costing something in time, psyche, or both. Rest in the knowledge that students will have another shot at information writing and that you can make plans for future conferences that feel big and important.

Instead, you will want to focus some of your energies on lean reminders and prompts. "Have you looked at any of the revision strategies your partner suggested you look at? Feel free to go over to the chart and check it out!" Or "I can tell you're getting ready to use your mentor text to really bump up the craft work you're trying. I can't wait to see what you do." Or something else along those lines. You might also want to encourage partners to work and give feedback to each other, or have students try teaching their topic, using their book as their guide to see if they've included everything worthwhile.

You might also find yourself wanting to move some students toward more grammar, conventions, and spelling work that, while being addressed all unit long, will be addressed in the end stages in another session. If you notice there are things that students can easily independently address (editing for sight words, domain-specific language, end punctuation), you might opt to push some students to begin that process.

On the whole, you want to talk to as many kids as you can today, making sure almost everyone feels that they have a personal tip from you, as well as making sure they feel the excitement and urgency that comes from drawing near to the close of a piece of writing.

MID-WORKSHOP TEACHING
Integrating Technology to Enhance Text Features

"Writers, can you put down your pens for a minute and look here?" I interrupted the class and moved to stand next to the classroom computer. "I realized that some of you are spending a lot of time coming up with the absolute perfect sketches, diagrams, maps, and other images to use as text features in your books. And some of you love that, because you feel comfortable with visual work. Still others of you want to either work faster because your deadline is coming, or else just don't feel comfortable doing all this artwork.

"If you feel that way, I'd like you to consider using technology." I tapped the computer beside me. "If you want to jump online to look up images or maps you can print out and include with your own captions, or use clip art or create diagrams or charts on the computer, please feel free to do so. I'm going to leave it as first-come, first-serve. But if we have too many people waiting, I'll either create a sign-up sheet with time slots or I'll see if I can get the laptop cart in here for a little while. For those of you who have access to computers at home, you might want to ask a grown-up at home if you can create or find some of those images and bring them to school to include in your book."

Studying Mentor Texts for Possible Text Features

Tell students that mentor texts can help them with text features by giving them ideas of what they might include, as well as how to best use them effectively.

"Writers, when you come and join me in the meeting area, can you bring your draft and your mentor text if you have one?" As I waited for the students to gather, I got ready to display my copy of *Deadliest Animals*.

"I noticed quite a few of you were working on text features today, which is really fantastic. But what was a little bit funny to me is that I saw hardly anyone looking at their mentor text for possible ways text features could go. We can look at our mentor texts not just for qualities of good writing but also for design and layout."

Model looking at a text feature in the class mentor text. Name what kind of feature it is. Comment on what you notice about how it helps the piece.

"Let me take a look at *Deadliest Animals*." I flipped the pages until I saw what I was looking for. "Look at this little yellow triangle—like a yield sign you'd see on the street. It says, 'Deadly Definitions,' and then right underneath it says 'Predator: An animal that hunts and eats other animals.' So that's kind of cool. It's a text box and a sort of mini-glossary, but it also catches the reader's eye because of the sign. And these signs are all through the text. Maybe we could do something similar. Instead of just saving definitions for the glossary at the end of the book, we could sprinkle them throughout with a little way of making them stand out in a text box."

Ask partners to share a mentor text to locate an eye-catching text feature, name it, and discuss why it is effective and how they might use it in their own writing.

"Will you and your partner gather any mentor texts you have on hand and see what you learn by studying the different text features you see?" Students turned and talked about various mentor texts, noting things such as hidden riddles, mini how-to sections, quick facts, pullout quotes, and other interesting text features that they hadn't yet tried.

Fact-Checking through Rapid Research

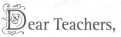ear Teachers,

Much of what you teach today will depend on the resources you have available. If you have access to a computer lab or laptop cart or can in another way offer Internet access to all of your students in one sitting, then that would be the ideal way to do today's work. If, however, you have only a single or a few computers for student use, you might want to organize this session in research centers where students can take turns using the computers or hard copy resources (books, articles, artifacts, and so on) that you likely have had available in your class all along. You might also consider bringing in, or enlisting students' help acquiring, additional general resources such as general-interest reference books, text books, or even encyclopedias. Sometimes these newer resources are exactly the thing to get students' energy flowing.

MINILESSON

In today's connection you will want to be sure that students understand that the act of fact-checking is not the same as the earlier research work they did. They are looking not to add new facts to their research, but rather they are making sure that the facts they have included are accurate. You might think of an analogy that helps them to understand this subtle distinction, such as the difference between checking your backpack to make sure you didn't forget anything (fact-checking) and actually deciding what to put in it and packing it (researching).

Your teaching point might go something like this: When information writers get close to the end of their projects, it is important that they check the major facts that they've included to make sure they are as accurate as possible. Readers need to be able to trust the things they are learning. One way writers do this is to scan their own drafts for facts that feel as if they might be shaky and then quickly look to another source (or two) to confirm that these facts are true. If they are not, the writer revises those facts.

COMMON CORE STATE STANDARDS: W.3.2, W.3.7, W.3.8, RI.3.1, RI.3.2, SL.3.1, L.3.1, L.3.2, L.3.3

The way you teach this lesson will depend entirely on the resources you have at your disposal. If your students have access to computers, you will almost certainly want to model your own fact-checking by showing students how to use a student-safe search engine quickly and efficiently. You will no doubt want to model how tempting it might be to go back and add additional information or to get lost on a trail of learning more things about one's topic, and how a writer might need to refocus at times. If you have a variety of resources, you will want to spend a little time modeling ways to use each resource. For example, you might model that when using print sources, we can't always find the answers in the first place we look and might have to search through multiple resources before finding the fact that we want confirmed. Or you might model how to sift through the thousands of sources that the Internet spews for each search query, to select the one or two best ones to look at further. No matter what your resources are, you will want to include a chart that students can refer to for remembering steps to take while fact-checking.

Again, this will depend on your resources. Ideally, if you will be using computers, each student would be able to work with a partner to conduct a quick online search with you as their guide. If, however, your resources are varied, you might also opt to create a practice resource, riddled with errors, and channel children to practice fact-checking using whatever resource you do have on hand.

You will want to let students know that they should double-check most facts, since even facts that everyone thinks are true can turn not out to be accurate.

CONFERRING AND SMALL-GROUP WORK

Much of your work time today will likely be spent nudging students to move along to check as many facts as possible. It is important to keep an eye out also for other, non–fact-check-related issues or needs you might see as you are moving around the classroom. Do students still have structural issues? Are there writers who could still use a quick tip about elaboration? Are there students who are feeling overwhelmed by the amount of work and could use your help with prioritizing?

MID-WORKSHOP TEACHING

Depending on how many text features your students included, they might not be thinking about fact-checking those as well. You will want to make sure they understand that all parts of their books need to be as factual as possible. This includes the labeling and details on diagrams, glossary definitions, the facts mentioned in charts, the categories referred to in tables, and so on.

SHARE

You might encourage students to take their fact-checking home if they did not have time to finish in class. If you know they have additional resources at homes, encourage them to follow up there. You might also want to let them know that tomorrow you will be moving on to editing, so if there are any other last-minute revisions they want to do, they might want to take a stab at doing them before writing workshop tomorrow.

Enjoy!

Lucy and Colleen

Session 16

Punctuating with Paragraphs

YOU'LL ALWAYS WANT TO WEIGH OUR RECOMMENDATIONS for sessions against what you see in your classroom. For example, in the third- and fourth-grade checklists, students are required to punctuate as they compose, not just adding end punctuation as one might scatter Easter eggs on a field of grass. They are also required to use spelling patterns to help them tackle unknown words—meaning that the word wall provides help not just with those words but with scores of other words like those.

You could absolutely decide to add a minilesson on these skills or to alter this one. The youngsters we were teaching had particularly pressing needs around paragraphing, however, so that's the direction we chose for this minilesson.

"Teaching paragraphing in expository writing is a way to teach structure, which is critical in the CCSS."

Whenever you want to make editing more glamorous, it helps to offer students special editing tools such as fancy pens, highlighters, correction tape, electronic spell-checkers, and so on. It's amazing how just the excitement of using these fresh tools can get even the most reluctant editor fired up.

Although paragraphs are not mentioned in the Common Core State Standards for third grade, it is very difficult to imagine not addressing paragraphs when so much of

IN THIS SESSION, you'll teach children that when information writers are editing, they keep a close eye on the way they use paragraphs.

GETTING READY

✔ A chapter from your demo information book that contains long paragraphs that can be broken into smaller chunks (see Teaching)

✔ Sample anecdote that illustrates pronoun-antecedent confusion, perhaps Abbott and Costello's "Who's on First?" (see Mid-Workshop Teaching)

✔ Colored pens for editing (see Link)

✔ Multiple small white boards, pads of chart paper, or easels and writing supplies to go with them (see Share)

COMMON CORE STATE STANDARDS: W.3.2, W.3.5, W.4.2.a, RI.3.8, SL.3.1, L.3.1.f, L.3.2, L.3.3

what students have been writing in their chapters has been in paragraph form. Additionally, teaching paragraphing in expository writing is a way to teach structure, which is critical in the CCSS.

Noah Lukeman, author of *A Dash of Style* (2007), teaches us that paragraphs can be viewed as a powerful form of punctuation. Students can look to see where larger chunks of text can be broken up into smaller paragraphs, as well as when to connect smaller paragraphs that feel like they would be better in a larger chunk of writing.

The mid-workshop teaching aligns directly with Common Core Language Standard 3.1.f, where students are asked to begin the work of ensuring pronoun-antecedent agreement. The Common Core does not require third-graders to master this usage, but we'd rather begin the journey early, because grammar becomes more complex as they move up the grades.

It is also worth noting that directly after this session, students will begin a new project. You might feel it is important to spend another day or so doing additional work on editing, based on your assessments. After this editing work is complete, there is no session set aside for publishing or copying over students' writing to fancy it up. We found in our work on this unit that for many students, there was so much drafting and revision work, and so much attention paid to text features, that the idea of copying the whole thing over was too daunting. If you decide it is work that your students are ready for and can handle, know that it might take a few days, and you will want to account for that. You might also consider having volunteers type the students' pieces while the students illustrate them (either with pen and paper or with computers) or else to work with a computer teacher or technology specialist in the building who can help with this work.

Punctuating with Paragraphs

CONNECTION

Assess what students already think about paragraphs.

"Writers, I know I told you yesterday that we would be working on editing today. I thought one of the best places for us to start would be to think about paragraphs. To warm up your brains, can you turn and tell your partner what you know about paragraphs? How do you make a paragraph?"

I listened to the students talking and heard them say things like "Paragraphs are about one thing," and "They have to have a couple sentences," and "You put spaces in front of them."

"I'm so glad to hear that you have already noticed and have thought a bit about paragraphs!"

❖ **Name the teaching point.**

"Today I want to teach you that informational writers edit with a laser focus on one of the most important organizing structures: the paragraph. Writers look at the paragraph as the most powerful punctuation there is. Paragraphs separate not just words into sentences, but also whole groups of sentences into topics."

TEACHING

Explain that when writers choose to start a new paragraph, they are often making that choice in much the same way they decide to end a sentence.

"There are many different beliefs that people have about paragraphs. People will even tell you there are rules. But I'm going to let you in on a little secret. Mostly, the rules aren't true. People paragraph more by feel, by look, than by rules.

"The main reason writers start new paragraphs is because they want to say, 'This chunk of thought is over. I'm now moving onto the next chunk of thought.' Do you remember hearing that you put a period at the end of a thought? Well, you put a new paragraph at the end of a bigger thought. And just like a writer can decide to write short sentences or longer ones for a certain reason, writers make similar decisions about paragraphs. The trick to paragraphing information

Of course, children learned to paragraph during the narrative unit, so this minilesson stands on the shoulders of that work.

Your goal is for your students to write in paragraphs of thought, not sentences of thought. Over time, their ideas will become complex enough that they do not fit into the confines of a sentence. As writers become more sophisticated, they'll use the whole paragraphs not so much to elaborate upon a one-sentence idea, but to lay that idea out in the first place.

texts is to think about when you have said enough about one chunk and are ready to move on, and when you want to make a chunk a bit longer."

Demonstrate looking back through the model text, looking for places with long chunks of text that might need to be broken up into paragraphs.

"So, let me see. I'm going to flip back through my pages to see if I have any big chunks of text that are a little hard to read because there's no break at all," I said, turning the pages on my chart tablet to find the page I was looking for. "This page looks okay. There are three nice paragraphs here, all indented and everything. And this page looks good too," I said, acting as if I was talking to myself.

Model this revision of a paragraph, thinking aloud about meaning, pace, and purpose.

"Ah! Here's one! Look at how big this chapter is! There's a whole page of writing and only one paragraph. That can't be right. I know I had a few different things going on in the chapter. Let me go ahead and reread it to see if there's a way I could paragraph it to make it more readable." I pulled out a pen and held it at the ready. "When I see a place where I should start a new paragraph I'm going to make a little paragraph symbol so I know that's where I'll indent." I sketched a quick image of the editing symbol for a paragraph.

> Killing cockroaches using natural methods is not the only way to keep cockroaches out of your life. There are many ways that you can keep cockroaches from ever becoming a problem in your home. You would want to keep them from even walking in to begin with by plugging gaps. Some cockroach exterminators suggest using steel wool to plug those holes. Other people recommend using plaster. You can also make the space uncomfortable for cockroaches by making it drafty and bright. According to the book <u>Cockroaches</u> by Nancy Dickman, cockroaches like places that are warm and dark. Another way to keep cockroaches from being a problem in your home is to be sure they can't survive in your home. Clean up all food and store foods in cockroach-proof containers to accomplish this.

I stopped reading abruptly after the last sentence, before I moved on to the next. I indicated that I was noticing something. I scratched my head, then held my pen at the ready. "You know, I'm feeling two things here. One thing is that this paragraph is starting to feel *really* long. The other thing is that I'm noticing that the whole first part was all about keeping cockroaches from coming into homes in the first place. This next part is about a different chunk of ideas—about making the environment uncomfortable. I'm going to make a paragraph there." I modeled placing a paragraph symbol right before the sentence that starts, "You can also make the space . . . "

Debrief.

"Writers, did you see how I looked for a big long chunk of text and then reread it carefully so that I could think about using paragraphs as super strong punctuation to break that chunk up? Do you see how much easier my piece is going to be to read now because it's broken up into paragraphs?"

When you shift from the demonstration to debriefing, students should feel the different moves you are making just by the way your intonation and posture changes. After most demonstrations, there will be a time for you to debrief, and that's a time when you are no longer acting like a writer. You are the teacher who has been watching the demonstration and now turns to talk, eye to eye with kids, asking if they noticed this or that during the previous portion of the minilesson.

ACTIVE ENGAGEMENT

Give students an opportunity to chop up another demo text into paragraphs.

"Now it's your turn to try. Can you look back at Jeremy's piece that you read before about where turtles live and see if you and your partner can decide on places to chunk the text into paragraphs?"

As students discuss possible paragraph breaks, listen in and guide them to notice that there are different ways paragraphs can go.

"I think there's only two paragraphs in this part. One paragraph is about turtles living on land or in the ocean. The other paragraph is about if they are in the zoo or the desert," said one student to her partner.

"I completely disagree. I think there are three paragraphs. Putting everything up to the zoo part together makes the first paragraph too long," replied the partner.

"But if we make three paragraphs, the first one is too short!" was the passionate comeback.

I leaned in, "I'm wondering about that. Do paragraphs have to be a certain length? Or is it okay as long as what's in the paragraph goes together?" I left the girls to ponder this.

LINK

Reiterate the teaching point and remind the class that they know about additional editing moves besides paragraphing.

"Today we talked about paragraphs and how important it is to use this particular form of punctuation and to edit for it. But you also know other things about conventions that you can edit for. You also know what things you struggle the most with. Can you turn to your partner right now and tell him or her at least three things that you are going to be on the lookout for when you edit today?"

Introduce a new editing tool.

"Writers, one last thing before you go off to edit. It is very helpful for writers when they edit to be able easily to see the changes they're making so that these changes stand out clearly. One way to do this is to use a different-color pen. Today, if you are ready to edit, you can grab one of the new colored pens from the basket on the writing shelf. Use it for editing today and anytime in the future in our class when you are editing."

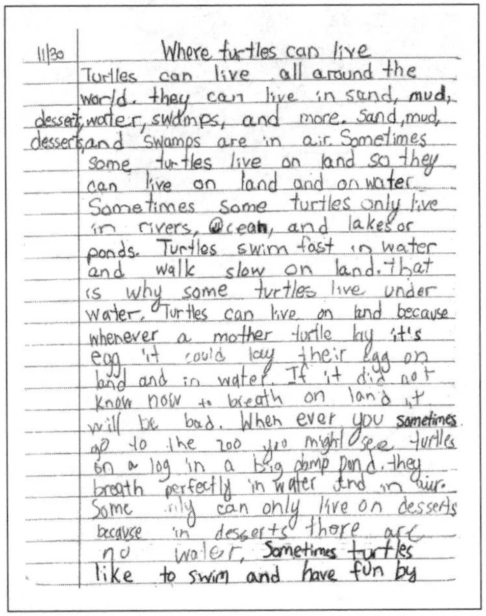
11/30
Where turtles can live
Turtles can live all around the world. they can live in sand, mud, water, swamps, and more. Sand, mud, and swamps are in air. Sometimes some turtles live on land so they can live on land and on water. Sometimes some turtles only live in rivers, ocean, and lakes or ponds. Turtles swim fast in water and walk slow on land. that is why some turtles live under water. Turtles can live on land because whenever a mother turtle lay it's egg it could lay their egg on land and in water. If it did not know how to breath on land it will be bad. When ever you sometimes go to the zoo you might see turtles on a log in a big damp pond. they breath perfectly in water and in air. Some only can only live on desserts because in desserts there are no water. Sometimes turtles like to swim and have fun by

FIG. 16–1 Children use Jeremy's article on turtles to practice paragraphing.

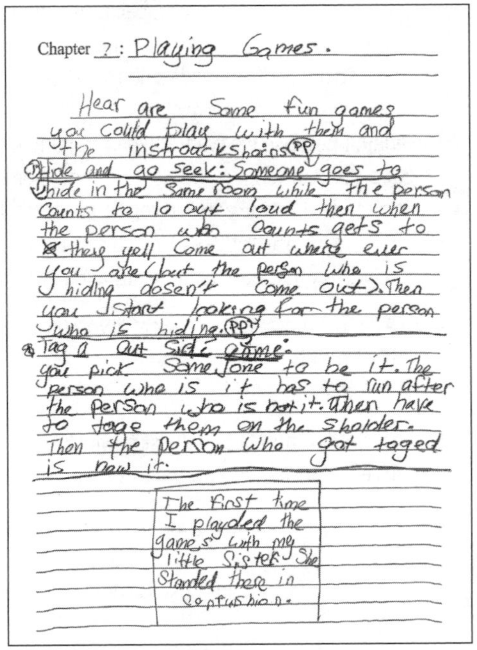
Chapter 2: Playing Games.
Hear are Some fun games you could play with them and the instroackshoins (PP)
Hide and go seek: Someone goes to hide in the Same room while the person Counts to 10 out loud then when the person who Counts gets to there yell Come out where ever you are (but the person who is hiding dosen't Come out). Then you Start looking for the person who is hiding. (PP)
Tag a Out Side game:
you pick Some one to be it. The person who is it has to run after the person who is not it. Then have to tage them on the Sholder. Then the person who got toged is now it.
The First time I played the games with my little Sister She Standed there in conftushion.

FIG. 16–2 Kayla marks places in her chapter where she wants to create paragraph breaks.

Grasping the Logic in Children's Work to Inform Teaching

AS YOU CONFER TODAY, make sure that your first goal is to understand the intelligence in what students are doing with spelling and conventions. For example, if a child's spelling seems to you to be especially unusual, ask the child to spell as he sits beside you. You may then hear the child say a word—say, *bucket*—and you may watch him progress along in the spelling. The child comes to the final /t/ sound and he says, 'bucket—t—tuh' and then writes *uh* at the end of the word. Check through his text. Does he often seem to add extra letters at the ends of words? Presto! You've found logic in the child's errors and can teach in a way that unravels his misunderstanding.

MID-WORKSHOP TEACHING **Making Pronoun-Antecedent Connections**

"Writers, I hate to stop you, because I know you are all working so hard right now," I said, indicating that I wanted them to put their pens down for a minute to focus on me. "So many of you have said to me while you're working that you were trying your best to catch 'all your mistakes,' which is great. But here's the thing. We're not only editing because we want to keep from making mistakes. We're also editing to make sure that our readers are not confused. Sometimes they might be confused because we made a mistake. However, other times it's just a place where our wording is a little weird or just doesn't make sense. We want to make sure that nothing gets in the way of our readers understanding what we are trying to say.

"A long time ago there were two comedians who performed a very famous skit about baseball. The two comedians were named Abbott and Costello. Here's a little piece of it."

I showed a short clip of the skit, which I had downloaded from the Internet, and also placed chart paper with the transcript right alongside the screen.

"You see, what makes it so funny is that *who* is a pronoun, but it is also the baseball player's name. So as much as Abbott is trying to explain it, because the name is the same as the pronoun, Costello doesn't understand.

"This skit reminded me of some of the writing in this classroom. A lot of us like to use pronouns like *he, she, they, it, what, who* all the time. Here's the thing. If a writer isn't careful and doesn't first introduce who the pronoun is referencing, readers can go, 'Huh? Who is he? Is he the dog or the dog owner? Or who?'

"See if you can tell why my pronouns are sort of confusing in this part of my writing."

Cockroaches love to eat a lot of different kinds of food that people like to eat. When they eat this food they often share it with their children.

"I underlined the confusing pronouns. I could be talking about either the cockroaches or the people. What I meant to say is not that *people* share their food but that *cockroaches* share their food with their children. So, if I want to fix this so readers aren't confused, I need to spell out who my pronouns are referencing. My new section reads like this."

Cockroaches love to eat a lot of different kinds of food that people like to eat. When cockroaches eat this food they often share it with their children.

"Right now, will you and your partner switch papers? And when you get your partner's paper, read it over and make sure you know who's who and what's what. Tell each other if you are confused."

Then again, you may see that a child tackles long complex words in a letter-by-letter fashion. This youngster might write *evaporation* by saying letter sounds /ē/ /v/ /ă/ /p/ rather than in chunks, leading to a tangle of sounds.

If you can grasp the logic in what a child is doing, then you'll be able to teach in ways that address the root of the problem. To do this, try to train yourself to look at a page that seems, at first glance, to be riddled with errors and to see instead a few repeating kinds of errors. Be able to say to the writer, "It looks to me like you have a few main things that are messing you up."

Ask the writer why she struggled with some things. "I notice you don't use capitals correctly. Is that because you don't know the rules about when to use capitals—do you need to be in a small group on this a couple times a week—or do you know this perfectly well and you are just being lazy?" If the child admits she is lazy, congratulate her for saying so, and ask what it will take for her to turn a new leaf.

In this sort of way, you'll use every minute of today to make a lasting difference.

Celebrating by Teaching

Ask students to come to the meeting area with their pieces. Congratulate them on finishing their pieces.

"Writers, the time has come to set aside your pens and pencils and come celebrate all that you've done," I called from the front of the classroom. "Can you all tear yourselves away from your work, grab your pieces and join me on the rug?" I headed over to my chair, set beside a blank piece of chart paper. I uncapped my marker with a flourish.

Explain to students that one of the best ways to celebrate new learning is to teach. Remind them that they started this unit by teaching others. Now they will get a chance to teach a new group of students, this time using their informational writing as a sort of lesson plan.

"As you all know, today is the last day we'll be working on these projects. Tomorrow we will start on something new that we will apply everything we learned so far to. However, it feels only fitting before we jump over to begin that work that we should take some time to celebrate. What might be a fitting way to celebrate?" I gave the students a few seconds to contemplate this rhetorical question, knowing full well that what they had in mind and what I had in mind would be very different.

"You probably remember that at the very beginning of this unit we took turns teaching each other about our expert topics. You might even have looked back somewhere along the way and thought to yourself that you know even more now and could definitely teach it even better. As a teacher, I can tell you, one of the best ways to celebrate new learning is to teach it. So that's exactly how we're going to end today's session. You might have noticed that in the four corners of the room there are some easels with white boards and chart paper. In a few minutes I'm going to break you up into small groups. You're going to take your books with you and gather with your small groups. Using your teaching tools (easels, whiteboards, chart paper, voices, gestures, and your informational books, of course) you will try your hand at teaching your classmates about your topics. Take a minute or two to prepare by looking through your informational book before you begin teaching so that you can follow it as a guide for what and how to teach."

After taking a few minutes to plan, the students headed off to the corners of the room. I moved from group to group admiring their informational writing and their teaching styles.

FIG. 16-3 Prachee's published piece, "Migrating Monarchs"

Migrating Monarchs

1

2

Chapter 1: Monarch Butterflies are very important

Monarch butterflies are very important, there are many reasons why. One of the reasons are that monarch butterflies help pollinate the world. Another reason is that they kill dangerous predators. I'm really glad that we have monarch butterflies around to help the world.

Pollinating is important because, when a monarch butterfly goes to a flower to drink the necter, some of the pollen gets stuck to their body. When they fly to the next flower the pollen drops on the little eggs inside the flower. Then the flower starts to die and fruits and vegetables start to grow. That's where stores and living thing including us get food. Also while monarch butterflies are migrating, they pass over some areas where pollination is a problem. They help pollinate those places. Without them plant life may suffer.

Monarch butterflies kill predators by using the chemicals in their body. Some of these predators can be very dangerous to us. Red ants bite, big spiders can also bite. and who knows what the other predators can do.

Chapter 2: Parts of a Monarch Butterfly

Monarch butterflies have lots of body parts. All of the parts are different. Like all the other butterflies, a monarch has three body parts.

The head is the first part. It holds the proboscis. The proboscis is like a straw, that sucks up the necter from flowers. It also holds the compound eyes. The compound eyes have lots of vision. The head also holds a pair of antennae. Some moths don't have antennae like monarch butterflies do. Moth's antennae are feathery and monarch butterfly's antennae are strait with a curve at the top.

The second body part is the thorax. It is right in the middle. It holds some its legs and part of it's wings. The abdoman holds the rest.

The abdoman is the last part of the monarch butterfly. It is leathery, so it's harder for animals to bite. Like I said, the abdomen holds the other half of the wings and part of its legs. since monarch butterflies don't have mouths, they breath through their spericals. Spericals

are little holes on the abdomen. You can't really see them, because they are very small.

Monarch butterflies have six legs. It has 3 on one side and 3 on another. The wings are attached to the Thorax and the abdomen. The wings need to be warm to fly. If they are frozen they can't fly. That is why the go before winter.

Chapter 3: The Colors of a Monarch Butterfly

A monarch butterfly has many different colors. The wings are the most colorful part of the butterfly. The wings have six colors. The six colors are orange, black, white, yellow, sunburst, and chocolate. Those colors warn predators not to eat the monarch. The colors tell the predator that the monarch tastes bad.

The color orange takes up most of the space in the wings. It is the middle part of the wing. It kind of traces the wing, but it's smaller. The orange is broken into 2 peices by the black.

The black traces the orange and fills up the blank spaces. The black is thick, but also thin. The black is like the outhline of the orange. The head, thorax, and abdomen are also black. The black has some orange and sunburst dots on it.

The color white occurs less. The white is just white dots on the black. It is on top of the black. It could be on the orange, but it's mostly found on the black

FIG. 16–3 (Continued)

6

The color yellow is on the other side of the wings. If you flip a monarch butterfly you will see the yellow parti. It takes up 2 of the 4 parts of the monarch butterflies wing.

Don't forget the sunbursd yello. That is also the middle part of the wings. Some monarchs has orange in the middle and others have sunbursd yellow. sunburst yellow is sord of, like light orange.

Another color is chocolate. Choclate is like brown. Some monarchs have chocolate instead of black. The orange or sunburst dots go on the chocolate, instead of black.

7

Chapter 4: Adaptations of a Monarch Butterfly

Monarch butterflies have lots of structures and each structure has an adaptation. The adaptations help the monarch butterflies survive the invirnment.

The probosci's helps the monarch butterfly suck up the necter from flowers, so it can drink it. Since they don't have mouths, they use the probosci's to suck up the necter from a flower and drink it.

Migrading is another adaptation a monarch has. Migrating is an adaptation because, the monarchs migrate to stay away from the cold winter. If they didn't migrate they would be freezing and won't be able to survive the cold. So that is why migrading is an adaptation. It helps the monarch butterfly, stay warm and not frozen.

The wings are an adaptations too because, the wings help it fly. Without the wings the monarch wouldn't be able to fly. In fact they wouldn't be called a butterfly any more. The

Another adaptation is the chemicals inside

the monarch butterfly's body. The chemicals make the monarch taste bad. So when a predator tries to bite the monarch, it will spit it out. If the predator is lucky, it will survive, but it is possible that the predators could die.

Another adaptation is a leathery abdomen. It is so leathery that when a predator tries to bite it, the predator can't rip it apart. The abdomen is hard for the predator to bite.

FIG. 16-3   (Continued)

9

Chapter 5: Migrating to Mexico

Monarch butterflies have to fly a long journey to Mexico. That is where they migrate. Mexico is warmer then new york. They get a head start at fall because it takes them a long time to get to Mexico. They fly in groups, so they don't get lost.

Monarch butterflies migrate in fall and spring in Mexico. Their journey to mexico begins in september. By november they reach texas. They take a rest because they still have a long way to go. When their rest is over, they start flying again. In early december they reach Mexico. They have traveled for more than 2,000 miles.

When they are in Mexico, hundreds or thousands of monarchs hang on trees and go to sleep. They cover theirselves with their wings. They use it as a blanket. They hibernate, take a deep sleep during the cold weather, in forests in Mexico.

There are many reasons why monarch butterflies migrate to Mexico. They migrate

to Mexico because it gets so cold at where they live. If they live in the cold and don't migrate, their wings will get frozen and they can't fly. The monarchs can't stand heavy snowfalls, or lacks of plants in the winter, so they move to the southern part of the united states.

FIG. 16–3 (Continued)

Plan Content-Area Writing, Drawing on Knowledge from across the Unit

IN THIS SESSION, you'll teach children how to transfer the skills they've learned in this unit to plan and draft for a content-specific information text.

GETTING READY

✔ Charts from previous sessions posted around the room as resources and reminders, including "Teaching Moves that Information Writers Should Borrow" (Session 1), "Strong Tables of Contents" (Session 2), "Strong Information Writing" (Session 5), and "Informational Writers Bring Their Writing to Life" (Session 8) (see Teaching)

✔ Main ideas and details about your content-area topics to brainstorm with class (see Teaching)

✔ Writer's notebooks (see Link)

COMMON CORE STATE STANDARDS: W.3.2, W.3.4, W.3.5, W.3.8, W.3.10, RI.3.2, SL.3.1, L.3.1, L.3.2, L.3.3, L.3.6

128

THIS SESSION STARTS THE FINAL BEND OF THIS UNIT. In this final portion of the unit, students are given an opportunity to transfer what they have already learned from their deep involvement in an extended effort to write information books to a quick, intense effort to plan and flash-draft a short text, which they will then revise so that it is written in a new form. That is, the goal of this final bend is to teach students to transfer and apply all they've learned to some fast-drafting in a content area, in hopes that they leave this unit able to draw often on all they have learned.

Educational researcher Douglas Reeves has reported on research by Schomaker showing that 73% of students claim that they never write in social studies or science classes. Schomaker observed 1,500 classrooms and found almost no opportunities across the curriculum for writing ("Making the Case for Writing," 2010). Your classroom can be a dramatic exception! Now that you have taught students to write information books, it is important that your students should bring their newfound skills into discipline-based classrooms.

For students to write often and easily in their social studies class, you'll want to be sure they know how to draw on all you have taught them, applying those skills and strategies to briefer, quicker information pieces. Today you specifically help them to draw on what they learned about planning and structuring information texts to write a nonfiction text on the topic they've been studying in social studies. We've written the minilesson as if students have been studying China, but you could just as easily alter that to any other topic. Because the students will be writing a short text and not a book, you'll help them understand that when an information text does not begin with a table of contents, there are still ways to plan the text that are tremendously important. In fact, it is almost as if one creates a simplified version of the table of contents for texts that do not have an actual one. You will emphasize that just as, earlier in the unit, your students did not commit to the first table of contents they created but instead explored several options before settling on a plan, so, too, your students will now want to explore a few different options as they weigh possible ways to structure the text they'll write today and this evening, for homework, before revising the text tomorrow.

Plan Content-Area Writing, Drawing on Knowledge from across the Unit

CONNECTION

Tell writers that you are going to teach them how to bring the nonfiction writing skills they've developed into social studies.

"Writers, will you pretend this isn't writing time at all? It is social studies class. You know what we are studying—China. Right now, think about what sort of work we usually do during social studies time." I gave children a minute to do this. "I'm pretty sure you said we read books, and we talk, and we map, and we watch videos, and we take notes. Here's the thing: from this day on, in social studies class, we're also going to write nonfiction."

❖ Name the teaching point.

"Today I want to teach you that when writers move on to other subject areas, writers don't just leave their writing skills at the door. Writers carry those skills with them when they become scientists, anthropologists, and mathematicians. Specifically, writers make sure that they use what they know about planning well-organized information texts, whether they are writing a book in writing workshop or writing an article or a paper or a feature article in the social studies classroom."

TEACHING

Drawing on the boxes-and-bullets (main idea and details) planning that students did earlier in the unit, demonstrate two alternative ways you could imagine structuring a text on a topic from the class's recent social studies unit.

"So I was thinking about one thing I find particularly fascinating about China, and that is shopping. There are just so many things in the world that are made there, and there are so many different ways to shop in China! But I know from our information work that I can't just write a blob all about my topic. I need to plan the parts of my writing. We're going to be writing a short text, not books, but we can still plan in almost the same way as we used to plan if we make a bulleted list of how a piece of writing might go. Let's see. If I want to write a text about shopping in China, how could I chunk that whole topic into parts? Hmm. I know! I could try this," I said and picked up a marker pen.

◆ COACHING

The Teachers College Reading and Writing Project has been helping teachers in thousands of schools accelerate students' achievements to meet the new demands of the CCSS. For us, it has been especially important to explicitly teach students to transfer what they learn in one discipline to another discipline. We need to be able to say to students, "Bring your charts and your work from the writing workshop with you across the school day—and we'll teach you how the writing you'll do in other disciplines is both a bit different, and also very much the same, as the work you've already learned to do."

You may notice that it isn't exactly clear what kind of text this will be that you (and the children) are writing. You can, if you like, refer to this as an article. But in another two days, the work will involve rewriting this text into a particular form, such as a brochure or an article in a travel magazine or a speech. So we're keeping the precise form of this a bit vague for now.

Places for Shopping in China

- Malls
- Outdoor markets
- Small shops

"As I'm writing that, I'm thinking of *another* way I could chunk the topic of shopping in China." I scrawled.

Things to Shop for in China

- Toys
- Tea
- Jewelry
- Accessories

Recall other ways to structure information writing, and mention quickly at least one other possible way to partition the overall topic into parts, such as ways the topic is the same as or different from something

I referenced the charts that showed the various structures we explored in Session 5. "I could also play with other ways to structure information writing, such as maybe comparing and contrasting, or writing about ways things are the same and different. I could compare shopping in China with shopping in the United States, for example.

"Remember, we're pretending this is the social studies classroom. That might be hard to remember, because do you see that I'm using a lot of what we just learned in the writing workshop and applying it to our study of China? I tried a few different organizational structures, and already I'm getting closer and closer to what I think I really want to write about. I've also got in mind a few different ways to organize my writing."

ACTIVE ENGAGEMENT

Channel students to quickly think of a topic they would like to explore more and to share it with a partner.

"Can you, right now, just think for a minute? When you think of everything we have learned about and studied so far about China, what topic do you feel particularly drawn to? Choose something you know a lot about that you could explore a bit more." I left a bit of silence. "Thumbs up when you have a topic in mind." I waited for a majority of students to signal that they'd settled on a topic before moving on.

You may wonder what, exactly, the students will be writing. Do you refer to this writing as an article? A research paper? A feature article? Do you leave the genre open? The truth is that this decision is up to you. We decided to call this a feature article because we imagine that such texts may or may not boast subheads, and we think some students will want and need that structure.

Ask students to plan one possible way they might chunk their topic into parts, organizing the writing they intend to do, using their fingers as a graphic organizer.

"Now would you do what I did when I thought about the different things I could address in writing about shopping in China? Think about the different parts of the topic that you could address in a piece of writing, and list them across your fingers." Again, I let the room become quiet. "Use your fingers as your bullet points," I clarified. After a minute, I channeled children to talk to their partners.

LINK

Encourage students to hold in mind what they have learned about information writing as they write about their social studies topic. Suggest they keep their writer's notebooks out as reminders.

"Today you'll write a text about your China topic: you'll start it, and you'll either finish it, or you'll finish it at home tonight. Keep in mind as you work what you know about your China topic," I gestured to show this is on the one hand, "and, also, what you know about information writing.

"For example, you have a tentative plan for how your information writing on China might go. Think back to the work you did way back at the start of this unit. What do you know about how information writers get ready to write that might help you figure out the work you should be doing today?" I left a moment for children to think. "Are you remembering that some of you found it helpful to teach each other about your topic before you wrote about it? Some of you made draft after draft of your table of contents, each time making sure that there was a logical progression for the way you'd like your chapters to go. Think right now about what you will do to get started writing—keeping in mind that you will need to do that quickly, so you also have time to write. Give me a thumbs up if you have a plan for what you'll do first."

As thumbs went up, I signaled for children to get started. "You may want to keep your writer's notebook out on your desk, because it can remind you of the sort of work you did during the unit of study. That way, you'll remember to do similar work right now. Get going!"

It's important to recognize that any phase of this entire process can be as complex or as simple as you decide it should be. You'll see that I approach the prospect of drafting the essay in a breezy, no-nonsense fashion, conveying the impression that a writer will find it no big deal to go from a bulleted plan to a full-blown text. As a writer, I also know this work can be infinitely complex. But for a child's first journey through this process, I think we need to simplify and condense the steps so that the writer can get into the swing of this kind of writing. During a second, third, or fourth cycle of nonfiction writing, a teacher can help writers realize that nothing is as simple as it may seem.

- one way I can orginize it is like where did they live then what do they eat, how do they survive, like a table of content.

94 <u>table of contents</u>

- where do they live.
- what do they eat.
- how do they survive.

- a other way is start with the most important then end with the less with the most important, like.

- how do they survive thats important then.

95

- what do they eat thats not so important

FIG. 17–1   Mickey reflects on ways he's learned to try tables of contents.

Anticipating and Responding to the Predictable Challenges

I T IS HELPFUL TO ANTICIPATE THE PROBLEMS STUDENTS will encounter. Because this final bend is a brief one and the whole idea is for students to do some efficient work, you will want to help students who are stymied find ways to move forward.

Some children will have chosen topics that are interesting to them but that require research time, and you are asking students to alight on topics they can write about today. Suggest that children record the topics that will require research in a safe place so they can return to them once they've had a chance to learn more, and suggest that for now, children think, "What do I know a lot about?" Chances are good that this will mean selecting a broader topic. For example, if your class actually was tackling the broad area of China, it is likely that one of your children could write a feature article about the geography of China. One look at a map could remind that youngster of a host of things to say. Granted, the writer might not have a lot of tiny details at his disposal—but there would be no shortage of information. You'll want to think of other similar topics that overlap with the class's studies and that might be accessible for your students—and more than that, you'll want to think of resources that children can turn to nudge them to recall such topics. Might they scan classroom charts? The textbook? Their social studies notes?

Then, too, you'll want to be ready to teach students ways to generate information related to a topic. That is, when writing about personal knowledge, the challenge is to choose a topic. When the topics are ones on which children have firsthand, personal knowledge, coming up with information is the easy part. But when the topic is a more distant one and the writer's knowledge base is less secure, coming up with information, with content, isn't so easy. You might, for example, teach children questions they can ask to help themselves recall what they know (who, where, when, why, and how, for example, are good for a start.) You might teach children to generate lots of words related to the topic and then to cluster those words into related clusters and talk at length about each word, each concept. That can help the writer recall what he or she has to say.

You will also want to be ready to channel children to do some quick research. This may surprise you. You may ask, "Is there really time to conduct research?" But the truth of the

---

MID-WORKSHOP TEACHING Consider Different Structures, Then Move Rapidly to Drafting

"Writers, can I have your eyes and your attention? Right now, will you consider reorganizing your writing—or part of it—into a compare-and-contrast book where you write about how your topic is mostly similar to another topic but is partly different. Talk to your partner to try to imagine doing this." After children talked about this for a minute, I said, "Now will you imagine writing your piece in chronological order, telling about what happened first, next, and so on." Then, after a minute, "Will you try thinking about pros and cons." Again I let a few minutes of talking time go by. "My hunch is that one of these has seemed like a good idea for you. Once you find yourself with a plan for how your writing will go, will you jot down that plan?"

Many children began recording plans, and I said, "You'll need to start your writing today, because you have just a few days to write the whole text. You won't be writing a book, but a short text, so if you have planned chapters, think of those as subsections. You'll probably want to start with an introduction, which you may revise later. Use all our charts. I have them displayed."

---

matter is that a single photograph can support an entire piece of writing. If children can find a few photos related to their topic, that will be an incredible resource to draw upon.

As always, when children tell you things about their topic, be sure that you listen raptly. You'll find that the force of your attention primes the pump and leads youngsters to say more, to remember more, to rise to the occasion of teaching you.

By a third of the way into today's workshop, you'll need to be sure that all your students are writing up a storm. From this point on, some of your teaching will take the form of voiceovers as you prompt students to write fast and furiously, to keep their hands moving, to remember to paragraph (and perhaps to use subheadings) and so forth.

Taking Stock of Where We Are and Moving Forward

Get a sense of how far students have gotten in their projects so far.

"I know everyone has been working very hard. I would love to get a sense of where you are in the process. Raise your hand if you have an informal table of contents in mind that you plan on following as you write." Most of the students raised their hands. "Raise your hand if you have started drafting your new piece." All the students raised their hands. "Raise your hand if you have written almost a page, or a whole page, and will soon be onto the next page." Lots of hands shot up in the air.

Channel students to set themselves up to finish their drafts for homework or at least to get it done first thing tomorrow.

"Well, it looks like most people are in good shape. I'd like to give you a choice of your next steps. Tomorrow you can finish and then revise these drafts. Some of you are completely ready for that, some of you are almost ready, and some need more time. If you would like to finish your draft at home, please do. If, however, you'd rather not do that, plan to use any free time you have today in class, and tomorrow before writing time, to finish your draft. One way or another, bring a completed draft to tomorrow's workshop so you can spend the whole day revising and editing it, because it needs to be done tomorrow."

Revising from Self-Assessments

IN THIS SESSION, you'll teach children that writers need to compare their plans for their drafts, reminding them of different strategies to revise either the original plan or the writing.

GETTING READY

✔ Charts from previous sessions posted around the room as resources and reminders, including "Teaching Moves that Information Writers Should Borrow" (Session 1), "Strong Tables of Contents" (Session 2), "Strong Information Writing" (Session 5), and "Informational Writers Bring Their Writing to Life" (Session 8)

✔ Your own plan for a content-based informational piece (see Teaching)

✔ Mentor texts from previous sessions (see Teaching)

✔ Excerpt or quote on revision from a professional writer (see Share)

✔ "Questions Writers Ask Themselves as They Get Close to the End of a Project" chart, prewritten (see Share)

COMMON CORE STATE STANDARDS: W.3.2, W.3.5, W.3.10, RI.3.1, RI.3.10, SL.3.1, L.3.1, L.3.2, L.3.3.a, L.3.6

Y ESTERDAY'S SESSION WAS A WHIRLWIND of activity and transference. You probably alternated between being thrilled and being disheartened when you saw how much of what you'd taught in the preceding unit your children were able to apply to a new context. Today will again feel like a whirlwind. After completing the drafts they began yesterday, your students will try their hand at revising that draft.

Your teaching won't be too different today than it was yesterday. You'll again remind children of what they know and teach them that they can draw on all they know again and again. Specifically, you'll remind them of what they know about qualities of good information writing. You'll then teach them that when writers know a lot about an effective piece of information writing, writers use all that knowledge to assess their own rough draft writing. They see where the rough draft is stronger and where it is less strong. When writers spot places where their drafts don't demonstrate their best knowledge of how effective information writing goes, writers revise to apply their knowledge.

As students reread and revise, then, they hold their draft up against their knowledge of good writing and note the differences. They also hold their draft up against their intended plan. If they planned to follow an implicit tables of contents, did they do so? If not, was this a deliberate choice? If not, might they want to rewrite the piece, this time adhering more closely to a planned structure?

All throughout the session you will want to remind your children to draw on all that they already know, directing them to refer to class charts, mentor texts, and their own writing as a photo album of sorts to help them work at their highest possible levels on this project. This is also the last day they will be writing this piece. Tomorrow they will be asked to think about all the forms that nonfiction comes in and to consider writing in one of those forms—although they'll probably use this same content as the basis for that writing. That is, they may take what they have done so far and reimagine it as a brochure or a speech or a feature article. For now, children will just be told that their aim is to finish this second piece today.

Revising from Self-Assessments

CONNECTION

Congratulate students on how much they accomplished in one day, and set them up to make plans for next steps.

"Congratulations on all the amazing work you did yesterday! I know some of you doubted me when I said we would have a draft finished in one day, but so many of you did pull it off. And from your writing, I have learned so many things I didn't even know about China! You are probably already expecting the work that you'll need to do today."

 **Name the teaching point.**

"Today I want to teach you that nonfiction writers assess their own writing to see what works and what doesn't work. One way they do this is by thinking, 'Did I do what I set out to do?' They reread to see whether the draft matches the plan for it—and if it doesn't, they decide whether the plan it does follow works or whether the piece needs to be rewritten."

TEACHING

Explain that to assess what you did, you first need to read over what you wrote yesterday, trying to read as someone who has never seen the piece before.

"So, here was my plan for my informational piece. Let me make sure I still like it."

Things to Shop for in China

- Toys
- Tea
- Jewelry
- Accessories
- Silk

This connection, on a minilesson that is almost at the very end of this unit, harkens back to the first minilesson in the unit, where children taught one another what they knew about their topics.

"So far, so good." I placed a section of my draft alongside my plan. "Here's a piece of my draft. Will you help me see if I followed the plan? And let's think, too, whether I drew on everything we have learned together about writing information texts." I began to read aloud.

> China is a great place to go shopping. There are so many things to shop for in China because so many items are made in China.
>
> One great thing to shop for in China is toys. There are plenty of toys to buy in China that you can buy in the United States. However, there are also lots of toys that you can only buy in China or that are hard to find in the United States. For example, kites and shadow puppets are often handmade and beautiful, and very easy to find in China.
>
> Another thing to buy in China is jewelry. A lot of it is handmade too! You can buy pearls and jade for very inexpensive prices. You can also buy hand-painted beads.

Demonstrate that you refer to charts, previous pieces of information writing you've written, and other materials in the classroom as you assess your writing and make further plans.

"Hmm, what do you think? I think it's a good first draft, what I've read so far. Are you thinking what I am thinking about the introduction? I need to do something to make it more interesting. I'm going to revisit my mentor text to see if I can get ideas for how to do that. I'm also noticing that I started out following my plan, but then I skipped writing about tea and jumped right to jewelry. I need to make sure that I include tea somewhere and don't leave it out. There's more, but let me jot a little list for myself on this Post-it note so that I can have a list of things to work on for my revisions."

ACTIVE ENGAGEMENT

Set students up to try the assessment work looking at another student's writing from another class.

"I know it can be tricky to see how a piece of writing matches or doesn't match the initial plans, so I thought we might practice doing this on this sample of a student's work from last year's class. This writer had planned to write about food, one of my favorite subjects. Let's pretend that it's our plan."

Food People in China Eat

- Breakfast
- Lunch
- Snacks
- Dinner
- Dessert

"That sounds like a very logical, well-organized plan. I think we're in good shape. Now let's see if the draft follows the plan." I began reading aloud.

> People in China eat a lot of different foods. Just like Americans, Chinese people have different mealtimes. People in China eat a lot of noodles, vegetables and some meat. They also eat fruit. They also eat different kinds of rice. People in China use chopsticks to eat.

Ask students to talk to their partners about what they notice. Suggest they make a plan of things the writer needs to work on, using the resources in the room as a guide.

"Writers, talk with your partner about whether the writing follows the plan, and about what you'd do to revise if this was your piece."

I leaned in and listened to few partnerships as the children talked. Frank said, "Hmm, so I'm noticing that it starts out strong. The introduction is clear. But then in the third sentence, it's almost like the categories are lost. Now it's just all about Chinese food."

His partner nodded. "I agree. If this was my piece I would make at least one new paragraph for each of the bullet points. Or something . . . ?"

LINK

Ask students to begin today's work by self-assessing.

"Most of the time, after a lesson like this, I tell you to think carefully about what you want or need to do during work time. Today I'm going to make a request. I'm going to ask everyone to spend the first several minutes of class time looking over your writing and assessing it. Ask yourself, 'What have I done well here? What work still needs to be done? What can I improve upon?' Then jot down a quick To-Do list for work time today. I know for a few of you, your list may include finishing the draft—or deciding not to, since you could go right into rewriting it."

Stress that students already know a plethora of strategies for revising informational texts.

"When you are making that To-Do list, it might be helpful to remember that we learned a lot about revision while we were working on our information books. You will likely want to revisit some of our charts that offer revision strategies to remind yourself of all that you know. And as a special bonus, you might even be inspired to try some things that you hadn't even included on your original list!"

Encourage them to get as far as they can with their pieces.

"I can tell by your wiggling that you are ready to go. I don't want to keep you here much longer. The last thing I want to mention to you is this: you want to use every precious minute of writing time today. You know revision strategies and you even know a whole bagful of editing strategies to use if you manage to get some editing done today. I can't wait to see how you use all of what you know today!"

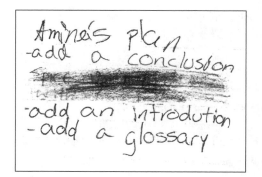

FIG. 18–1   Amina creates a plan for what she needs to do.

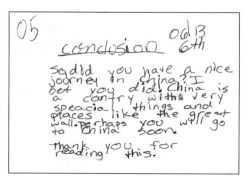

FIG. 18–2   Amina follows through on her plan by crafting a conclusion.

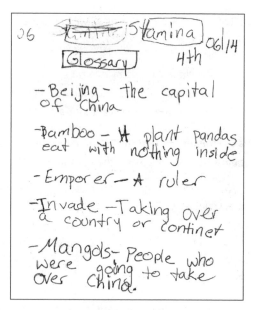

FIG. 18–3   Amina includes a glossary as part of following her own plan for revision.

Integrating Resources and Skills

FOR MANY TEACHERS, DAYS LIKE TODAY CAN FEEL OVERWHELMING: there are many different projects going on; two subjects (social studies and writing) are at play; there are lots of materials in use; charts are covering every free inch of space. You are probably tempted to just roam your classroom, putting out fires and handing out quick, generic compliments. While there are certainly worse things you could do, a better way to face the challenges of today is to think of your students not as twenty-eight (or so) individuals, but as four or five groups. Since your students are sitting at tables, gathered around resource baskets, the most efficient and effective way to teach today may be to move from group to group, using the built-in structure of table groups.

As you approach a group, quickly assess what needs to be taught. Chances are that the decision will relate to the timing for your visit. At the first group, you will probably be coaching students to get started immediately rereading their draft and jotting a quick plan for themselves. You'll want the students to see that as a three- or four-minute activity, not as one that involves fifteen minutes. You'll probably want to quickly scan their initial drafts, noticing children whose first drafts didn't have the all-important structure, and you'll want to channel those students to plan on rewriting an entirely new draft, doing work similar to the work the class just imagined for the author of "Chinese Food."

Presumably the second group will be just starting to work on their revisions, and so you'll be able to channel some of them into more ambitious plans—into a whole new draft. You'll probably want to encourage this group to use resources such as mentor texts and charts—also their previously written pieces of writing—to remind them of all they know (and to make their plans more ambitious).

By the time you get to the third group, you may need to light a fire under some children. If they're progressing slowly, remind children that they have just this one day to get their work done, and they need to work like the wind. You might find it necessary to do a little content-area instruction, such as showing them how to read a map if they are struggling with it or studying artifacts to gather additional information.

No matter what you end up teaching, it is important to try to reach each of your table or study groups so that each of your students has an opportunity to work with you.

MID-WORKSHOP TEACHING
Use Voiceovers to Rally Writers to Work Fast and Furiously

"Writers, the work you are doing right now needs to be done by tonight. You can take your writing home and continue to work on it, but I know you'll want to leave today's workshop with an almost completed, almost revised draft so that tonight can mostly be for polishing and editing. So watch the time. You just have twelve more minutes. You can get an amazing amount done in twelve minutes if you push yourself. Get going."

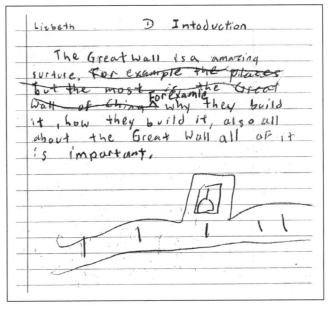

FIG. 18–4   Lizbeth revises her introduction.

Asking Questions to Help Revise

Teach children that they can ask themselves a set of questions to determine if their draft is ready to be declared done.

"Writers, Janet Burroway, author of a book on writing, suggests that authors can ask themselves questions to see if they are done. This list contains some of her questions, as well as a couple I added."

Questions Writers Ask Themselves as They Get Close
to the End of a Project

- Is the language fresh?
- Is it clear?
- Where is it too long?
- Where is it too short?
- Will the reader learn everything I want the reader to learn?

I pointed to each question on the chart as I talked through each point. "So, the first question, 'Is the language fresh?' is asking if I said anything in boring ways. Could I have used better vocabulary words? The second question, 'Is it clear?' is simply asking if the piece makes sense all the way through. The third question, 'Where is it too long?' is looking for balance. Are there any places where the writing goes on and on and doesn't say much? The question after that is the opposite, 'Where is it too short?' In other words, are there places where I could elaborate more? Say more? If so, I need to do something about that. And the last question is connected to our teacher selves: 'Will the reader learn everything I want the reader to learn?'"

Give students an opportunity to use the questions to make decisions about their pieces.

"I noticed that some of you were nodding and exchanging looks with your partners as I was going through these questions. You already know which ones you need to address. For the rest of you, I want to make a suggestion. Don't worry about trying to answer every question. Instead, choose a question that you think will help make sure your piece is the

140

best it can possibly be. You might decide that by thinking a bit about how your last information piece went and what you know you needed to work on in that piece. You should work on a similar thing here and answer any questions that might support that work."

Let students know that writers and anthropologists are always asking themselves questions.

"I know we're doing this today as we near the end of a project. But writers, anthropologists, or really anyone who is trying to convey information to other people, consistently check in with themselves by asking themselves questions. This isn't something you might do just today and tonight when you get home, but it's something you want to do whenever you write something for other people to read. Tonight, at home, will you finish revising your writing and bring it in, completed, tomorrow?"

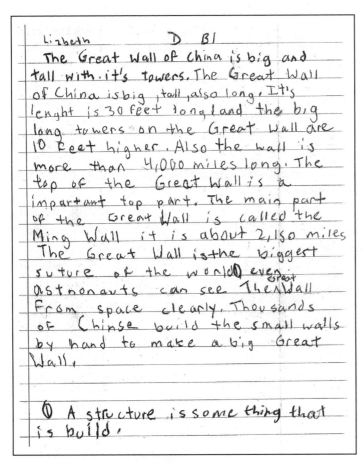

Lizbeth   D   B1
The Great Wall of China is big and tall with it's towers. The Great Wall of China is big, tall, also long. It's lenght is 30 feet long, and the big long towers on the Great wall are 10 feet higher. Also the wall is more than 4,000 miles long. The top of the Great Wall is a important top part. The main part of the Great Wall is called the Ming Wall it is about 2,150 miles. The Great Wall is the biggest suture of the world even astronauts can see the Great Wall from space clearly. Thousands of Chinse build the small walls by hand to make a big Great Wall.

① A structure is some thing that is build.

FIG. 18–5   Lizbeth uses her self-assessment to work on focus, vocabulary, and fact inclusion.

Crafting Speeches, Articles, or Brochures Using Information Writing Skills

IN THIS SESSION, you'll continue to teach children that the skills they used to write their information books can be transferred to other sorts of information writing and can be used quickly, on the run. Specifically, you'll give students the opportunity to reimagine the text they have already written as a speech, a brochure, or an article.

GETTING READY

✔ Anecdote that illustrates transference of one informational text to another (see Connection)

✔ One to three mentor texts to model structure and informational writing strategies, which could include a speech, article, or brochure (see Teaching and Active Engagement)

✔ "Writers Use Informational Writing Skills in Lots of Different Genres" chart (see Teaching)

✔ Your "Things to Shop for in China" plan from Session 18 (see Teaching)

Y OU AND YOUR STUDENTS MAY BE BREATHLESS at the pace of all this, and you may want to call "Uncle" and bring the unit to a close. If that's the case, you can move forward to the celebration. This session, however, will be a lot of fun for your students, and also gives you a chance to help those students who need an extra buffer day to catch up. In your minilesson today, you teach children that the skills and qualities of good information writing apply whether a writer is writing an article, a brochure, a lecture, or a nonfiction book.

You let students know that it is helpful to think about the audience and the context in which writing will be shared, and to choose a form that seems suitable. If they are writing for social change, they want to craft a speech, whereas if they are trying to promote a topic, they might create a brochure. To support students working with independence in a range of genres, it will help for you to gather a handful of mentor texts that are written in the different forms you can imagine your students selecting. A few possibilities include speeches, lectures, articles, brochures, guidebooks, and, of course, informational books. The overarching goal is to show students that once they understand how to organize and craft an informational text, they can take those skills on the road and apply them to virtually any type of information writing that exists. In just this one day, students won't be able to embark on a deep, all-consuming study of the genre they are trying on for size, but they can look quickly at the genre and notice some of its defining features. Brochures are often done on paper that has been folded in a really cool way, and there are photographs and headings. Speeches need to be delivered, perhaps through a videotape. Many of the finer nuances of these genre will get a little muddied or lost in this quick work, but the larger principle should nevertheless be clear. For this stage in their development as writers, it is especially important for children to realize that they know a lot about writing and that every time they grow new muscles in one type of writing, they can use those new muscles many times over and in many different ways—a powerful understanding to have in third grade!

COMMON CORE STATE STANDARDS: W.3.2, W.3.4, RI.3.1, RI.3.4, RI.3.8, RI.3.10, SL.3.1., SL.3.3, L.3.1, L.3.2, L.3.3

Crafting Speeches, Articles, or Brochures Using Information Writing Skills

CONNECTION

Tell a story that illustrates that you came to an understanding that knowing how to write one sort of information text allows writers to write all kinds of texts.

"Last night I was sitting on my couch, reading your pieces from yesterday. The news was on in the background. I wasn't really paying attention to it because I was reading. But then, all of the sudden, something caught my attention. I looked up and really tuned in to what the newscaster was saying. Well not really *what* he was saying—much more *how* he was saying it. All at once I realized that the way the newscaster spoke relied upon the same sort of structure and crafting that you have been using to write information pieces. I jumped off the couch, so excited because I realized that now that you are so good at writing information texts, you can become newscasters. Or you can write travel brochures. Or you can plan new companies. The truth is—once you know how to write information texts, you can write any text that aims to teach others information."

 **Name the teaching point.**

"Today I want to teach you that information writers can use their skills at structuring and elaborating, introducing and closing, to create all sorts of information texts."

TEACHING

Show a sample of something that has many of the same qualities of information writing that your students studied.

"Let me show you what I mean. I want to share an excerpt of a speech written by Mary Pope Osborne, the author of *The Magic Treehouse* books. She gave a speech at the United Nations about the need for children all over the world to have access to books. Will you listen while I read a bit of this speech? Let's look for the places where she uses skills we know from our study of information writing. Here's a part of the speech." I shared an enlarged copy of her speech. "The part I am sharing comes just after she spoke about working at a homeless shelter."

One of the most important ways to accelerate students' progress is to deliberately teach toward transfer. We know from a lot of research that if students are not explicitly taught to transfer and apply skills from one context to another, they often don't. The powerful thing is that the very act of applying skills allows a person to understand those skills at a deeper level. You have probably found that there are times when you realize that what you do as a teacher of writing can support your teaching of reading or of social studies. Once that aha is made, there is a rush of adrenaline as all that prior knowledge is brought to bear on new content. That's what you are after in these final sessions.

Every child is capable of using imagination. Every child has a hunger to know things. But not all children live in an environment where their imaginations might be stimulated or their thirst for knowledge satisfied. Nearly all the children at the shelter came from extremely impoverished neighborhoods. Most likely there were no books in their homes—and hardly any in their schools.

Studies show that in low-income neighborhoods in this country there is approximately 1 book for every 300 children . . .

It's obvious that we need to find better ways to teach all children to read. But I believe that literacy alone is not enough. We need to give children a passion for reading. Once ignited, this passion can be a fierce motivation for a young person to try to change his or her life for the better . . .

Usually we recommend that students first listen to or read a text as readers of it, responding to the content, and that thinking about the craft is a secondary move, done in a reread. In this instance, you are jumping past responding to the content. We apologize!

After giving children time to think to themselves about aspects of the text that reflect what they have learned information writers do, name a few of these yourself, jotting them on a chart.

"Wow. Powerful stuff in that speech! I could talk for hours just on what that speech is *about*. But instead, can we think about what Mary Pope Osborne did as a writer. Are there things she did that you do when you write information texts? Hmm." I was silent, rereading the text and thinking, and giving children time to think as well.

"One thing that jumps out at me is that she says something and then she elaborates on it right away. Almost in the same way we pushed ourselves to write a few sentences in every section. I also noticed that she included different kinds of details, like facts and descriptions. And . . . wait . . . Yes! She also used information from her experiences and also from outside sources. These are all things we did when working on our informational books. Let me start a chart to record some of the things."

You'll feel as if you are rushing here, and you are. This minilesson is a long one, and the expectations for the work that kids will do today are especially high, so you don't have time to tarry. Be very brisk. Also consider cutting out a portion of the minilesson.

Writers Use Informational Writing Skills in Lots of Different Genres

- Elaborate in various ways:
  - Include a few sentences for each point.
  - Use a variety of details (facts, descriptions, definitions, and so on).
  - Balance between personal experiences and research when backing up points.

"I know we could study this for hours, but I want to move on to another kind of text."

Show a sample of another type of text, perhaps one related to your content-area study or a hot topic of interest for your students.

"Another kind of writing that falls into the territory of information texts is the article. Let's look at this *TIME for Kids* article,* doing the same sort of thinking. In what ways is the writer of this text using moves we already learned to do as information text writers? You ready to think about that with me?"

The Tube, Food and You
by Alice Park

Excerpt from TIME for Kids

What you see is what you eat, according to the latest study to confirm that watching TV encourages children to eat more junk food. But the researchers say there may be an easy way to stop unhealthy snacking in front of the tube: put healthier foods within easy reach.

Leah Lipsky and Ronal Iannotti are staff scientists at the Eunice Kennedy Shriver National Institute of Child Health and Human Development. They worked on the study, which was reported this week in the Archives of Pediatrics & Adolescent Medicine. The report says that for every hour of television children watch, they are 8% less likely to eat fruit every day, 18% more likely to eat candy, and 16% more likely to eat fast food. Those results are similar to previous studies that have linked TV viewing with unhealthy eating habits among kids.

Cite and chart ways in which the writer of the article has used moves that students studied when writing their information chapter books.

"Just like we saw when we studied Mary Pope Osborne's speech, this writer elaborates in various ways." I looked back at the chart and ticked off the first two items. "The author of this *TIME for Kids* article also includes percentages, which are a fancy kind of fact and evidence. How many of you have done that as well?" Many kids signaled that they'd done this. "Let's see if there are any new things we can add to our chart." I reread the article in a stage whisper, then stopped to talk through what I noticed. "I see two big things here. There is a lead that gets our attention, and the writer is grouping information together. There are no chapters, for sure. But this section is all about the research." I added to the chart:

> - Use a logical structure:
>   - Write a lead that gets people's attention and introduces the topic.
>   - Group similar information together.

* "The Tube, Food and You" by Alice Park, from *Time for Kids* Magazine, May 14, 2012, ©2012 Time Inc. Used under license. "Time for Kids" and Time Inc. are not affiliated with, and do not endorse products or services of, Licensee.

"I also noticed that the writer connected each section to the next, like the way we tried to make paper chains between our different paragraphs. I'm going to add that to the chart under the structure section."

> • Connect sentences and sections together.

List possible forms for information writing, and stress that writers need to choose among these forms.

"This makes me realize that there are tons of different kinds of writing that you can do now because you know how to write information texts. Things like travel guides, brochures, letters, blogs, lectures, reports, newscasts. The list goes on! So that means when you want to teach someone some information, you need to decide: what form should my information writing take?"

This is, in a way, a second teaching point. It could easily have supported an entirely new minilesson, or been taught in the share, but for today's session to work, you need children to think about this prior to writing time.

Demonstrate your own process for deciding on a form and then beginning to draft.

"Let me show you how I think about form with my topic—shopping in outdoor markets in China. I could write this for people who might be visiting China and want some tips to make their shopping experiences go better. So I need to think about possible forms. Let's see. What about a speech? Hmm. I don't think giving a speech is very helpful because I doubt that people who are getting ready for a trip to China want to go to a speech. But they might want to read an article, maybe in a travel magazine. So, my job now is to take the writing I did yesterday and think about how to turn it into a snazzy article in a travel magazine. I think the structure can stay the same." I reviewed the plan for the article.

Things to Shop for in China
- Toys
- Tea
- Jewelry
- Accessories
- Silk

"But the lead needs to make this sound like an article. And I will definitely want subsections, with subheadings. I'll work on that later, but do you see how I am taking the text I already wrote and trying to think about a form into which it can go?"

You won't have time to write this in the minilesson, but if you later want to show students how you rewrote the original into an article, you might hang this up as an example, or use this in a small group.

Almost everywhere you go in the United States you will find things that were made in China. So why would you want to shop in China? Because there are things you can buy in China that you can not buy back at home. These are often traditional Chinese products made in small shops and factories that never get sent out of the country. Below are the top 5 things tourists should consider shopping for when visiting China.

Toys

Many toys were first invented in China. Probably the most famous example is the kite. There are many small shops where the shop owners hand make their own kites. These aren't just the rectangle kites we see here. They are often in the shape of traditional Chinese symbols for good luck, wealth, and happiness such as the dragon and the goldfish.

ACTIVE ENGAGEMENT

Ask students to consider yet another form and to spot some of those information text moves.

"Let's look at one more popular information form—the brochure. Here's a travel brochure I got about family vacations in Costa Rica." I displayed a copy of the brochure. "Let's look at this carefully with the lens of expert informational writers. What are some things the writers of this brochure have done that we also know how to do. You might want to look back at our charts in the classroom if you are looking for reminders."

> *Vacations for Everyone*
>
> *There is a growing worldwide demand for family vacation options. Costa Rica, with a long and strong tradition of peace and democracy, sees the family as the nucleus of civilization where such values can be fostered. So, this country has developed a series of family recreation activities and specialized programs: hikes, guided visits, group games, interaction with several communities and cultural groups, food tasting activities of Costa Rica's variety of cuisine, and beach sports, among others.*
>
> *You can choose among many options that will make your family vacation time a memorable one.*
>
> *Sports, adventure, nature, relaxation are part of the special family tourism you can enjoy in Costa Rica.*
>
> *Most of this country's coasts have the advantage that their water remains lukewarm the whole year round, which gives you the chance to profit from them whenever you like.*

The students turned and chatted to their partners, often referring to things similar to the ones I noticed on the other texts we studied. I helped guide a few to notice some of the vocabulary and word choices the author made, because we hadn't yet covered those things yet.

Break down what they noticed and add new items to chart.

"So a lot of you were noticing that this brochure has a lot of the same things the other two texts do. Which is so exciting! Some of you also noticed some new things that we learned when writing our informational books that would fall under the category of language. Let's add those to the chart."

Hopefully you will have a way to display an enlarged text to your kids. If you don't, then scoop up a whole armload of these brochures while you are at the travel store! Obviously it will be best to use a brochure you actually have on hand rather than the one we've put into the minilesson.

> - Use language carefully
>   - Include vocabulary specific to the topic
>   - Get the readers' attention by using fancy language or talking directly to them

Prod students to think about what form they could imagine working in while considering their content-area topic.

"I think you are realizing that when you wrote your information books, you learned skills that you can apply to speeches, articles, brochures, lectures, letters, and reports. Right now, think a bit about your content-area topic. Once you have it in your mind, think about your audience and about the context in which the writing could be shared. What form do you think your writing could take? When you have an idea, put your thumb up." I waited until I saw a majority of thumbs in the air.

LINK

Let students know that they'll have two days to rewrite their writing, putting it into a new form and angling it for an audience.

"Today, writers, you will begin putting your writing on your content-area topic into a new form. You will need to finish this work within two days. Choose a genre that best fits your audience and is one you know you can finish within that time.

"Writers, because you are planning and drafting today, you will want to get right to work."

Max

> The clay army was first found by a farmer who dug up a head then bodys were found, ponys were found.
> But the rest of the clay army was found in different pits, pit1, pit2, pit3 and pit4.
> Pit 1 was the biggest it could fit up to 6000 soldiers pit 2 could fit about
> Pit 2 was found empty, Pit 2 was the 2nd biggest.
> Pit 3 was the smallest
> Pit 4 was the 3rd biggest.
> The pits were organized by rows. There were about 20 rows with 100 soldiers and 10 horses.
> In some rows there were broken soldiers
> There were also emplers.

FIG. 19–2 Max crafts an article.

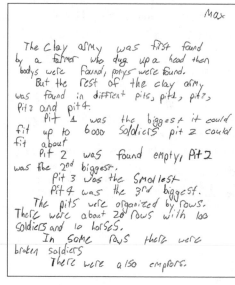

FIG. 19–1 Alessandra tries writing a speech to teach people about pandas in China.

Using Direct Quotes from Texts

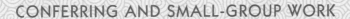

WHEN CONFERRING AND LEADING SMALL GROUPS TODAY, you'll probably want to first circulate and see if you can encourage students to take on some ambitious work. If it seems like many of them are going for the form that will require the least amount of revision, say what you see and suggest they can be the kinds of workers and learners who don't just take the easiest way out. You might say, "What about turning this into a speech, and perhaps we can video tape you doing it! Or you could pretend to be a travel guide, talking to a group that is just about to head off to visit something in China. Try something exciting."

For others, you may want them to use this invitation as a chance to think carefully about design, even helping others consider this as well. Increasingly, a big part of composition involves design. Which words should be enlarged, and why? What photos can be brought into the document. Where? Why?

For your more sophisticated writers, you may want to show how to directly quote a text. You will want to teach them how to refer to the title and author and how to punctuate the quotation. Practice it first with your demonstration text, and then coach the students through their attempts.

If you opt to teach this, make sure to be on the lookout for common pitfalls: overlong quotes, too many quotes, or including quotes that the students do not really understand. It might be helpful in this work to refer to mentor texts, particularly ones that are not on the same content-area topic you are working on (choose Canada if you are studying China, for example) so that students can see clear examples without getting distracted by the quotable content.

MID-WORKSHOP TEACHING   Writers Use Power Tools

"Can I stop all of you? I am pleased you are trying new types of writing. I saw some of you pull out your information writing checklist to use it as a guide. That's a wise use of resources.

"But there are lots of resources you aren't using. Look around this room and think about all the things we have here that could make your work better. Do you see the books about China, the computers loaded up with digital bins, the walls plastered with charts, maps, and artifacts? Writers, in life, human beings are made more powerful by the tools they use. If you hired me to build an addition to your home and I arrived with just a hammer and a hand saw, you'd wonder whether I could really do the job. Your work will be vastly better if you make use of all the power tools we have. For example, you don't need to feel as if you should draw all your information on the topic from memory. In fact, as we learned, most experts surround themselves with lots of resources so they don't have to try to remember every little thing, but rather, they can look some of these things up. This is especially true when you are working on a topic like social studies or science. Right now, point to one resource you will be going to sometime today."

Including Everything We Know Every Time We Write

Channel writers to use partners to double-check that they've got the basics in place.

"Writers, I'm a little confused. I know we have talked about and practiced using paragraphs, but as I look around, I see a lot of you are writing big ol' chunks of text without a single paragraph break! And that's just one thing I notice. There are other ways you have gotten so absorbed with the fancy new stuff that you are forgetting the basics. Right now, will partners exchange work, and will you help each other check that you've got the basics in place? If not, hurry to fix your work."

D   Introduction
Razia   5/18

There are several different kinds of festivals. For example. The Chinese New Year, Lantern Festival and lots of more holidays. If you want to learn more about China's holidays then you would want to read this S.A essay, you could learn a lot of holidays and festavils from this essay.

essay

FIG. 19–3   Razia makes a first attempt at trying her topic as an essay.

D
B1
Razia   5/18

The Chinese New Year is a wonderful holiday. In schools children have breaks for Chinese New Year, three weeks off. The Chinese New year is a important holiday. It is also a joyful holiday. On the first kids went to see relatives. Everyone is nice and friendly to each other to get goodluck from the dragon. If people deos bad things they get real bad lucks during New Years one from the dragon. For Chinese New Year Chinese people has a specail cake. It is not only called cake it is called Nia Gao in China. Chinese New Year is centries-old spring festival. There are four important animals of Chinese New Year, they are Rabbit, fox, dragon, and lion. Loin dancers and music players

D   Body 2
Razia   5/18

Did you know that in October 1 is the day of National day? There is lions and dragons dance at the end. There are other holidays too. Celebraitions start with a holiday and end with a festival. People in China get gifts and food for the holiday. There are special foods for special. The Chinese belive in the dragon giving good lucks and bad lucks during Chinese National day New Year. China come alive, for example. It come alive by music, drums, fire works and when it is every bodnye birthday. In every celebraitions people go to see relatives and give gifts also to get goodluck not bad lucks. If people deos bad things they get bad lucks.

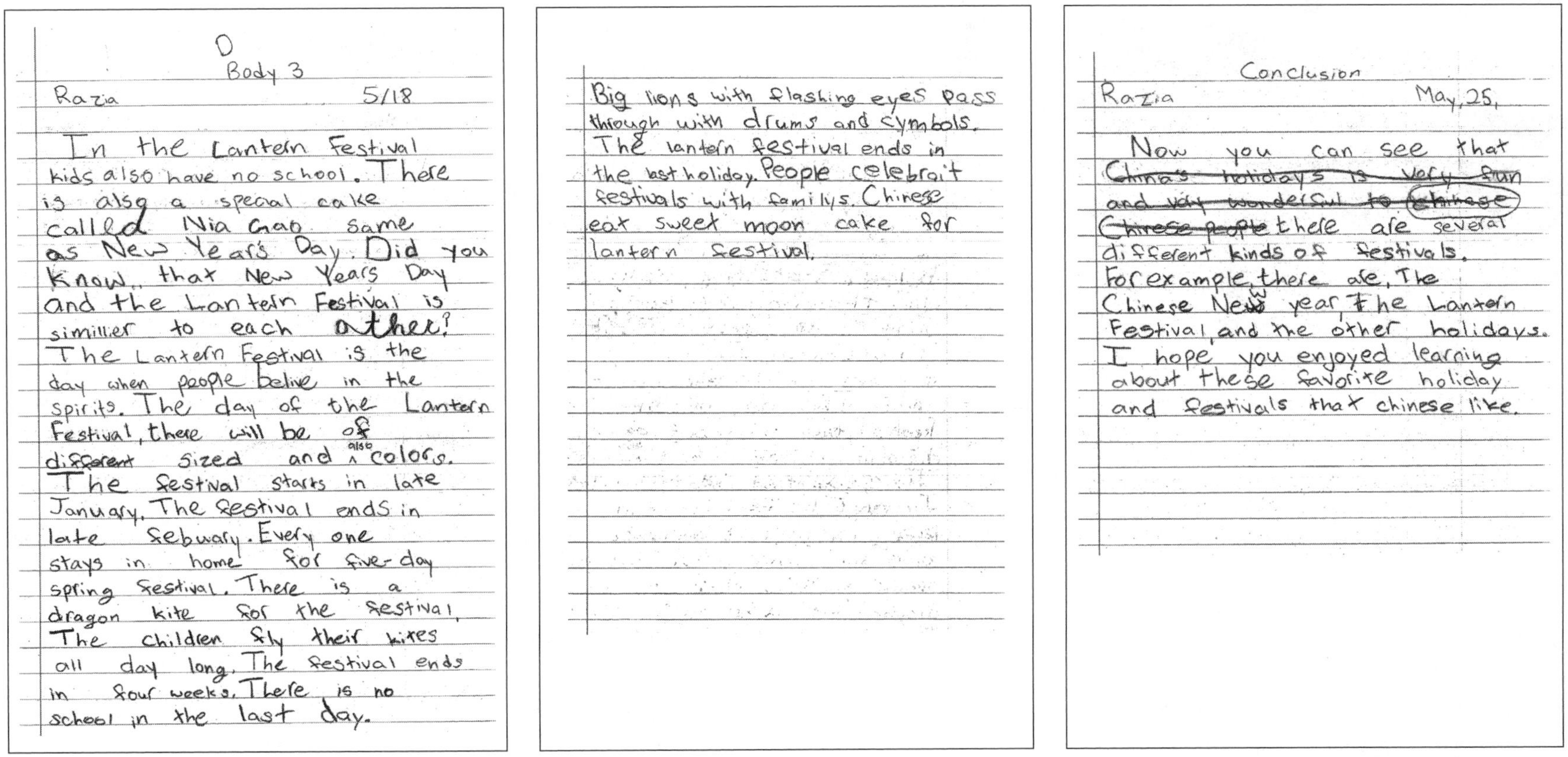

O

Body 3

Razia   5/18

In the Lantern Festival
kids also have no school. There
is also a special cake
called Nia Gao same
as New Year's Day. Did you
know, that New Years Day
and the Lantern Festival is
similier to each other?
The Lantern Festival is the
day when people belive in the
spirits. The day of the Lantern
Festival, there will be of
different sized and also colors.
The festival starts in late
January. The festival ends in
late Sebwary. Every one
stays in home for five-day
spring festival. There is a
dragon kite for the festival.
The children fly their kites
all day long. The festival ends
in four weeks. There is no
school in the last day.

Big lions with flashing eyes pass
through with drums and symbols.
The lantern festival ends in
the last holiday. People celebrait
festivals with familys. Chinese
eat sweet moon cake for
lantern festival.

Conclusion

Razia   May, 25,

Now you can see that
China's holidays is very fun
and very wonderful to chinese
Chinese people there are several
different kinds of festivals.
For example there are, The
Chinese New year, The Lantern
Festival, and the other holidays.
I hope you enjoyed learning
about these favorite holiday
and festivals that chinese like.

FIG. 19–3   (Continued)

Bringing All You Know to Every Project

IN THIS SESSION, you'll guide children to draw on all they know as they finish up their projects.

GETTING READY

✔ Your own story that illustrates the value of carrying knowledge with you everywhere you go (see Connection)

✔ Student information writing from the unit (see Teaching and Active Engagement)

✔ Clipboards for students (see Mid-Workshop Teaching)

✔ Copies of Information Writing Checklist, Grades 3 and 4 (see Mid-Workshop Teaching) 🖥

YOU ARE IN THE HOME STRETCH NOW! Today is the last day for your students and you to do work that might still be needed for an in-depth understanding of information texts. You'll see that in the mid-workshop teaching, you channel students to look again at their information checklists, comparing what they do now with what they did earlier in the year, so they can notice ways they have grown. The minilesson, then, is brief, and really just rallies youngsters to work like crazy in preparation for that final assessment. We know from experience that the final few minutes before the whistle blows are important moments. Notice that the teaching point is not worded, "Today I want to teach you . . ." Using words with precision is important when you teach, and the truth is that today's minilesson doesn't offer new content. This is a reminder minilesson. Your job is to make it a bit fresh—hence the little story at the start—and to make it engaging—hence the opportunities for kids to be actively involved. And to make it short!

"Rally youngsters to work like crazy in preparation for that final assessment."

COMMON CORE STATE STANDARDS: W.3.2, W.3.5, RI.3.1, SL.3.1, L.3.1, L.3.2, L.3.3

Bringing All You Know to Every Project

CONNECTION

Tell a story that illustrates the value of carrying knowledge with you everywhere you go.

"The other day I was at friend's house. She was having a cupcake-decorating party and had made dozens of cupcakes and had sprinkles and candies and little decorations. Just as we all settled down to start decorating, she realized that she forgot the frosting at the store! She was mortified. Everyone started to volunteer to go to the store to pick up frosting. Then I realized that I actually know how to make frosting. My mom taught me how to make frosting for cakes when I was little. I said to my friend, "Do you have powdered sugar, butter, milk, and food coloring?" She said yes. So I was able to make the frosting in just a few minutes, and no one had to leave the party. That was because I remembered something I learned a while ago—and remembered to use what I knew."

 **Name the teaching point.**

"Today I want to remind you that writers draw on everything they know to make their work the best it can be."

TEACHING AND ACTIVE ENGAGEMENT

Let students know that today's minilesson is different. They will do the teaching. Suggest students leaf through their work and find a place where they did something they could remind others to do.

"Writers, over the past few days you have all tried to bring what you know about good writing and about information writing to your current work. One of you may have remembered that it can be powerful to include small stories inside of information writing. Another one of you may have studied ways that visual design can make a piece better. Some of you almost forgot to paragraph and then remembered to do so at the last minute. Will you look over your work and think about what you remembered to do that some of the other writers in this class may have forgotten to do, and get ready to teach—to remind—each other? In a minute, you'll tell and show each other what you did that might remind others to do that was well.

"I've got a big chart up here of the information checklist, because in another fifteen minutes, you'll be assessing your writing using that checklist, so if you did something that is on the checklist, that might be what you choose to share."

◆ COACHING

You've seen that we often use an interesting story to catch children's interests and then teach them—through metaphor. This is not the best kind of connection for children who are just beginning to learn English. For those children, the story or metaphor may obscure the teaching point rather than enhance it. By all means, in these cases, delete entirely or substitute a new connection opener!

As children leafed through their writing, I said, "I can tell some of you are worried whether your writing is good enough to show everyone. Let me let you in on a secret. Most grown-up writing teachers worry about that too. It's a hard thing to put your writing out in the world as an example. But remember, I've shown you lots of stuff that's less than perfect. Sometimes I show stuff and tell what I am about to do, not what I have already done, and that's fine too."

Divide the students into groups and set them up to teach each other briefly.

"Teachers, let's divide the rug into four corners, as if there is a line down the middle here (from me to the back of the meeting area) and another line down the middle, sideways. Right now, turn to face the far corner of your corner. And will the student sitting nearest to that corner start and teach the others? Then a writer to the right of that person can teach, and so on."

As students taught each other, I eavesdropped, giving hints if needed. Before an entire round of teaching was completed, I gathered everyone back together, apologizing that there wasn't time for everyone to teach.

Name some of the great writing tips about structure and elaboration you heard from the teachers.

"I was so impressed by the quality of teaching in this room! And not only that, but I learned so many great things. Like Kayla had the idea of highlighting the different parts of her plan in different colors, then going back to her draft and using the same color to find each part. That way she can make sure she covered each part she planned to do and can see easily if some sections have too little information. And Anisa was saying that when thinking about elaborating, it can sometimes be nice to include lists of things that are important to your topic."

LINK

Cheer students on to bring every bit of effort all the way through the finish line.

"Today is our last day before the celebration. Think about everything you learned not just today, but for the past several weeks, and try to pour it into your writing work today. Don't let a second of work time or a sliver of what you know go to waste!"

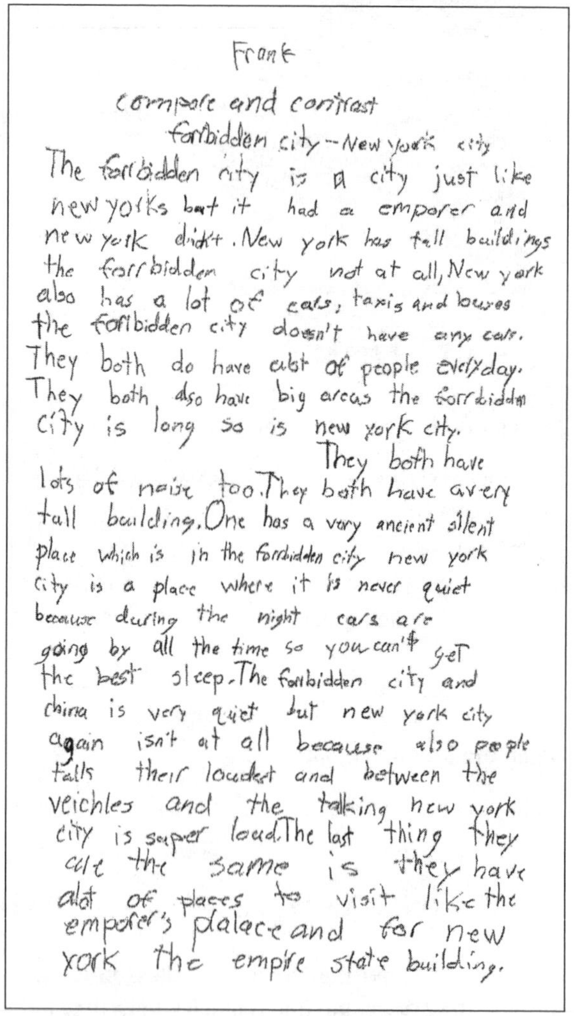

FIG. 20–1 Frank uses a compare-and-contrast structure in his piece about the Forbidden City.

Focus on the Positive

WHILE IT MIGHT BE TEMPTING TO RUN AROUND trying to fix one more problem, improve one last line, the truth is, today is not the day for that. There won't be much time for students to make any large-scale revisions to their pieces based on your conferences. So instead, you will be more productive if you use this time to give students compliments that will make a lasting difference. Remember John Hattie's research. He has found that nothing accelerates achievement more than feedback and claims that the feedback that matters most consists of what he refers to as "medals and missions." (We refer to this as compliments and teaching points.) For today, you will focus on the compliments. Hattie points out that a good compliment is informative; that is, it gives the learner information. You won't just be saying, "Nice work. You tried really hard and you did a good job. You should be proud." Instead, notice specific ways the writer has improved. To do this, you may want to draw on the checklist. You'll be able to say, "When you first worked on your information writing, you were . . . " and then read from, say, level 2. "But now you have really mastered . . . " and then read from level 3, "and I even see you starting to do . . . " then read from level 4. Show the learner more than one example of where he or she has done this good work. In this way, you help students to have a sense of themselves on a trajectory of progress. You let them know that in just a month, they can work deliberately toward a goal and achieve that goal.

When giving compliments, you might also think about the qualities of good work that do not appear on the checklist. For example, we all know that true success in life (and in writing) requires not just things like "writes with structure" or "elaborates using a variety of techniques." There has been research lately on the characteristics that make for success in college and elsewhere, and these include traits such as perseverance. If you see evidence of writers working with perseverance, or of writers being willing to learn from others, or of writers being willing to take risks, be sure to point those out and to help students know that you see and value those traits.

When complimenting writers, the more specific you can be, the better, and the more honest. Your compliments might sound like this. "Frank, I know you worked so hard on your book about dragons, something you feel very passionately about. I was a little worried that you might not have the same kind of energy around your content-area piece. But now I'm seeing that those little specific details that you included are just as rich and telling as anything you might have included in your dragon book. It's like you look at your topic with a magnifying glass, trying to see all the things that other people sometimes don't see because they don't look closely enough. That's a real gift you have. Never lose it!"

If you feel like you want to give one more teaching point to a student, limit it to a quick tip—something that might be enticing for the child to try, but the lack of which won't leave the child's piece flawed. It might sound something like this: "I was looking over your shoulder trying to squeeze my brain, trying to give you one little tip to make your great piece even better. And I could think of one thing—a little thing—but I'm not sure you even want to hear it. You do? Oh, well, it's just that I thought, since your introduction and conclusion are so strong, that you might want to think of some way to connect them. Like what we saw in some of our mentor texts, where a line or image was repeated." Then walk away.

Channel students to return to the information checklist to see how they have grown from the start of the unit until now.

"Will you gather in the meeting area, bringing your work, some Post-its, and a clipboard?" As students convened, I gave them each an information checklist and the initial on-demand information text they wrote at the very start of the unit.

"Before you do anything else, will you re-read the on-demand writing that you wrote long, long ago at the start of this unit? And as you do, think about how that piece of writing contrasts with the new work you've been doing. You should be able to see ways your writing has gotten dramatically better." I gave children some time to do this.

"Let's look really closely between your newest writing and the checklist to see what, specifically, you have learned to do. I'm going to read off one item—the first—and then will you look at your piece of writing, and check if you see evidence of this? Use a Post-it to point to the place where you did that work.

Information Writing Checklist

	Grade 3	NOT YET	STARTING TO	YES!	Grade 4	NOT YET	STARTING TO	YES!
	Structure							
Overall	I taught readers information about a subject. I put in ideas, observations, and questions.	☐	☐	☐	I taught readers different things about a subject. I put facts, details, quotes, and ideas into each part of my writing.	☐	☐	☐
Lead	I wrote a beginning in which I got readers ready to learn a lot of information about the subject.	☐	☐	☐	I hooked my readers by explaining why the subject mattered, telling a surprising fact, or giving a big picture. I let readers know that I would teach them different things about a subject.	☐	☐	☐
Transitions	I used words to show sequence such as *before*, *after*, *then*, and *later*. I also used words to show what didn't fit such as *however* and *but*.	☐	☐	☐	I used words in each section that help readers understand how one piece of information connected with others. If I wrote the section in sequence, I used words and phrases such as *before*, *later*, *next*, *then*, and *after*. If I organized the section in kinds or parts, I used words such as *another*, *also*, and *for example*.	☐	☐	☐
Ending	I wrote an ending that drew conclusions, asked questions, or suggested ways readers might respond.	☐	☐	☐	I wrote an ending that reminded readers of my subject and may have suggested a follow-up action or left readers with a final insight. I added my thoughts, feelings, and questions about the subject at the end.	☐	☐	☐
Organization	I grouped my information into parts. Each part was mostly about one thing that connected to my big topic.	☐	☐	☐	I grouped information into sections and used paragraphs and sometimes chapters to separate those sections. Each section had information that was mostly about the same thing. I may have used headings and subheadings.	☐	☐	☐

"I'm also going to read off the fourth-grade version of that item, and some of you may find that you are starting to do, or even mastering, some of the fourth-grade standards. If so, mark these off. But writers, here is the thing. You could easily go through and say, 'Check, check, check, I do all these things, la de dah,' and it might not be the case at all. The whole reason to do this is that the checklist can be a way for you to find the goals that you still need to work toward. You are going to be doing lots and lots of information writing in social studies and science even when the writing workshop turns to different kinds of writing, and your real hope is that you leave this work with some very clear goals. So don't cheat your own learning by saying 'Oh yes, I have mastered this' if you know you just barely do it, a little but, with a lot of help. Only check 'Yes!' if you have truly mastered something."

I then read through a few items on the chart before suggesting the children continue reading through them on their own and annotating them on their own.

Partners Engage in Close Reading of Each Other's Work, Holding Each Other Accountable

Channel writers to share their checklists with each other, rereading and talking back to each other's self-assessments.

"Will you share this work with partners? Partners, will you look together at each other's checklists, going first to the traits you think are most important? Talk back to each other. Say things like, 'Show me the evidence,' and question each other's assessments. Be hard on each other."

Channel writers to identify and celebrate goals they will hold onto as they continue working on information writing.

After about five minutes, I distributed colorful markers, suggesting writers make fireworks or stars beside their goals, because the goals were going to be the magic that helped them get better. After children did this for a bit, I said, "Let's also talk about what you learned and how you grew. What do you think you especially learned? How will your information writing be different because of this unit?" The children talked, and I took notes.

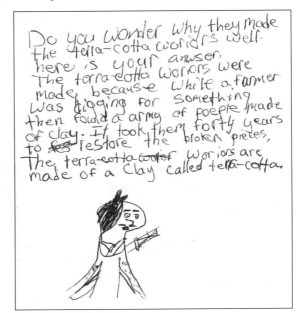

> Do you wonder why they made the terra-cotta worirs well. here is your anwser. The terra-cotta worirs were made, because while a farmer was digging for something then found a army of poeple made of clay. It took them forty years to restore the broken pieces. The terra-cotta worirs are made of a clay called terra-cotta.

FIG. 20–2   Francesco makes sure to organize his information in his draft.

> Amina
> The mongols were going to invade china. The emperors was going to fix all the walls in china and put them together to make it the "Great wall of china". It took more then 1000 years Just to build the great wall. They build it to protect themselfs, You can see it from the moon! It streches across the north of china.

FIG. 20–3   Amina researches facts and fills in blanks as she revises.

A Final Celebration

Using Knowledge about Nonfiction
Writing to Teach Younger Students

Dear Teachers,

When considering the best ways to celebrate this unit, we thought about many options. The most obvious option was to have an expert fair where students could place their publications out on tables and invite students from other classes to spread out among the displays. If there are twelve displays, each featuring two projects, visiting students could look over the two texts, and then, on cue, one of those two authors could give a brief lecture on his or her topic to the two or three listeners at that station before visiting students move to a second table and hear a second mini-lecture. We continue to feel that such a fair would be a great option, especially if your students are particularly enamored with their topics and if other classes would be willing to participate. Of course, parents could also be invited. If you decided to do that, you might add a day of instruction in public speaking, because there are important skills to learn.

We thought we'd toss another idea into the hopper. Students might teach younger students not about their topic, but about all they have learned about information writing, and if they do this, they might use all that they (and their classmates) have written as illustrative examples. Across the country, there has been some discussion about what "above standards–level" work might look like. In math, especially, some have been suggesting that students' work can be rated as above standards if they not only can do the work, but can teach others to do it as well. There are lots of advantages to such a view of excellence. For one, we all know that understanding something well enough to teach it to another learner, especially a younger one, is a powerful way to deepen one's own understanding. Then, too, this image of excellence supports notions of schools as communities of learners and values collaboration and shared accountability. Of course, the opportunity to teach a younger student about information writing would require your students to do yet another sort of application of their knowledge—an added bonus.

COMMON CORE STATE STANDARDS: W.3.2, W.3.6, RFS.3.4, SL.3.1, SL.3.6, L.3.1, L.3.2, L.3.3

PREPARATION

Choose a younger class (first or second grade would be perfect). It would be great if the children are also involved in information writing—and this is likely to be the case. Tell your students that they'll be working in pairs to make short presentations to the younger children (in small groups) in which they teach them what they've learned about information writing. Remind your students that they need to begin by planning out the subtopics they will address. Remind students that they should pick just a couple of things they think are the most important for the younger writers to learn and to be sure to repeat those two things as often as possible. If students are having a hard time prioritizing, suggest they start by thinking about structure and elaboration. Guide students to refer to a few examples to support each subtopic. Presumably most of the examples will come from the students' own writing. Suggest that both students plan the presentation and that the texts that both students have written be used as examples throughout the presentation, but one of the two might be the actual spokesperson.

Give your students time to rehearse, and give teaching pointers as you listen to their rehearsals. You will probably want your students to keep the props to a minimum. The simpler their teaching, the more easily it will be executed, and the more likely that the little ones might pick up a few ideas they can try in their own writing.

THE DAY OF THE CELEBRATION

Make sure each teaching team has a special space to work. Some teachers have found that simply hanging sheets of chart paper near a pair of chairs can create the sense of a mini–meeting area for your young teachers. You will probably want many teaching sessions to occur simultaneously, so that each pair of students is teaching at the same time. Make sure to take plenty of pictures of your students and their young charges as they work. You might also to have a table set aside with your students' finished pieces displayed so that the younger kids, and even your students, have a chance to ooh and ahh. (See examples on the following pages.)

AFTER THE CELEBRATION

After the younger students have left, you might want to gather your class back into the meeting area. Perhaps have them kick off their shoes and pass out some snacks. You're trying to re-create the reflective attitude that great teachers take after a job well done, when they spend some time with their respected colleagues, reviewing all that they've done and learned. Encourage your students to talk about what was good about the teaching and what was hard. Then shift gears to talk more about what they learned about information writing that they will carry with them, not just throughout the year, but throughout their lives. Celebrate those declarations most of all.

Enjoy!

Lucy and Colleen

FIG. 21–1   Kayla's final expert piece, "The Guide on Babysitting"

Table of Contents

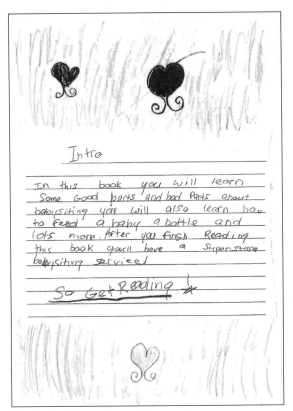

Intro

In this book you will learn
Some Good Parts and bad Parts about
babysiting you will also learn haw
to feed a baby a bottle and
lots more. After you finsh Reading
this book you'll have a Super-stare
babysihing serviec!

So Get Reading! *

T-Shirts
Pants
Shoes
Socks

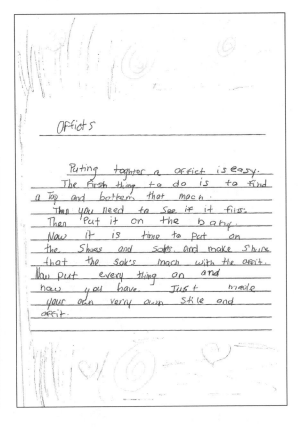

Offic+s

Puting togther a offict is easy.
The First thing to do is to find
a Top and bottom that mach.
Then you need to See if it fits.
Then Put it on the baby.
Now it is time to Put on
the Shoes and soks. and make Shure
that the sok's mach with the offit.
Now Put every thing on and
now you have. Just made
your own verry own stile and
offit.

FIG. 21–1   (Continued)

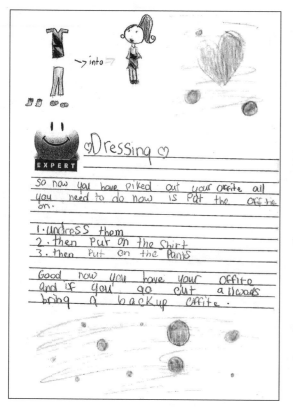

♡Dressing ♡

EXPERT

So now you have piked out your offite all you need to do now is put the offite on.

1. undress them
2. then put on the shirt
3. then put on the pants

Good now you have your offite and if you go out allways bring a backup offite.

♡Making a bottle♡

EXPERT

So the first thing you need to do is find a clean bottle.

Then take out the milk paur the milk into the bottle make Shure the milk does not over fill. Then put the bottle into the micuave for 30 seconds. A trp: Do not put the bottle into the micuave without the top parts. When the bottle comes out of the micuave put the top parts on. Then tie the bottle upside-daun for 1 second and let the drip go on you rist. If it is like that you couldent fell the milk drip the milk is Just right to give to the baby. Then if the drip stings do not give it to the baby. Now when it ys the right teptuate give it to the baby.

rember to warm the baby while it drinks the bottle so the baby won't choke on the milk it is given.

a digram of a **Bottle**

feeding part or nipple part

ounces

milk

Danceing Games

My favorite danceing game is frezz dance
this is How you Pray.

Someon sits on the side while
the others dance. Then the person on
the side hits the pause Booten.
The dancers frezz, if a dancer moves
they are out. Then the person who
sits to the side hits Play. And
then you Play it to all the
dancers are out.

Fawow the leader
Then you could Play Fllow the leader

1) first pick some one to Be a leader.
2) The leader dose a dance
move.
3) Then the other kids copy
the dance move. And thats how
you Play.

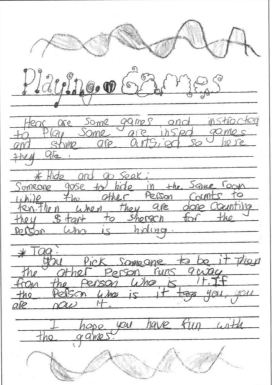

Playing Games

Here are some games and instractions
to Play. Some are insed games
and some are outsied so here
they are.

* Hide and go seek:
Someone gose to hide in the same room
while the other person counts to
ten. Then when they are done counting
they start to shorach for the
Person who is hiding.

* Tag:
You pick someone to be it Then
the other person runs away
from the person who is it. If
the Person who is it tags you, you
are now it.

I hope you have fun with
the games.

Misstakes you Shouldn't Do

1. Never take a eye off them.
2. Never be super mean.
3. Never tell them that there is a
monster under there bed.
4. Never put them to bed without
Reading them a bedtime story.
5. Never put them to bed without
a bottle.
6. Never be strict.
7. Never be bossy.
8. Never be mean.
9. Never describe the monster.
10. Never scarer them.

FIG. 21–1 (Continued)

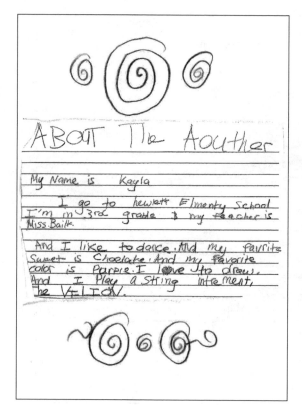

FIG. 21-1   (Continued)

Anisa

All about Color

HOW to make colors

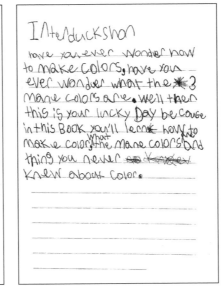

Tabe of contents

Interduckshon

have you ever wonder how to make colors, have you ever wonder what the 3 mane colors are. Well then this is your lucky Day be couse in this Book you'll lern how to make color what the mane colors and thing you never knew about color.

The Pimemary colors

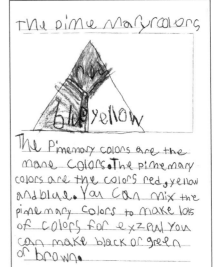

blue yellow

The Pimemary colors are the mane colors. The Pimemary colors are the colors red, yellow and blue. You can mix the pimemary colors to make lots of colors for exzpul you can make black or green or brown.

The secittary Colors

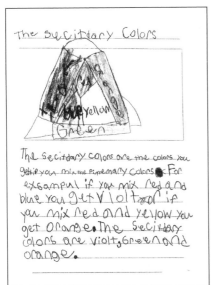

yellow
Green

The secittary colors are the colors you get if you mix the pimemary colors. For exsampul if you mix red and blue you get violt or if you mix red and yellow you get orange. The secittary colors are violt, green and orange.

Shades

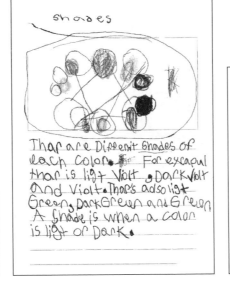

Thar are Different shades of each color. For exapul thar is ligt Violt, Dark violt and violt. Thar's adso ligt Green, Dark Green and Green. A shade is when a color is ligt or Dark.

4 Fun Fact's About color

Wite means Detn in inda

In inda wite is the color of Detn.

Togers int's Baby blue with a Different name Baby blue is made with wite and blue but togers is made with blue wite and orange.

Red Violet Pink

Everysingwe color has a sade family like the red sade family

Gold ligt orange

Gold and ligt orange look sisters

5

FIG. 21–2   Anisa's final expert piece, "All about Color"

PINK and BLUE

Pink and blue are colors
that are very populer for baby
kids, espeshully BaBys. PoePul
+oday say that Pink is for grels and
blue is for Boys, tot but back
Then they said Pink was for
Boys and Blue was for greils.
x but Both of those Sayings
are not ture

because blue is 4 Just for Boys
and Pink is4 Just for Grels. some
times Boys waer Pink and some
times grels waer Blue, that's
why those saxings
aren't true

Wite is not a pime mary
color but you can't make it
out of eney ather color. snow
is wite and the clodes are wite,
than are a lot of things and colors we
need wite for. some colors are made
with wite. Pink, Baby Blue, lit green
and ligt volet all need wite
to be a ligt color.

In Conclushan,
qll of the things in the
werod have color. from the
lest popexter color to the most
popexer color. thar is so much
you can lern about
color.

colors you can make

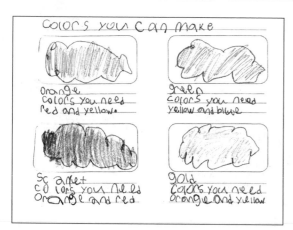

orange
colors you need
red and yellow.

green
colors you need
yellow and blue

sc arlet
colors you need
orange and red

gold
colors you need
orange and yellow

colors you can make

pink
colors you need to
make it. red and wite

puerpul
colors you need to
red and blue.

trange
color you need
blue, wite and green

ras berry
colors you need
Pink, red and puerpl

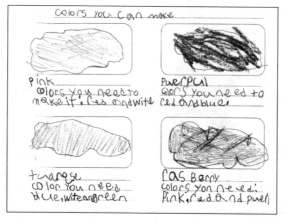

dark pink
colors you need
pink and red

ligt puerpul
colors you need
puerpul and red

ligt green
colors you need
green and yellow

FIG. 21–2 (Continued)

Name _Frank_

Topic: _Dragons_

(look for the Dragon's eye in each chapter)

Table of Contents

Chapter One: _What am I?_

Chapter Two: _Where am I?_

Chapter Three: _look at my sharpeners_

Chapter Four: _Its dark in here but not for long_

Chapter Five: _Oh—Oh food_

Chapter Six: _egg years_

Chapter Seven: _Dragon vs. trex_

Chapter Eight: _I am famous?_

Chapter Nine: _real or fake_

Chapter Ten: _About the Author, Glossary, index_

by _Frank_

FIG. 21–3 Frank's final expert piece, "Awesome Dragons"

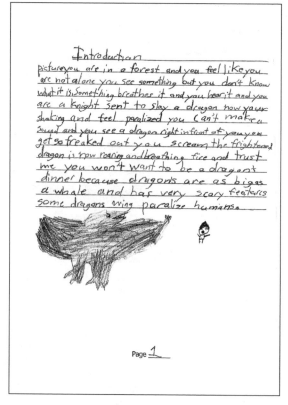

Introduction

pictureyou are in a forest and you feel like you are not alone you see something but you don't know what it is,Something breathes it and you hear it and you are a knight sent to slay a dragon now your shaking and feel paralized you can't make a sound and you see a dragon right infront of you,you get so freaked out you scream the frightened dragon is now roaring and breathing fire and trust me you won't want to be a dragon's dinner because dragons are as big as a whale and has very scary feeters some dragons wing paralize humanse

Page 1

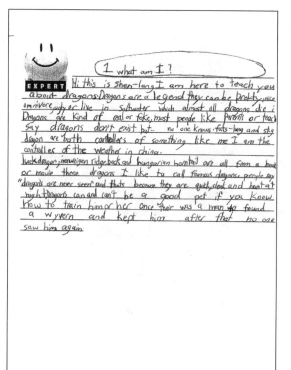

1 what am I?

Hi this is Shen-long I am here to teach you about dragons.Dragons are a legend they can be pretty nice omnivore,ugly or live in saltwater which almost all dragons die i Dragons are kind of real or fake,most people like parents or teach say dragons don't exist but. no one knows facts-long and shg dragon are both controllers of something like me I am the controller of the weather in china.

luskdragon,norweigen ridgeback and hungarian horntail are all from a book or movie these dragons I like to call famous dragons. people say "dragons are never seen" and thats because they are quick,sleak and hunt at night.Dragons can and can't be a good pet if you know how to train him or her once their was a man to found a wyvern and kept him after that no one saw him again

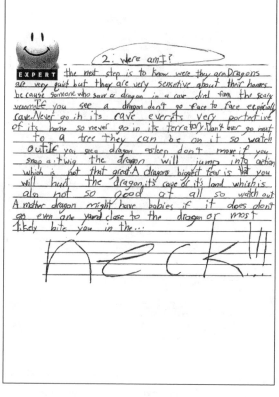

2. were am I?

the next step is to know were they are.Dragons are very quiet but they are very sensetive about their homes because someone who saw a dragon in a cave died from the scary vroom.If you see a dragon don't go face to face espinaly cave.Never go in its cave ever its very portectire of its home so never go in its terratory.Don't ever go next to a tree they can be on it so watch outif you see a dragon asleep don't move if you snap a twig the dragon will jump into action which is not that great.A dragons biggest fear is that you will hurt the dragon,its cave or it's land which is also not so good at all so watch out A mother dragon might have babies if it does dont go even one yard close to the dragon or most likely bite you in the...

NECK!!!

FIG. 21-3   (Continued)

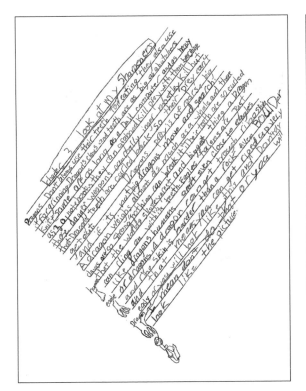

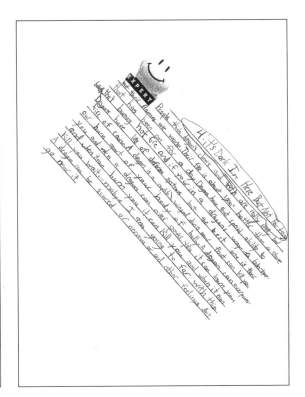

FIG. 21–3 (Continued)

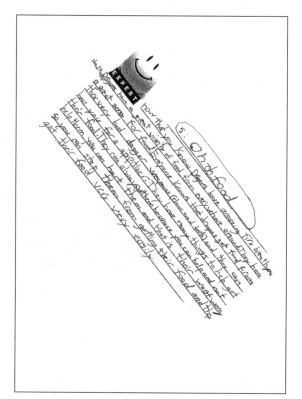

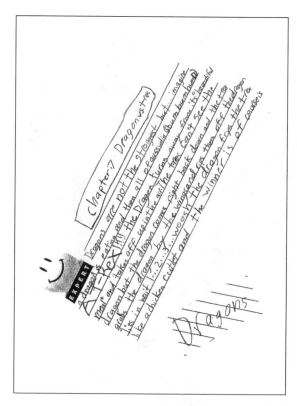

FIG. 21–3 (Continued)

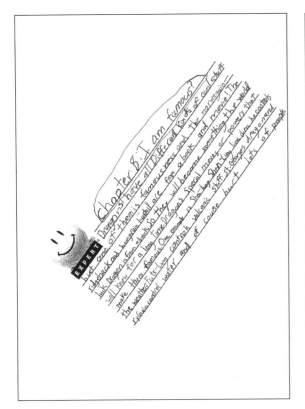

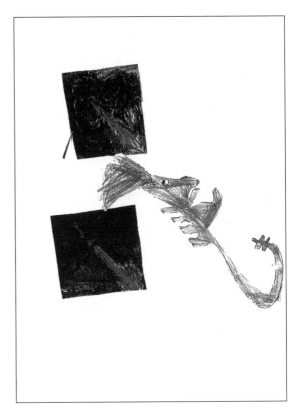

FIG. 21–3 (Continued)

About the author

So who is behind a of this funny chapters and great writing it is frank, I am in thipd grade and I always make people laugh (I love to) also I hoped you would enjoy the as much as I love writing it.

glossary

dagger-very very sharp weapon
cranky-tired and yell or scream as a dragon would roar appitizer little something (food)
Knight-someone who has metal armor or works for a king.

index

A Apoleda p.3
B B tattle Dragoreats
C conclusion p.1 cover p.frontcover
D Different Dragons p.1 and 8
E every dragon p.lands
F fofnir p.2
G Grey griack p.2

FIG. 21–3   (Continued)

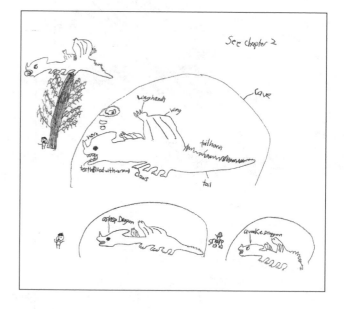

Conclusion

Its not over! but sadly this is my last page I loved writing this book but really I have to go I want you to read more books! and some are mine. Also read J.k. really books they are very good so is harry potter witch is by her she is a very good author if you think I was good read her books they are so so soooo ooo good. I love them hope you liked them too.

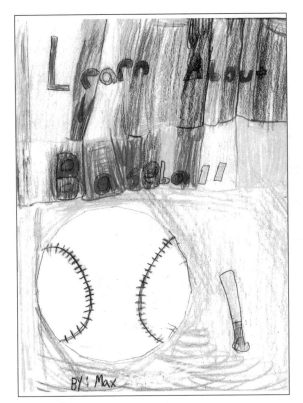
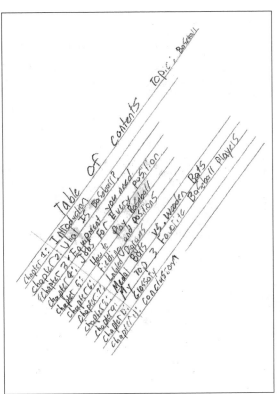

FIG. 21–4   Max's final expert piece, "Learn About Baseball"

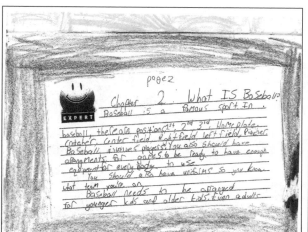
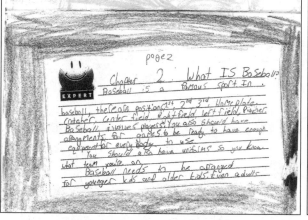
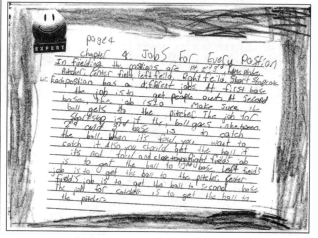

FIG. 21–4 (Continued)

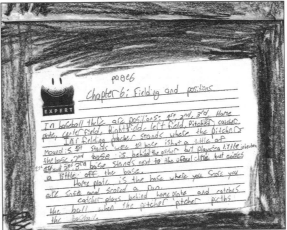

FIG. 21–4   Continued

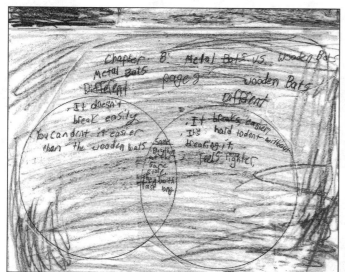

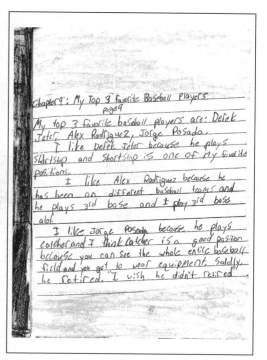

FIG. 21–4   (Continued)

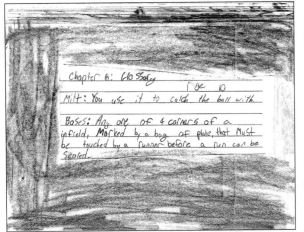

Chapter A: Glossary

Page 10

Mitt: You use it to catch the ball with.

Bases: Any one of 4 corners of a infield. Marked by a bag of plate, that Must be touched by a runner before a run can be Scored.

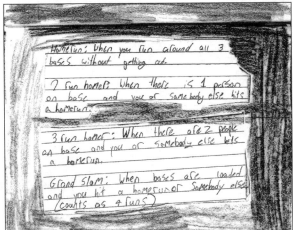

HomeRun: When you run around all 3 bases without getting out.

2 run homer: When there is 1 person on base and you or somebody else hits a homerun.

3 run homer: When there are 2 people on base and you or somebody else hits a homerun.

Grand slam: When bases are loaded and you hit a homerun or somebody else (counts as 4 runs)

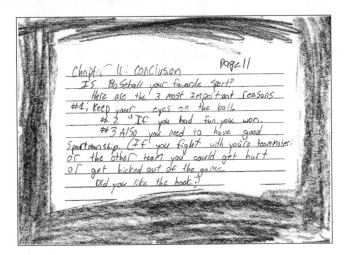

Chapter 11: Conclusion

Page 11

Is Baseball your favorite sport?
Here are the 3 most Important reasons
#1; Keep your eyes on the ball.
#2 "If you had fun you won.
#3 Also you need to have good Sportmanship. (If you fight with you're teammates, or the other team you could get hurt or get kicked out of the game.
Did you like the book?

FIG. 21–4   (Continued)

Table of Contents

Chapters	Pages
Chapter 1:	
What is soccer	1
Chapter 2:	
Uniforms	2
Chapter 3:	
Pastimes	3
Chapter 4:	
In 1980	4
Chapter 5:	
20 things about soccer	5
Chapter 6:	
Land of soccer	6
Chapter 7:	
Chapter 8:	
Chapter 7:	
Chapter 8:	

FIG. 21–5 Alessandra's final expert piece, "All about Soccer"

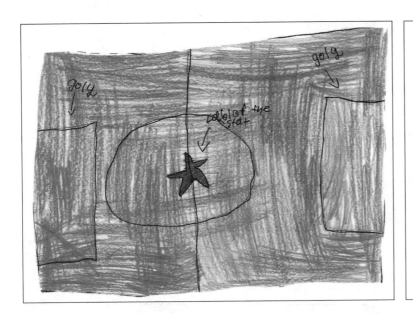

goly

goly

tablof the stat

EXPERT

Introducion 1

In my story you will be blown away by it. When you read the first chapter you will start to feel like you an expeart allready, So in my you will Learn and explor about soccer and ponfenshenals and if you play that sport you sand of an expert already, so if you now someone that is a panteshanal soccer Player maybe they will be in my story, so go Learn and explor in my book

EXPERT

What is Soccer? 1

Soccer is a game that can be aggressive. some times, sometime some Player get to aggressive and they can get a yellow card. or a red card. Those are bad and I will explan what they are. The yellowcard is when you get a Penalty. It happens when you push, kick, trip or even punct some one. You can be very aggreseve sometimes, sometimes if you are a goaly you th get kicked in the face to.

Cool but weard The feld i heidi is smaller than the one outside

FIG. 21–5   (Continued)

Chapter 2 Uniforms

Uniforms are important because if you dont have the right uniform youl get mixed up with the other team and then you will pass the ball to the other team player and they will get the ball. And the prestuh is on the golly. You have to have uniforms because one is your home uniform and one is your away uniform. Sometimes in indoor soccer they make you bring new uniforms because they dont now what the other teams color is.

cool but weard you can not slid takl in indoor soocer.

Chapter 3 Postions

Soccer isa agrasiv sport. In soccer there are 4 postions, Golly, defense, midfeld and otprec. The golly has a very iportent goh. Neris a personal story.

Once when my team scord a goal. Then the other team got relly mad and then they punch the rereand my team player and the golly.

so as I was saying goly is a very in portent goft. If you get sacand op the ball than goly is not the postion for you there are still other gobs. Sometimes you need to punt the ball. I bet you gise are like I dont know what its puts. Punts are. When you throw the ball up in the air than you kick it then it ether gos hig, or low. because some people are not so good at it. Now we are on defense. Its a iportent job because you have to stop the other people or team from geting a gore. If the other team gets behind the defece then they probuly will man a gore. Now we are on opene is wear most of the action because you scor gores or get the ball frome other people.

1980 Chapter 4

In 1980 thear was a very famous soccer player in the world. Her name was Rebecca Hamm she wone 5 cups in a rous. When her team got into t 6th world cup they lost because they where shooting from the line and the other team had a very good goli.

FIG. 21–5   (Continued)

To thinky about soccer chapter 5
In soccer there are a yellow cards and
red cardsA yellow crde means you can't play for
Do whit is than you can play by the way 2 yellow
cards = a red card. One red card meens that you can't
play for the game. What can case a yellow card is
tricing or pushing. What can sase a red card is kicing
punching and tribing

Land of scope
Land of scoor is a chaplen of how soccer is played.
soccer is the kind of game that is grasive
some times you are alowed to use you hede
when the Reffe calls it or when it is out.

Quiz!

What is the 4 postions

— — — —

PS do not wright in the
book. do it on a peic of
paper.

FIG. 21–5   (Continued)